The United States Military
in Latin America

ALSO BY GEORGE B. CLARK
AND FROM MCFARLAND

*The American Expeditionary Force in World War I:
A Statistical History, 1917–1919* (2013)

*Battle History of the United States Marine Corps,
1775–1945* (2010)

*United States Marine Corps Generals of World War II:
A Biographical Dictionary* (2008; paperback 2014)

*The Second Infantry Division in World War I:
A History of the American Expeditionary Force Regulars,
1917–1919* (2007)

*Decorated Marines of the Fourth Brigade
in World War I* (2007)

*The Six Marine Divisions in the Pacific:
Every Campaign of World War II* (2006)

*Hiram Iddings Bearss, U.S. Marine Corps:
Biography of a World War I Hero* (2005)

EDITED BY GEORGE B. CLARK

*United States Marine Corps Medal of Honor Recipients:
A Comprehensive Registry, Including U.S. Navy Medical Personnel
Honored for Serving Marines in Combat* (2005; paperback 2011)

The United States Military in Latin America

A History of Interventions through 1934

GEORGE B. CLARK

McFarland & Company, Inc., Publishers
Jefferson, North Carolina

LIBRARY OF CONGRESS CATALOGUING-IN-PUBLICATION DATA

Clark, George B., 1926–
　　The United States military in Latin America : a history of interventions through 1934 / George B. Clark.
　　　p.　　cm.
　　Includes bibliographical references and index.

　　ISBN 978-0-7864-9448-4 (softcover : acid free paper) ∞
　　ISBN 978-1-4766-1579-0 (ebook)

　　1. Latin America—History, Military.　2. United States—Armed Forces—Latin America.　3. Intervention (International law)　4. United States—Foreign relations—Latin America.　5. Latin America—Foreign relations—United States.　I. Title.
F1410.5.C55　2014
355.0098—dc23　　　　　　　　　　　　　　　　　　　　2014024050

BRITISH LIBRARY CATALOGUING DATA ARE AVAILABLE

© 2014 George B. Clark. All rights reserved

No part of this book may be reproduced or transmitted in any form or by any means, electronic or mechanical, including photocopying or recording, or by any information storage and retrieval system, without permission in writing from the publisher.

On the cover: The 6th Company of Marines in camp, Haiti, 1915

Printed in the United States of America

McFarland & Company, Inc., Publishers
　Box 611, Jefferson, North Carolina 28640
　　www.mcfarlandpub.com

Table of Contents

Acknowledgments — vi
Introduction — 1

1. Argentina — 3
2. Chile — 9
3. Colombia and Panama — 13
4. Cuba — 34
5. Haiti — 53
6. Honduras — 100
7. Mexico — 103
8. Nicaragua — 112
9. Paraguay — 137
10. Peru — 138
11. Puerto Rico — 140
12. Santo Domingo/Dominican Republic — 142
13. Uruguay — 167

Appendices
A. Biographies — 171
B. Officers of the First Provisional Regiment, Nicaragua, 1909–1910 — 178
C. Officers at Coyotepe and Barranca, Nicaragua, 1912 — 180
D. The Roll of Honor — 182

Chapter Notes — 190
Bibliography — 201
Index — 205

Acknowledgments

I wish to thank the following individuals who have rendered help with this and many other projects:

Retired Colonel Richard Camp, a former Marine. Actually there are no former Marines; as the slogan puts it: "Once a Marine, always a Marine." He supplied many of the photos from his personal collection. I wish he had been available to assist me in writing this; he has so many fine publications to his credit.

Retired Sergeant Major Jim Butler, who worked finding photos on my behalf.

Retired Marine and recently married Lieutenant Colonel Pete Owen, who during his honeymoon found pictures for me. Thanks Pete, and Mrs. Pete.

Retired Marine Lieutenant Colonel Curt Bruce, who took the time to make contact with Susan Hodges at the Marine Heritage Center in order to assist me. Thanks to both.

Retired Lieutenant Commander Neil G. Carey, USN, an old (very old) friend of so many years who has been alongside for every effort I've been involved with.

Retired Master Gunnery Sergeant Steve Hansen, USMC, a very knowledgeable Marine historian. He has been there when I needed him.

Former Marine Harry J. Tinney, who has read more books than anyone I know of, including me. He has also been there when I needed him.

Two men, both Marines and editors, have been helpful in many ways for many years. Bill White and Walt Ford are both editors of that great Marine magazine *The Leatherneck*.

I must not forget my helpful son, Patrick T. Clark, who is there when I need him, which is often.

And my great "old" friend, even though he was U.S. Army, James McIlwain, M.D., pride of Mississippi and Brown University.

Introduction

The United States began intervening in the affairs of its neighbors in the Western Hemisphere early in the 19th century. That was at a time when most of them were rebelling against their colonizer, Spain. Possibly the most important element in that process was the Monroe Doctrine created by President James Monroe when he delivered his message to Congress on 2 December 1823. In it Monroe proclaimed the separation between the Western Hemisphere and the rest of the world, namely Europe. No nation in Europe (the World) was to ever interfere in the affairs of the hemisphere, "or else" they would face a confrontation with the United States. No nation, that is, other than those already in possession of land, such as Spain, Britain and France.

The various Spanish colonies in the southern part of this hemisphere were in turmoil. Though the United States did not interfere in any of those engagements, at least not publicly, U.S. Navy ships were patrolling as far south as Argentina, observing each situation. Aboard each of those ships were small detachments of the Navy's fighting men, U.S. Marines. Those Marines, in the early years usually accompanied by sailors to back up the relatively insubstantial numbers of Marines, were sent ashore in various places to protect Americans or their interests. Frequently they were called upon by the local American representative, sometimes called chargé d'affaires or consul.

Spain gave up Florida to the U.S. in 1819 with the Florida Treaty. The first nation to question the establishment of that Monroe Doctrine happened to be Great Britain and it was regarding the settlement of the Columbia River and Canada. The next confrontation was with Russia about its claims to the northwest coast of North America. The czar gave up in 1823. For years following there were various negotiations with Latin America, and of course the estrangement with Mexico that developed over the relationship with Texas and eventually, we went to war. With that settlement the U.S. wound up with large, new territories and the nation is now all the way to the Pacific coast. To the victor went the spoils.

As the years went by the United States ever increasingly interfered in the affairs of its neighbors. Soon, after the turn of the 20th century, it was those nations lying just south of the U.S. that got the most attention. American citizens seemed to control much property in the island nations and those along the peninsula. And with that ownership went many landings to protect property holdings from locals who were usually in rebellion against their own government. Or sometimes the government against its citizens; or sometimes against the United States.

With the turn of the 20th century, the U.S. became involved, heavily, in Panama; in Cuba, many times; the Dominican Republic, from 1916 to 1924; Haiti, 1915 to 1934; Honduras several times in the 1920s; Mexico in 1914 (and again in 1916 in strictly a U.S. Army incursion); and Nicaragua, in 1912 heavily, and again in 1927 followed by an occupation until 1934. These actions, and many more, are covered in this book and are organized by nation, then chronologically.

The natives of each nation gave the Marines a run for their money, but none quite like Augusto Sandino in Nicaragua. The Marines believed in what they were doing because the U.S. State Department had issued the command to intervene. Some Americans denounced the action and even the Marines themselves; but the Marines did not order those interventions. The State Department and sometimes the president (Wilson at the time) were the order givers, and the Navy simply carried them out. Occasionally the U.S. Army would become involved, such as in Vera Cruz, Mexico, in 1914, but usually after the Marines and Navy had settled the immediate problem.

The election of President Franklin D. Roosevelt ended the United States' interference in the nations of Latin America until the end of World War Two and the creation of the United Nations. Occasionally since we have intervened in several Latin American nations, and plenty of others elsewhere. All for the betterment of mankind, so they say. Perhaps someday soon we will run out of manpower and have to stay at home?

1

ARGENTINA

Insurrection in what is now the Argentine Republic dates back to the 16th century, when Alvar Nunez, the Spanish governor, was deposed by the followers of Martinez Irala and later shipped to Spain as a prisoner. Since this early date many revolutions have taken place for the control of the government but the United States found few reasons to intervene.

The first encounter with the Argentine Republic took place off shore at the Falkland Islands, which Argentina claimed in 1829.

For several years, sealing around the Falkland Islands had been a profitable trade. American sealers, like those of other countries, had been engaged in this enterprise for some time. During the latter part of 1831, the American schooners *Breakwater*, *Harriet*, and *Superior* were so employed when seized by Luis Vernet, the political and military governor of the islands. President Andrew Jackson referred to this act in his annual message to Congress of December 6, 1831, as "a band acting, as they pretend, under the authority of the Government of Buenos Ayres," and he recommended the adoption of measures "for providing a force adequate to the complete protection of our fellow-citizens fishing and trading in those seas."

It was quite evident that Congress approved of the president's recommendation, inasmuch as the sloop *Lexington*, under Commander Silas Duncan, was ordered from Buenos Aires to the Falklands to release these American schooners. Commander Duncan arrived off Berkley Sound on the morning of December 28, and at 12:15 p.m. came to anchor in the sound (having taken in tow a small schooner a short way from the entrance), where he remained apparently inactive until 1 January 1832.

Early in the morning of the first day of the year, he stood in for the port of St. Louis and came to anchor at 11:30 a.m. Just prior to anchoring, he sent a landing party of two officers and 15 Marines ashore in the commandeered schooner to confer with the authorities, and, at 11:45, another party, well armed, in two boats, to augment the first. The three schooners were finally liberated and permitted to proceed.

Practically all of the American citizens in the islands desired to leave, and Commander Duncan agreed to give them passage to Montevideo in the *Lexington*. While they were preparing for their departure, he sent a guard of 12 Marines ashore to protect their property and to assist them in their preparations for the voyage. This guard returned at noon the following day, but a smaller guard went ashore each day until the 5th. On the 21st those Americans who wished to leave the Island came aboard the *Lexington* and were made as comfortable as conditions on board a man of war would permit. The following day this party of 20 men, 8 women and 10 children sailed on board the *Lexington* for their native land.

At about this time, British ships appeared and also claimed the Falklands, and added they had possession for the previous 60 years. Argentina requested that the United States impose the Monroe Doctrine and send Britain on its way, but, unfortunately, the U.S. acknowledged British sovereignty.

On 1 October 1833, an uprising was in progress, and it became so violent as to necessitate a landing by United States naval forces for the protection of American citizens and those of other foreign countries not represented by naval forces in these waters.[1]

Commander John P. Zantzinger, U.S. Navy, in place in the *Natchez*, was at Buenos Aires when this uprising took place, but was under orders to take his departure for another port. The United States was not represented in Argentina by either a diplomatic officer or a consular agent, and Daniel Gowland of the American firm of Daniel Gowland and Company assumed the responsibilities of representing all citizens of the United States who resided in the city of Buenos Aires. On 16 October he addressed a letter to Commander Zantzinger in which he expressed keen regret that the American man-of-war was to depart so soon, and the belief that if Commodore Melanthon T. Woolsey was aware of the local conditions, he would retain the *Natchez* in the harbor.

Commander Zantzinger gave Commodore Woolsey on the flagship *Lexington*, which was at Montevideo, a copy of Gowland's letter with a petition signed by American and English merchants suggesting that the *Natchez* be retained at Buenos Aires, at least until another American ship should arrive to relieve it, for the protection of the interests of the United States. The commodore set sail for the troubled area and arrived there on the 21st of the month.

After his arrival and upon familiarizing himself with all of the conditions in the city, Commodore Woolsey deemed it advisable to have someone on shore to look after the interests of his government, since the United States was not represented at the time by any political agent. He selected Commander Isaac McKeever of the *Lexington* as the representative and ordered him to reside ashore until further instructed. Commander McKeever took up his residence on shore the same day, called upon the president, arranged for a salute to be exchanged between the *Lexington* and the Argentine authorities, obtained such facts about the revolution as was practicable, and reported this information to the commodore.

Conditions ashore remained about the same from day to day, with occasional sporadic outbursts of musketry throughout the city until the 31st of October, when the outbreak became general, and the commodore deemed it necessary to order an armed party ashore to protect foreign interests. At 3:30 p.m. a force of 43 officers, Marines and sailors proceeded on shore, and were placed under the direct command of Commander McKeever for such disposition as he might deem necessary or advisable. This detachment remained ashore until 15 November when, tranquility having been restored, they returned to their ships.[2]

The year 1852 was ushered in by the advent of another revolution in the political affairs of the republic of Argentina. The city of Buenos Aires was invested (surrounded) by land by an allied army from the revolting provinces and from Brazil, while by sea a cordon of sloops of war hovered near, and all were in a state of readiness to turn their guns on the beleaguered city when so ordered by the allied leader.[3] The president (dictator) of Argentina, General Juan Manuel Rosas, the head of the Argentine army, had gone out to lead them against the allied forces. The situation was tense, and the populace was in a state of expectancy fraught with impending disaster.

About this time Commodore Isaac McKeever, in his flagship *Congress*, arrived at Montevideo, Uruguay, where he received dispatches from the American chargé d'affaires, John S. Pendleton, at Buenos Aires, acquainting him with the state of affairs in that city. Commodore McKeever felt that his presence at the latter place was urgently needed and that probably additional Marines might be necessary if a landing would be required for the protection of the interests of the United States. Accordingly, he ordered the Marine Guard of the *Congress* under Brevet Captain Algernon S. Taylor and Second Lieutenant George Holmes to proceed to Buenos Aires. The commodore also sailed for that city, and, upon arrival, transferred his pennant to the *Jamestown*, which was lying in the harbor off Buenos Aires at the time. On the 2 February a meeting was called of all the accredited diplomatic corps present to consider ways and means for the protection of their nationals. Commodore McKeever and the British admiral and senior naval officers of France, Sardinia and Sweden were invited to attend. At this conference it was decided to apply to the authorities to land such forces as might be necessary under the circumstances.

United States Marines and a few seamen landed in the city on 3 February.[4] Scattered forces of Rosas' cavalry also began entering the city, and a little later it was learned that they had been defeated by the allied forces from Uruguay now investing the city. Renewed alarm was now felt for the safety of foreign citizens, and an immediate answer to the application to land troops was urged—which orders were given. Commodore McKeever pressed into service the American steamer *Manulita Rosas*, loaded it with the Marines of the *Congress* and *Jamestown*, and ordered it into the inner harbor. The Marines landed by the use of flat boats from the frigate HMS *Centaur*, which had been loaned to the Marines through the kindness of British Admiral Henderson.

The Marines of the *Jamestown* were commanded by Second Lieutenant John R. F. Tattnall,[5] and combined with those of the *Congress*, formed guards at the residences of the chargé d'affaires, the Consul Joseph Graham, and that of Messrs. Zimmerman, Frazier and Company, who conducted the largest American mercantile house in the city, and in whose residence Commodore McKeever was a guest. The British and French forces were distributed in a similar manner, and the whole foreign detachment was situated so as to concentrate at a given point in a minimum of time when required.

Late this same evening, the 3rd, advices were received that General Justo Jose Urquiza of Uruguay, the allied commander, had defeated General Rosas, and that the latter's army was completely dispersed. Based upon this information, the authorities sought the services of the diplomatic corps to solicit a stay of the onward march of the conquering allied forces into the city. They agreed, and proceeded instead to Palermo, where they awaited General Urquiza. However, they were unable to communicate with him until the following day when he arrived at Palermo, and upon being advised of the state of affairs, readily agreed to withhold his army, sending only a small force to restore order.

In the meantime several stores had been rifled by a band of pillagers bent upon plundering the city. These mounted pillagers came upon a party of Marines and sailors, under Midshipman John G. Walker, who were patrolling the streets to prevent the sacking of the city. The pillagers charged and fired upon them but providentially none were harmed by their bullets or the charge. The Marines returned the fire of the pillagers and four of the robbers fell, two being killed outright and two seriously wounded who died later. This prompt retaliation dispersed the band, and apparently put an end to pillaging outrages in the city.

General Urquiza approved of the landing of the foreign troops and their action in firing upon those bent upon pillage, and requested that these forces remain until such time as he had perfected arrangements for the proper policing of the city and had reestablished tranquility. Commodore McKeever stated, "Great credit is due to our gallant Marines for their share in the restoration of comparative safety to life and property. They were under the command of Captain Taylor of the *Congress* and Lieutenant Tattnall of the *Jamestown*."

General Rosas, after his defeat at the hands of General Urquiza, is said to have entered the city in disguise and made his escape in the night to HMS *Centaur*, and later on a steamer bound for England. There he went into exile for the balance of his life as a farmer in Southampton.

On the 7th of February, believing that the allied force was in all respects able to maintain order and tranquility, the American chargé addressed himself to the provisional governor, Senor Vicente Lopez, concerning withdrawing the American Marines. Lopez replied: "The longer presence in the City of the United States Marines seems unnecessary, but ... you are at liberty to withdraw them to their vessels, whenever you may find a suitable opportunity." In accordance with the desires of the provisional governor, the Marines were withdrawn on 12 February aboard their respective ships.

Another outbreak occurred on 11 September which necessitated the landing of another detachment of American Marines. This new revolt was caused by General Urquiza deposing the officials of the provisional government whom he had previously appointed, and assuming the office of governor of that province himself. Just prior to this insurrection, Commodore McKeever arrived at Montevideo, and on the 3rd of August despatched Captain Samuel W. Downing, in the *Jamestown*, to Buenos Aires to observe conditions. He arrived and was present when the outbreak occurred. This affair did not reach the proportions that the earlier one had. Nevertheless, a Marine guard at the American Consulate was deemed advisable, and on the 17th of September a Marine guard was so landed for the protection of American interests. The exact date these Marines returned to their ship is not presently known. However, it is believed to be sometime in April 1853.[6]

Revolution, and revolutionary intrigue, had held sway in the greater part of Latin America for a number of years prior to 1855. Argentina had been the scene of several uprisings during prior years, and it is quite possible that the unrest manifested by the inhabitants of that state had been communicated to those of Uruguay. About mid-summer of 1855 an uprising of revolutionary proportions spread over this country, and attained a character so sanguinary and disastrous that foreign residents were beseeching their diplomatic representatives for protection for themselves and for their property. On 28 August, Marines from the *Germantown* went ashore in Montevideo, Uruguay, to protect American lives and property, but the upset ended almost immediately and the Marines returned to their ship the following day.

As had been the practice for a number of years, the United States had a squadron in South American waters whose duty it was to furnish protection to American citizens in cases of emergency. Brazil, France and Spain also had vessels of war in this locality to look after their respective interests. These vessels and the American squadron were at anchor in the harbor of Montevideo, Uruguay. The United States was represented by Commander William F. Lynch, who commanded the sloop *Germantown*, and the American Consul Robert M. Hamilton. The commanders for the foreign vessels, together with the diplomatic representatives of their respective governments, held a conference and decided to make a combined landing of a portion of their forces for the protection of their nationals and consulates.

The 25th of November was agreed upon for the landing. The force was composed of the Marine Guard of the *Germantown*, under First Lieutenant Augustus S. Nicholson, and Marines from the ships of the other three countries represented. On the 27th, owing to the seriousness of the conflict being waged between the different factions ashore, additional forces were despatched to reinforce the Marine detachments that were landed two days previously. These additional forces, as well as the first detachments, were placed under the direct command of Lieutenant Nicholson. The reinforcements, however, were returned to their ships the same date, but the original detachments still remained on duty ashore. The American Marines were withdrawn on the 30th after the revolutionists had capitulated and conditions had become tranquil.[7]

A short time before Lieutenant Nicholson and his Marines returned aboard their ship, an incident took place which indicates the resourcefulness, bravery, and ability of the American Marine to act in emergencies. The insurgents had capitulated to the government. After they had been disarmed, the nationalists charged them and a massacre would have ensued had not Lieutenant Nicholson and his Marines interposed themselves between the government troops and the insurgents. He forced the victors to place the matter before the courts, to which they agreed. Afterward, Nicholson was commended by his superiors for his humanitarian act.

In July of 1890 still another revolution was in progress in the province of Buenos Aires, Argentina. On the 30th a small detachment of Marines was landed for the protection of the American consulate and the residence of the minister, John R. G. Pitkin. These Marines were landed from the *Tallapoosa* and remained ashore most of that day, then withdrawn and returned to their ship.

2

CHILE

Chile had always been in a state of near or absolute conquest from the time of the Inca until later Spanish adventurers. After nearly three centuries had elapsed, Chile was in revolt in 1810. José de San Martín, at the head of a joint expedition of Argentine and Chilean forces, crossed the Andes and in a brilliant campaign freed Chile, whose independence was proclaimed on 12 February 1818. The United States recognized Chile as an independent state four years later. There were at least two factions who desired to head up the new, independent government, the Carreras brothers and Bernard O'Higgins. San Martín chose O'Higgins as political director, and headed this new government until he was deposed by a Carreras revolution in 1823. Following O'Higgins' deposition, mutinies, assassinations, and dictatorships took place in rapid succession.

This reign of terror was not concluded until the Battle of Lircai or Lircay, which took place on 17 April 1830, when the conservative faction triumphed. Succeeding years brought little change, for they, too, were marked by bloody contests and revolutions between the different factions; in fact the conservatives controlled Chile for the following 30 years. The United States would have little interest in interfering in that nation until 1890.

In the year 1891, the people of this revolution ridden republic were again in a state of open insurrection against the faction then supposed to be controlling the government. Conditions were deplorable due to the capture in August of Valparaiso by the forces of the congressional party. Foreigners residing within the boundaries of the republic, especially those living in the captured city, were in great danger of losing their lives and property. Even foreign legations and consulates were in danger of being violated.

During the course of this revolution, a bitter feeling against the United States arose, due, it is believed, to the false and malicious accusations put forth at Iquique and later at Valparaiso in reference to the action of the Navy of the United States and their Marines.

American Minister Patrick Egan concurred in the belief that foreign armed forces were necessary, not only for the moral effect on the insurrectionists, but more importantly as a means of protection for Americans and American interests.

In the latter part of March, Rear Admiral George Brown had been ordered to Chilean waters as the relief of Commodore William P. McCann, and was issued definite and detailed instructions for his guidance in view of the unsettled state of affairs in Chile.[1] Admiral Brown proceeded in the *San Francisco,* and in company with the *Baltimore,* was present at Valparaiso when that city was captured by the revolutionists.

The American minister applied to Admiral Brown for a suitable guard for the legation, and his request was granted. A detachment of 36 Marines and 36 sailors, under the command of Captain William S. Muse, U.S.M.C., was landed at Valparaiso on the 28th of August and remained until the 30th when they were withdrawn.[2]

About six weeks after the withdrawal of the Marine guard from the American Consulate, an affair took place which assumed grave aspects—one which merited the landing of Marines to again protect American citizens, and indicated in no unmistakable terms the extreme ill feeling that the Chileans harbored toward the Americans. The affair was the attack on 16 October in the city of Valparaiso on members of a liberty party off the *Baltimore.* However, Admiral Brown, because of this extreme ill feeling, and believing that the matter could be more appropriately handled through diplomatic representation by the United States Department of State, deemed it inadvisable to use the Marine landing force at his disposal.

On this date men from the *Baltimore* went on shore in uniform for liberty, in accordance with the universal practice prevailing on board the ships of war in foreign ports. Two weeks had passed since the surrender of Valparaiso, and the city was quiet. Other foreign war ships had already given liberty, and no reason existed for withholding a like privilege from the men of the *Baltimore.* At 6:00 p.m. the men had been ashore about four hours, and the testimony is that they were then orderly, sober, and well-behaved.

The first encounter appears to have taken place when a Chilean spat in the face of one of the members of the liberty party. The sailor knocked the Chilean down and was immediately set upon, with his companion, another of the *Baltimore*'s crew, by an angry crowd. The two sailors took refuge in a passing street car. They were dragged from the car by the crowd. One of them, Petty Officer Charles Riggin, was stabbed and left to die in the street. His companion, Talbot, an apprentice, escaped, but was afterwards arrested; catgut nippers were put on his wrists, and he was struck again and again by the police on his way to prison. Another Petty Officer, Johnson, then in a neighboring house, seeing Riggin lying helpless in the street, went to his assistance. The crowd now left. Finding Riggin still breathing, Johnson took him in his arms to carry him to a drugstore nearby. At this moment a squad of Chilean police, with fixed bayonets, came up the street. When at close quarters, they fired at Johnson, being so near that his face was blackened by this discharge. One shot entered Riggin's neck and shoulder, inflicting a death wound. Another shot passed through Johnson's clothing.

The affair of the street car was only one of many simultaneous attacks made upon the *Baltimore*'s men. The attacks lasted for an hour. They were not confined to one locality, but occurred at several widely separated points in the city. In many instances the American sailors were in restaurants and hotels quietly getting supper when attacked by crowds numbering from 25 to 200 men. The part borne by the police in these attacks is shown by the report. Thirty-six of the *Baltimore*'s men were arrested and taken to prison, being subjected on the way to treatment of the utmost brutality. Catgut nippers were placed on their wrists, and—in the case of one man—McWilliams, a lasso was thrown about his neck. Williams, another apprentice, 19 years of age, was arrested by a mounted policeman who put the nippers around his wrists and then started his horse into a gallop, throwing the boy down. Coal-heaver Quigley, in trying to escape from the mob, was struck with a sword by a police officer. Petty Officer Hamilton was dragged to prison dangerously wounded and unconscious, and his companions, attempting to relieve his sufferings, were threatened with blows from musket butts and compelled to desist.

Coal-heaver Turnbull received 18 wounds in the back, two of which penetrated his lungs and subsequently caused his death. Other men were seriously injured and several of the wounds were caused by bayonet thrusts, clearly showing the participation of the police. As a result of the attacks, two of the men, Riggin and Turnbull, died, and 18 others were more or less disabled by wounds.

At the examination of the prisoners immediately following the arrest, which was conducted secretly, a request was made of the authorities by Captain Winfield S. Schley to allow one of his officers to be present in court.[3] The request was denied. Before the men were discharged they were required to sign a paper in Spanish. A court official, whom one of the men asked what might be the meaning of the paper, declared that it was a mere form, stating that the signer had not been engaged in the trouble.

The members of the liberty party during the attack were without arms and therefore defenseless. Of the 36 men arrested and examined, all were discharged, there being no proof of any violation of the peace on their part. The judicial investigation into the conduct of the men failed to show that a single one was found drunk or disorderly. It is clear that their only offense lay in wearing the uniform of the country to which they belonged.

Secretary of State James G. Blaine demanded apologies and the firing of guns to salute the American flag as well as indemnity for the victims. The president, Jorge Montt, refused and the people were demanding Chile declare war upon the United States. The United States finally settled for $75,000 paid to the families of the dead.[4]

3

COLOMBIA AND PANAMA

One of the most important affairs in 19th and 20th century U.S. interaction was whatever was to happen to a canal in the Western Hemisphere. It certainly governed matters until the turn of the 20th century. There were two locations considered: one was the Isthmus of Panama in the state of Colombia, because of its narrowness, the other was Nicaragua via its rivers.

The importance of the Panamanian isthmus as a crossing point was apparent as early as the Spanish explorer Balboa. When gold was discovered in California in the 1840s it became more apparent. The U.S. entered into an agreement with New Granada, which was the name utilized by what later became Colombia, to allow an American firm to build a railroad across that narrow neck between east and west.

The railroad was completed and traffic, mainly east to west and the California gold fields, began in earnest. Other European nations were making attempts to get into the long Latin American stretch going south from northern Mexico to Colombia on the South American continent. But the U.S. would instantly find ways to interrupt every effort.[1]

As far as a canal was concerned, Nicaragua was regarded as the most feasible location.

In 1846 the United States government negotiated a treaty with Colombia, then called New Granada, by which the U.S. guaranteed the neutrality of the isthmus of Panama and the security of the Isthmian transit. As the result of chaotic conditions on the isthmus and in accordance with the provisions of the treaty, U.S. naval forces made a long series of interventions, which did not cease until several years after Panama had become a separate nation and the Panama Canal had been constructed.

Not long after the treaty was signed, gold was discovered in California, and gold seekers rushed westward over every possible route. Their most popular route from the Atlantic coast was by steamer to Colón, then across the isthmus, and then by another vessel from Panama City. The transit, as made at first, was up the Chagres River as far as possible and then by trail to the Pacific coast. General political chaos in New Granada and the presence of disorderly elements along the line of transit caused considerable concern to the American authorities. When available, one or more U.S. Navy vessels was in the vicinity during this early phase of isthmian transit.

The possibility of constructing a railroad across the isthmus soon appealed to American promoters, who with great difficulty built such a railroad between 1850 and 1855. Travel across the isthmus greatly increased. The construction work had attracted a great many laborers, who were left without employment when the job was finished; the disorderly elements on the isthmus were thereby greatly increased. In April 1856, while three shiploads of American passengers were making the transit, a serious riot occurred in which the native officials joined the rioters; a number of Americans were killed and about 50 were wounded. The rioting did not stop until the *St. Mary's* arrived at Panama on June 18. With that small vessel not having sufficient men to land and cope with the situation, and the government of New Granada refusing to act, Commander Theodorus Bailey of the *St. Mary's* determined to do all in his power without resorting to a landing. He had a landing force stand by in boats, ships in port, and made other shows of force. As a result of such measures, a semblance of peace was restored for the time. Rioting broke out again about three months later, but fortunately both the *St. Mary's* and the *Independence* were present. Commander William Mervine, fearing serious consequences, promptly landed a force of 160 Marines and sailors under Captain Addison Garland, U.S.M.C., who established a camp at the railroad station at Panama in order to protect the transit facilities from attacks by the hundred insurgents in the vicinity.[2] By means of parades and demonstrations Garland made a considerable show of force with his little battalion. Within three days the situation had sufficiently cleared up for the troops to be withdrawn. A similar naval force landed about a month later to protect the transit of the cargo of an American ship.

The transit situation was more or less critical for several years thereafter, and one or more U.S. naval vessels remained on scene for prompt intervention if necessary. In September, some Negroes started an insurrection in the vicinity of Panama and attacked the city. A British naval vessel landed a force for the protection of its nationals; the captain of the *St. Mary's* promptly followed suit by landing a force of sailors and Marines from his ship to guard the railroad station at Panama. Conditions gradually improved after the loyal forces had defeated the rebels. The landing force from the *St. Mary's* withdrew October 8. These interventions on the Isthmus of Panama were only the beginning of a series, the accounts of which will be given later.

The Panama mail steamer USS *Golden City* erupted in a riot and the captain requested that the Marine Guard detachment of the *St. Mary's* to come to his aid, which they did and quelled that riot.

Arriving at Panama on 7 May 1873, Rear Admiral Steedman found another period of disturbances and was told by the American consul, plus residents, that traffic across the isthmus had been interrupted. He sent 200 Marines and sailors ashore with four pieces of artillery from the *Tuscarora* and *Pensacola*. The disturbances quieted down and four days later part of that force was withdrawn. By 22 May problems among dissidents had been settled and all Marines and sailors were withdrawn to their ships.

Captain Albert G. Clary, commanding the *Benicia*, was the first to arrive at Panama; he was soon followed by Adm. Steedman on the 18th of September in the *Pensacola*. Steedman made contact with the American consul and the two men agreed that a landing was essential. One hundred thirty Marines and seamen, later increased to 190, with two howitzers, were landed at the Bay of Panama on 24 September from the *Pensacola* and *Benicia* to once again protect the railroad and American lives and property. They, too, were eventually withdrawn. The Marines were under the command of Capt. Percival C. Pope and 2d Lt. James V. D'Hervilly of the *Pensacola*, and 2d Lt. Henry G. Ellsworth of the *Benicia*. Additional officers and men were sent ashore on the 24th, 25th, 26th, 27th and 28th. Captain Clement D. Hebb, USMC, arrived for duty aboard the *Pensacola* on 1 October. On the 4th the crew of the *Benicia*, Marines and seamen, arrived back aboard. Then, on the 9th, those of the *Pensacola* returned aboard.[3]

A major landing, in fact the largest movement of the U.S. Navy and U.S. Marine Corps between the Civil War and the Spanish-American War, took place in Colombia (Panama) during the early months of 1885. The landing force of Marines was loosely titled a brigade of Marines, though a modern battalion would be more like it.

Again it was the protection of the American owned railroad from the always revolting Panamanians. There was no real trouble, the Colombian troops arrived and soon the "situation was well in hand."

The Landing at Panama[4]

Until 1914 transit to and from the Pacific Ocean for ship-board travelers required a passage through the terrible Magellan Straits or overland in the Isthmus of Panama. It wasn't far into the 19th century before it became apparent to many people in the United States and in western nations of Europe that a canal must be built. And the most likely place would be that narrow length of land stretching between North America and South America. That stretch of land we know as Central America. And at its narrowest point lies the Colombian state of Panama.

At that time the most aggressive of American nations was the United States. It was there that the thoughts of a canal began to seriously ferment early in the 19th century. Following the war with Mexico, the United States had expanded its territory to include California, which made the U.S. a Pacific rim nation. When the rush for gold in California began in 1848, travel across the plains and mountains by stagecoach was hazardous. Travel through the Caribbean by ship was less dangerous, so consequently another passageway had to be developed. Colombia, the nation which controlled Panama, and the U.S. signed a treaty which insured that the U.S. would have the right to traverse, protect, and preserve safe transit across the isthmus. The U.S. was not about to allow any interference with that right of passage. The U.S. had become a continental nation and safe travel to the western most parts of the nation was essential for continued communication and growth.

Like many nations in the Western Hemisphere in the 19th century, Colombia, especially in its northernmost state, Panama, was the scene of continual unrest. Efforts to control the unrest usually and eventually were successful. Most likely without outside interference, the uprisings, even the one that began in 1884, would have managed to settle down. And it might not have caused any great disturbance without assistance from the U.S. But that was not to be.

The U.S. had designs on Panama and on portions of its sister state to the north, Nicaragua, for the canal which the U.S. would oversee and control. Temporarily at least the U.S. had as much control as was necessary to insure its own continued growth so long as passage across the Isthmus of Panama continued without interference via railroad.

The political conditions in the isthmus were greatly affected by elections held in the summer of 1884. When the new president of the state of Panama proclaimed himself unable to protect foreigners or their property, the U.S. minister in Panama requested help from his government. The causes of the subsequent rebellion are very complicated and are made a part of this article only as believed essential. What is essential was the U.S. involvement.

The Political Situation

General Santo Domingo Vila, a distinguished Colombia military man, went to the isthmus in November 1884 as a fiscal agent of the general government to examine contracts between the Panama Railroad Company and the state. During the course of political instability Vila was chosen president of the State of Panama, 7 January 1885, by the Constitutional Assembly of Colombia. Señors Aresomena and Vivas Leon were chosen or appointed first *designado* and second *designado*. The office and duties of the *designado* were similar to those of vice-president, and in the event of death or the absence of the president they would succeed successively to the presidency. The other officers of the state government, such as secretary of state, governor of Panama, and prefects, were appointed by the president. The commander-in-chief of the Colombian (national) forces was appointed from Bogota, and that office was filled by General Gonima.

The steamer *Boyaca*, which later on performed valuable service for the national government, was lying off Panama; it formed part of Gonima's military force and was commanded by Colonel Antonio de Ulloa. Intended for the revenue service of Colombia, the vessel had been built at Wilmington, Delaware, by the Pusey and Jones Company in 1883 and 1884. It was about the size of sea-going revenue cutters of the U.S. Navy and consequently was a staunch craft.

In February a portion of the national forces of Colombia stationed on the isthmus was sent to Buenaventura, the sea port of the State of Canca, which was about 300 miles south of Panama City. The intent was that they should help in suppressing the revolution then on-going in that state. On 1 March 1885, General Vila sailed with more national troops for Carthagena, located on the northern coast of Colombia, to help suppress the revolution then brewing in the State of Bolivar. That effectively reduced the number of federal troops in Panama and the disaffected of that state took the opportunity to also attempt a revolution.

Arosemena had succeeded to the presidency of Panama during the absence of Vila. On 16 March a former president of Panama, General Aizpuru, a leader of the Liberal party in the state, led a demonstration against the government. Arosemena took flight and refuge aboard the British ship *Heroine*, then lying off Panama. The demonstrators then took destructive vengeance against the railroad, breaking open cars, blocking switches, cutting telegraph wires and generally making a nuisance of themselves and their cause, whatever it was.[5] The affair caused the railroad to close down, which is what the disturbers wanted in the first place. General Gonima, upon learning of the demonstration by Aizpuru and his followers of the national military forces, proceeded by railway nearly to Panama City. Aizpuru, rather than face Gonima's troops, retired from the city, and Arosemena returned from his refuge aboard the British ship.

Now Colón, the city just vacated by Gonima, was without troops and a Haitian black named Prestan, the leader of a faction of the Liberal party, took advantage of the situation and seized the city. Colón was the main base for most of the U.S. citizens in Panama. There was no love lost by any of the members of the Liberal party with the *Americanos*. Members of each of the other political groups liberally hated them also. This bitterness was a cause to unite the various dissident factions. Fortunately it didn't.

On March 20, Arosemena resigned and, although Leon was next *designado*, Gonima declared himself "military and civil chief of Panama. "On 30 March General Gonima sent Colonel Ulloa, commanding the *Boyaca*, to Colón by train with some troops to put down Prestan's revolution. Because of circumstances, Ulloa had to disembark from the train at Monkey Hill, about two miles west of Colón. The numbers of both Prestan's and Ulloa's forces were each about 150 men, and after a short conflict Prestan was forced to retire to Colón and to the barricades he had had built there.

Back in Panama, things went from bad to worse for General Gonima. The loss of the troops sent to Colón left him with only about 100 soldiers to defend the city against General Aizpuru. On the same day that Ulloa defeated Prestan, Aizpuru defeated Gonima and the city of Panama changed hands yet one more time.

Aizpuru declared himself president of the State of Panama and proceeded to install his friends in all the political offices. Meanwhile, Ulloa in Colón with 100 troops held that city, but the rest of the zone of transit in the isthmus was held by the insurgents under Aizpuru.

This, then, was the situation when the U.S. naval force, with Marines aboard, arrived at Colón on the 11th and 15th of April, in two Pacific Mail Steamship Company vessels, the *City of Para* and the *Acapulco*. The main force for intervention was to be commanded by Commander Bowman H. McCalla, USN (see Appendix A).[6]

On 2 April 1885, McCalla had received orders to assemble a force of Marines and bluejackets, and then to proceed to the Isthmus of Panama to protect American lives and property. The most important piece of American property was the railroad. It was essential for continued passage, east-west and reverse. Otherwise crossing through the dense jungles of the isthmus was impossible for anything other than animal drawn carts, and the dangers inherent in that precluded normal human passage. Without that railroad, ships, crews and passengers would be forced to make the long and dangerous voyage around the tip of South America through the Straits of Magellan. There really wasn't much choice about whether the U.S. should intervene. By the year 1885, economic and political conditions made it mandatory.

3. Colombia and Panama

It was the first large armed intervention in Latin America by the United States and it would not be equaled in size for another 13 years. Before the entire project terminated, three Marine battalions would be formed and grouped into a brigade, the first such in Marine Corps history.[7] In 1885 a battalion was composed of about 250 Marines, with companies in the range of 50 officers and men, more or less. So the manpower numbers weren't enormous by today's standards, but they were for 1885. That was a time when the Marine Corps' total manpower was fewer than 2,000 officers and men. Additionally, in most landings, as was to be the case in this, they were supported by sailors from the various U.S. Naval ships in the area. The sailors usually managed the rapid firing guns of various types and calibers. Most landings by the U.S. in the 19th century utilized large components of sailors to support the always limited numbers of Marines.

United States naval forces, including Marines, had intervened in the isthmus twice before 1885 and would again in 1895, 1901, and 1902, while Panama was still a part of Colombia.[8]

McCalla was a rising star in the U.S. Navy. A graduate of the Naval Academy in 1864, he had served briefly in the Civil War and at sea for most of his naval service. In his final report on this intervention, he stated, "I proceeded to New York and reported to the commandant of the Navy-yard as the commanding officer of the force to be sent to Aspinwall, United States of Colombia." It was common to place a senior naval officer in charge of sea-borne interventions during the period. Fortunately, McCalla was that kind of officer who was very capable in any situation, including land operations. Marine officers were not considered, by the Navy, to be capable of more than mere troop handling on land and not much of anything aboard ship. Even at that, it was all too customary to assign a naval officer to command ashore over a Marine officer of equal rank, regardless of the situation.[9]

Major and Brevet Lieutenant Colonel Charles Heywood (see Appendix A), a future commandant, was the officer assigned to command the brigade of Marines. He was ably supported by Marine officers and enlisted men, many whose names had already or would later become legendary in the corps. Three hundred Marines were formed up in Florida, most coming from ship and shore companies, and later more from ship detachments in the vicinity of Panama. Within a few weeks they were reasonably well organized into units and they were ready for any eventuality. The sailors carried three-inch breech loading artillery and Gatling guns ashore to support the Marines in their appointed tasks. All in all, it was a very large enterprise for the corps at the time. Only the landing in Korea in 1871 came close to its size, but then only 109 Marines with 542 sailors took part.

Rear Admiral James E. Jouett, the operations overall commander, had already arrived on 10 April and his forces had immediately set to work to get the railroad running again. The following day Colonel Heywood and his battalion arrived at the isthmus. He received an order from Jouett dated 11 April 1885.

>Sir.
>
>Proceed to Panama with the battalion of Marines under your command, for the protection of American lives and property in that vicinity. The details of this service are left to your discretion.
>
>Panama is now in the hands of the revolutionary forces, and it is feared that if the place is attacked by the regular Colombian troops these revolutionists will attempt to destroy the city, or portions of it, by burning. As the burning of Panama would involve the destruction of much American and other foreign property, you will prevent it if possible.
>
>Please advise Captain Norton, commanding the United States ship *Shenandoah* now at Panama, of your arrival there.
>
>I enclose herewith a copy of my telegraphic instructions from the department, and also some extracts of a sworn protest by Mr. George A. Burt, general superintendent of the Panama Railroad Company, for your information.
>
>I have detailed a Gatling gun and a 12-pounder S.B. howitzer, with officers and crew, for service with your command.
>
>The officers are directed to report to you.
>
>>Very respectfully,
>>Jas. E. Jouett,
>>Rear-Admiral, Commanding U.S. Naval Forces on N.A. Station.
>
>Major Charles Heywood, U.S.M.C., Commanding Marine Battalion, Isthmus of Panama.

On the following day, 12 April, Heywood's Marines landed and immediately went to work establishing a strong defensive position. By the 13th Heywood had occupied the entire city of Panama and had Marine guards on the now running trains of the Panama Railroad. Though some rebels attacked some trains, a few well directed shots rapidly brought that activity to a close.

McCalla and his detachment had left New York on 7 April aboard the *Acapulco*, a Pacific Mail steamship. While at New York over 500 Marines and nearly 300 sailors were gathered together by McCalla. His orders were to proceed to Aspinwall (also known as Colón) and report to the senior naval officer present in connection with opening the transit and protecting the lives and property of American citizens.

Once at sea he immediately established a routine aboard ship for the troops. First were floating targets for rifle and rapid fire gun practice, followed by instructions by an assistant surgeon in first aid with bandaging and tourniquets, and in recommended sanitary procedures ashore. Each man carried 40 cartridges, a blanket roll with one change of clothing, a canteen, and a haversack. They were prepared for an immediate landing almost from the time the troops went aboard the *Acapulco*. As luck would have it, and it was good luck, after eight days at sea, on 15 April 1885, the ship was able to tie up at wharf No. 1 of the Panama Railroad Company at Aspinwall, which made unloading all that much easier.

Upon their arrival Jouett inspected McCalla's command and expressed himself as well pleased with its appearance. Admiral Jouett's flagship, the *Tennessee*, had carried the former Pensacola, Florida, Marine garrison which was led by Captain Robert L. Meade.[10] This force included Second Lieutenant Arthur H. Clarke, seven non-commissioned officers, 28 privates and two musicians, all of which were added to the force under McCalla's command.

By 15 April, the date McCalla's ship arrived, the trains were again running with Marine and Navy guards from Jouett's squadron. Two cars with armor plates, prepared under the direction of Lieutenant William W. Kimball, USN, were attached to the 11:00 hour train, in each direction. Each of the cars was armed with a Hotchkiss revolving cannon, one Gatling gun, and one 12-pounder howitzer.

Captain Meade's company of Marines and a force of bluejackets from the *Tennessee* were stationed at Matachin, a very turbulent center under the overall command of Lieutenant Robert E. Impey, USN. Then they were removed to Panama City.

Under orders issued by Admiral Jouett, dated 15 April, Commander McCalla assumed command of all the naval and Marine forces ashore. He also relieved the temporary forces at Colón and Matachin that same day in order that they might return to their respective ships. As he states in his report, "The force assigned to duty on the Isthmus was distributed as follows":

Aspinwall [Colón] Garrison

Captain John H. Higbee, U.S.M.C., in command of naval forces at Colón.

Post 1, Captain Richard S. Collum, U.S.M.C., Commanding.[11] This post commanded the water approach from the eastward, and the garrison was quartered in the building occupied by the mechanics of the Panama Railroad Company, near the hospital.

Post 2, Captain Francis H. Harrington, U.S.M.C., Commanding. This post was on the beach near the church, an eighth of a mile nearer the center of town than post 1.

Post 3, Lieutenant Theodore B. M. Mason, U.S.N., Commanding. This garrison was quartered in a series of six houses.

Post 4, Lieutenant Charles O. Allibone, U.S.N., Commanding. This garrison was quartered at the Pacific Mail Steamship Company's wharf and guarded the causeway or approach by land to Colón, and the wharves and property belonging to the steamship company.

The quarters for posts 1, 2, and 3 were furnished by the Panama Railroad Company, and those for No. 4 by the Pacific Mail Steamship Company.

The District of Matachin.

Matachin.

Post 1, Captain Robert W. Huntington, U.S.M.C., Commanding. The garrison was quartered in the railroad station, the officers having the paymaster's car on a siding assigned to them.

San Pablo.

Post 2, First Lieutenant George F. Elliott (see Appendix A), U.S.M.C., Commanding. The garrison at San Pablo was quartered in a fine house loaned by the courtesy of the director-general of the Panama Canal Company. The post at San Pablo was an important one, as it commanded the approaches to the Barbacoas iron bridge over the Chagres River. A guard tent was put up at either end, and a small earthwork commanded the bridge and approaches.

This post was established on the 16th of April, in compliance with the following telegram addressed to Captain Huntington, viz:

[Telegram]

Colón, April 16—4 p.m.

Captain Huntington,
Matachin:
Send 25 men and two officers back to San Pablo by special [train] to-night to guard Barbacoas Bridge over Chagres River. Commanding officer at San Pablo garrison must ask Chief of canal what barracks he is to occupy, as agreed to-day with the director-general.

B.H. McCalla.

The main garrison at Panama city was commanded by the brigade commander, Heywood. It was quartered in old freight buildings and the passenger station. The buildings all belonged to the canal company. The four companies of Marines were commanded by 14 officers distributed as follows:

Lt. Col. Charles Heywood, Commanding; 1st Lieut. H.G. Ellsworth, adjutant.
Company A. Capt. Edward P. Meeker, 2d Lieut. T.G. Fillette, with 51 men.
Company B. Capt. Louis E. Fagan, 1st Lieut. Jesup Nicholson, with 51 men.
Company C. Capt. Henry C. Cochrane, 1st Lieut. Frank L. Denny, 50 men.
Company D. 1st Lieut. Ottway C. Berryman, 2d Lieut. James A. Turner, 49 men.
Company E. Capt. Robert L. Meade, 2d Lieut. A.H. Clark, with 37 men.
First Lieutenant Allan C. Kelton, Brigade Quartermaster.
Assistant Surgeon Frederick N. Ogden, U.S.N.

Pacific Squadron

Shenandoah's Marine guard, 1st Lieut. Thomas N. Wood, with 20 men. An armored [railway] car, Hotchkiss Revolving cannon, one Gatling, one 12-pounder howitzer.

Lieutenant E.M. Hughes, U.S.N., Ensign J.H. Oliver with 60 bluejackets, from *Shenandoah.*

From the *Alliance,* Naval Cadet C.P. Plunkett, with 24 bluejackets.

From *Sawatara*, Junior Lieutenant F.E. Sawyer, U.S.N., with 24 bluejackets.

A total of 19 officers, 258 Marines, and 108 sailors; 385 in all.

Back at Pensacola, Captain James M.T. Young, USMC, was forming a third Marine battalion with help from the various ship detachments in the area as well as those still remaining at the station. When completed they would be added to Heywood's command, making the first known existence of a Marine brigade.

McCalla tells in his report of how he and two aides rode the train on the 17th of April, inspecting the rails and the garrisons of Matachin, San Pablo, and Panama, with Huntington, Elliott, and Heywood in command, respectively. While near Panama City, McCalla sent for the American consul-general, Mr. Adamson, to come to Camp Jouett, the site of the naval force at the railroad station. McCalla came to the conclusion that so long as Aizpuru remained in power no harm could be expected to the railroad, even though anarchy reigned along the line of transit. He speculated that when a large force was gathered together and sent to reclaim Panama City, the rebels, mainly made up of "men of bad character" from the various islands of the Caribbean, especially Haiti, would probably fire the city. Without a water supply the city would suffer greatly, as would the railroad buildings, and a disaster would seriously impede the transfer of freight traffic for several months, at least.

McCalla further relates that the day he visited the various posts, "a Spanish Negro had been seen hanging about within the lines at San Pablo" and that Elliott, who was told of the man's threats to blow up the garrison, promptly had him arrested. He was discovered to have a package of dynamite in his possession and was sent to Colón for confinement. On the 20th of April, McCalla transferred his headquarters from Colón to Panama.

That same day Captain Higbee was directed to order Captain Collum to proceed to Panama with his two companies, B and D, by the 3 o'clock train. After the arrival of these companies, they, with a Gatling from the *Alliance* and a howitzer from the *Swatara*, all under the command of Captain Collum, were quartered at night in cars at the new passenger station, extending their lines to the bridge crossing the railroad. The following day, 20 April, Captain McCalla and his two aides reconnoitered the city in order to become better acquainted with it. On the 22nd instructions were issued to the garrison at Camp Jouett detailing what his command was to do "in the event of it becoming necessary to occupy Panama." Condensed, the order simply stated that the Marines and sailors under Collum were to advance upon the city in three columns with dispersals of the force along the way. In the event of arson they were to put out the fires; in the event of resistance they were to disarm the rebels unless they happened to be of the national Colombian force or any units from the various foreign ships in the harbor which might be landed to protect their nationals.

Colombian national troops, about 700 of them, were approaching Panama City by the steamship *Boyaca* plus several other vessels. And General Aizpuru and his rebels were building barricades to receive them. McCalla notified Adamson, the consul-general, that his force would occupy the city in half an hour but put that off a bit "in order that the men might have their dinner comfortably." Within the next few hours he sent two telegrams, one to Lieutenant Allibone, his aide in Colón, requesting that Captain Higbee release all the force at Colón with all the guns to Panama, with "the utmost despatch." The second went to the force commander, Admiral Jouett, also in Colón, which said "send the reserve battalion of Marines to Panama by special [train]."

As soon as the landing boats from the *Shenandoah* appeared the signal was given for the entry of the Marines and Navy landing troops into Panama City. Equipped with powder and fuzes the U.S. forces were well prepared to blow buildings should that course seem necessary. "The several columns advanced without music, the Marines in two lines deployed for street fighting, the Gatling and field guns between the lines of Marines." Marines carried 40 rounds of ammunition. Probably enough to eliminate any interference they might have run into. The instructions given by McCalla were followed to a certain extent but with modifications as follows: "Captain Collum's force marched directly to the Plaza Santa Ana; Captain Reid's company and the Gatling were left to occupy the junction of the Chemin de la Savane, with the road leading to the hospital. The left column, which was to advance along the beach was cancelled."

The Gatling gun was mounted behind a sand bag constructed barricade in the Carrera de Ricuarte and trained on the curatel, a building which housed soldiers. Company C of the 1st Marine Battalion was at the Cable Company's office; Company E of the 1st Battalion under Ensign Horace M. Witzel, with 20 men and a Gatling, were at the sand-bag barricade; Company B was stationed at the consulate; Company A, 1st Battalion, was stationed at the Pacific Mail Company's office; and Lieutenant Hughes, USN, with 20 bluejackets and another Gatling, were stationed at the junction of the Carrera de Sucre and the Cathedral Plaza. Ensign James H. Oliver, USN, with 20 sailors and a 3 inch breech loading rifle, were stationed at the junction of Carrera de Sucre and the Carrera de Cordova. Captain Collum occupied the Plaza Santa Ana, the most important position in the city, with Company A, 2nd Battalion and Company D, 1st Battalion, and 40 bluejackets with two pieces of artillery. Lieutenant Junior Grade Frank E. Sawyer, USN, and Naval Cadet I. K. Seymour were in charge of the latter. First Lieutenant Ottway C. Berryman, USMC, being relieved of his post at the depot, then marched his command to the Plaza Santa Ana.

Lieutenant Allibone arrived with the garrison from Colón late afternoon, nearing 5 p.m. This consisted of Companies C and E, 2nd Battalion, and two sections of sailors with Gatling guns and small artillery. Company C was commanded by Captain George C. Reid, and E by Captain Francis H. Harrington, both USMC. The Gatlings were under the command of Lieutenant Badger, Naval Cadet Plunkett, and Gunner Walsh, all USN. The entire force was under the overall command of Lieutenant Allibone, USN. In the meantime, Marine Company A under Captain Edward P. Meeker and Company C, Captain William S. Muse, reinforced Colonel Heywood's column, and was quartered in the Pacific Mail Company's office. The second platoon of Meeker's company was sent to the Shuber Hotel.

In the early evening, some civilians in the Cathedral Plaza engaged in an argument in which several shots were exchanged. That altercation was smoothed out when the Gatlings were fired, albeit into the air, clearing the plaza in moments. Major Heywood organized patrols and no further disturbance was noted during the balance of the night.

Captain James M.T. Young arrived at 10:00 p.m. with the 100 Marines from the North Atlantic Squadron, the reserve battalion McCalla requested earlier in the day. The next morning that group relieved the various detachments at the barricade and the cable office. The morning of the 25th, Captain McCalla was approached by a representative of Aizpuru requesting that the naval force be withdrawn to Camp Jouett provided a guarantee was given that no barricades would be erected and that no street fighting would be permitted. At Aizpuru's request McCalla spoke with him that afternoon. An agreement was drawn up which basically outlined the following points: withdrawal to the railroad station and yards; guarantee by Aizpuru to protect civilians, Americans as well as other foreign nationals, no barricades to be erected, and finally that McCalla would take no part in any "political contest." McCalla signed and by 8:00 p.m. most of the naval force was withdrawn. The Plaza Santa Ana and the consulate were occupied, at the request of General Aizpuru, until 9:00 p.m., when they too were withdrawn, as agreed.

After the signing of the agreement, McCalla had the force in the Calle Sucre moved into the Carrera Narino; the barricade of sandbags was moved one block westward, and the 12-pounder howitzer was moved to the junction of the Carreras de Caldas and de Acevedo Gomez. The rest of the force in the Cathedral Plaza was formed into a parallelogram embracing the bay on two sides, the Carrera de Camillo Torres and Carrera Narino. Afterward, McCalla had published an order congratulating his troops on their "excellent conduct under trying circumstances."

On Sunday the 26th, a fight broke out between Jamaicans and Colombians at Paraiso, about 8 miles from Panama. On Monday the British Consul called upon Captain McCalla to help the British subjects, stating that 13 had been shot during the disturbances and that the "calaboose" was loaded with wounded men. Captain Reid was sent with his company to Paraiso on the 27th. It was found that the claims were greatly exaggerated, only three Jamaicans had been killed in a drunken brawl, a racial fight, and all parties had been drinking and carousing. The entire matter was soon settled.

On Tuesday morning, the 28th, the 700 members of the Colombian National Forces arrived in the bay aboard their various vessels. McCalla immediately prepared and sent a message to the commander-in-chief advising him that in order to protect U.S. citizens and protect the transit, his naval forces occupied the railroad station, and described the bounds. He asked that the National Forces not be landed within McCalla's lines, otherwise "I shall be most happy to place my personal services at your disposition."

Colónel Montoya, military and civil chief of the State of Panama, along with his subordinate, Colónel Reyes, the commander-in-chief, discussed potential landing sites with Captain McCalla's messenger, Lieutenant William H. Reeder. Later that afternoon, Admiral Jouett arrived at Panama and the day following held a conference with Reyes, Montoya and Aizpuru at the railroad office. The outcome of the meeting was an agreement for Aizpuru to surrender and dispersal of his rebel forces. That was accomplished, and on the 30th the National Force landed and marched into the city, receiving a salute from the assembled Marines and sailors of Captain Collum's force. Reyes halted his troops and returned the salute, then proceeded to the Presidential Palace where the Colombian national flag was raised, as it was also at Camp Jouett.

That same day the various naval forces from the U.S. ships returned to quarters. The following day, May 1, the four companies of the Second Battalion of Marines, two sections of the rifle battalion, and the Gatling battalion returned to Colón, Lieutenant Allibone relieving Lieutenant Charles E. Colahan of the command of the force at Colón. On the 7th of May elements of the First Battalion of Marines were sent to San Pablo and Colón. That night McCalla and the units under his command sailed for New York on the Pacific Mail steamship *Colón*, which arrived at said city on the 16th of May.

In McCalla's final report, dated 8 June 1885, describing the adventures of his forces during the period of the intervention, he followed it with his conclusions, which were a result of his observations "upon the Isthmus." It was a highly detailed report in which he enumerated the activities of practically everyone that took part in the expedition. Some of his directives, citations and rosters of Marines officers have been made a part of this article.

Regardless of the many accuracies of McCalla's report, the commandant, Colonel Charles G. McCawley (see Appendix A), was incensed at the attacks upon his beloved corps. His response was rapid and to the point. His men were designated as ships' guards mainly, with little if any money for training as gunners or for field training as infantry. Both men were correct and in a few years with more men like Charles Heywood, the ninth commandant, in place, the Marine Corps became what it had to be in the new age of the twentieth century.

The period of assemblage, approach, landing and completion of the task was from 2 April 1885 to 16 May 1885, when all sailors and most of the Marines boarded ship and sailed for New York to resume the duties they had been engaged in prior to sailing for Panama. A small detachment from the First Battalion of Marines was sent to San Pablo and Aspinwall as a continued presence and guard. For now it was all over; it covered a period of barely more than a month. And now over 100 years later it is barely mentioned in history. But it was an important milestone in the growth of the corps.

Mistakes were made; there was more movement than actual fighting; few Americans were hurt and within a very few days all serious problems were corrected. The so-called "brigade" was never really completed though formulated. What is important is that the Navy was planning big things then and for the future. Perhaps the landing and operation was small "peanuts" but it loomed large at the State Department, and if it hadn't been settled satisfactorily it would have continued to be a festering problem for some time in the future. As in so many instances before and after, the problem was suitably laid to rest by a combined Navy-Marine team.

Bocas del Toro

On March 7, 1895, Captain Bartlett J. Cromwell, aboard the cruiser *Atlanta*, anchored in the harbor of Bocas del Toro, Colombia, for the purpose of observing conditions, as fighting was in progress among government troops and some insurgent forces.

The following morning Captain Cromwell received a request to furnish an armed landing force for the protection of American lives and property. He granted this request and selected a "Sergeant's Guard of Marines," together with a company of bluejackets and a Gatling gun under Commander Edward D. Taussig, and despatched them ashore with instructions to protect the lives and property of foreigners. This uprising soon quieted, and the landing force was withdrawn the following day, the 9th, but the *Atlanta* remained in the vicinity for more than a month before leaving for other waters.

Slightly over six years had elapsed since the last landing by American armed forces on the isthmus before their presence was required because of a new revolution: or should one say a new outbreak of a continued revolution occurred in this troubled area. Apparently many residents of Panama were determined to gain its independence regardless of the number of years it took or the number of revolutions necessary.

In late 1901, the Liberal and National troops were engaged in a fierce struggle for the supremacy of authority, in the matter of establishing the State of Panama as a separate republic. This conflict endangered the lives and property of all foreign residents. Great Britain and France despatched naval vessels to the area for the protection of their nationals. The United States also sent several vessels of the navy to the isthmus for the same purpose. British interests were represented by HMS *Tribune*, while those of France were in care of the *Suchet*. The interests of the United States were entrusted to the *Iowa*, Captain Thomas Perry; the *Concord,* Commander Gottfried Blocklinger; *Marietta*, Commander Francis H. Delano, and the *Machias*, Lieutenant Commander Nathan Sargent.

The British and French ships were at Aspinwall (Colón), as were two of the American vessels, the *Machias* and *Marietta*, while the *Concord* and *Iowa* were on the opposite side, at Panama. The *Marietta* and *Concord* arrived on November 23, having been preceded by over a month by the other two ships. Captain Perry, having consulted with the American Consul, Hezekiah A. Gudger, and other officials, concluded that a landing force was necessary to protect the interests of his government. He therefore directed a battalion of Marines and seamen to make ready and, at 1540 on the 24th, they left the ship and proceeded on this duty. The Marines of the *Iowa* were under the command of Captain Albert S. McLemore, with Second Lieutenant Edward A. Greene as second in command, while those of the other ships were in the charge of noncommissioned officers. On the 25th the *Concord* also sent a battalion of Marines and seamen ashore, and both forces remained on this service until December 4, when they were withdrawn.

While these landings were taking place at Panama, other landings were being made at Aspinwall (Colón) from the *Machias* and *Marietta*. These forces landed on the 26th, and their composition—Marines and sailors—was the same as the force landed at Panama. Captain Perry, after despatching the landing forces ashore at Panama, proceeded to Aspinwall and, on November 28, held a conference aboard the *Marietta*, which was attended by the commanding officers of the British and French vessels, General Alban of the Colombian troops, and General de la Rosa of the Liberal army. At this conference it was agreed that the Liberal forces should demobilize, turn their arms over to the foreign naval authorities then present, and the city relinquished to General Alban's control. The transfer of authority took place the following day at 2:00 p.m., and was accompanied by appropriate ceremonies.

During the time that the American landing forces were ashore, they furnished guards of Marines for all trains of the Panama Railroad crossing the isthmus, the last guard being withdrawn at 10:00 a.m. on the 4 December 1901.

The cessation of hostilities brought about by Captain Perry in the previous November, was of short duration. Hardly six months had passed before the Liberal and government forces were again engaged in open warfare. Commander Henry McCrea, in the *Machias*, was ordered from Santo Domingo to the Isthmus of Panama, where he arrived on 12 April 1902 at Aspinwall. Here Commander McCrea visited the American consul, David R. Hand, and the same evening proceeded to Bocas del Toro, arriving there the following day. The Liberal forces were quite active in this vicinity, and Commander McCrea despatched several messages to the commander of these forces relative to the protection of American interests. An attack on the town being momentarily expected, which if carried out would endanger the lives and property of Americans, a guard of two officers and 28 men were landed on the 16th to furnish the necessary protection.

Early the following morning heavy firing was heard from shoreward, and that evening a boat was despatched ashore containing Surgeon F.M. Began and others to assist in carrying wounded Colombian soldiers within the lines established by the American landing force and in dressing their wounds. During the same afternoon the Liberal commander requested Commander McCrea to communicate with the government leaders, and if practicable arrange a capitulation for the Liberal forces. About 7:30 that evening the leaders of the opposing forces repaired aboard the *Machias*, and with Commander McCrea drew up the necessary agreement for the cessation of hostilities. Early the next morning, the 13th, the Marines and a company of sailors were sent ashore to be present at the surrender of the Liberal forces, which was done in accordance with the agreement signed the previous day, and the landing force, with the exception of the Marines, were withdrawn, the latter remaining until the 19th before returning to their ship.

About mid-afternoon on the 19th, the Colombian gunboat *Pinzon* and the transport *Marcellus* arrived, and it appeared that they were loaded with government troops. Their commander, General Gomez, was informed of the negotiations entered into by the Liberal and government forces ashore, and warned of the necessity of giving the required notice before beginning a bombardment of the town. As General Gomez did not order the Government ships to leave the harbor, Commander McCrea deemed it advisable to send another force ashore as a precaution in case fighting should be renewed. Accordingly, a party of two officers and 28 men were again landed in the town shortly after noon on the 20th. About 5:00 p.m. the Colombian transport went alongside the dock and disembarked its troops. The following morning, the 21st, the German steamer *Hercynia* arrived with additional Colombian troops, and they were landed at Old Bank. At the request of General Gomez, Commander McCrea sent his Marine guard ashore on the evening of the 21st to guard foreign interests during the evacuation of the Liberal forces. This unit returned aboard the following morning.

On the 23rd, Commander McCrea sailed for Aspinwall, where he remained until May 16, when he received cable orders to return to Bocas del Toro. He sailed immediately and arrived at the latter place about noon the 17th. However, this new difficulty was straightened out without the landing of another armed force, and the *Machias*, after cruising along the coast and stopping at different places, sailed for Cape Haitien on July 23. Before it sailed, however, Commander William P. Potter, in the *Ranger*, had arrived at Panama. Conditions in this city remained quiet until the middle of September, when it was necessary to send a landing party ashore for protection of foreigners. This party was first landed on the 18th, but withdrawn each night thereafter until the 23rd, when it was entirely withdrawn.

Conditions at Aspinwall were by no means tranquil. Commander Thomas C. McLean, in the *Cincinnati*, arrived at the latter place on the 15th of September. He found conditions such as to require the landing of an armed force to protect American interests. This force was landed on the 17th, and part of it was diverted to guard the trains crossing the isthmus, while the remainder protected lives and property in the city. It returned aboard each night and went ashore each morning until the 21st.

In the meantime the Navy Department had ordered the commandant of the Marine Corps to furnish an expeditionary battalion of his corps for service in Panama. This battalion, organized under orders of September 11, consisted of 13 officers and 325 enlisted men under the command of Lieutenant Colonel Benjamin R. Russell, USMC. It sailed on the *Panther* the 14th and arrived at Aspinwall on the 22nd.[12] The following day the battalion was landed, went

3. Colombia and Panama

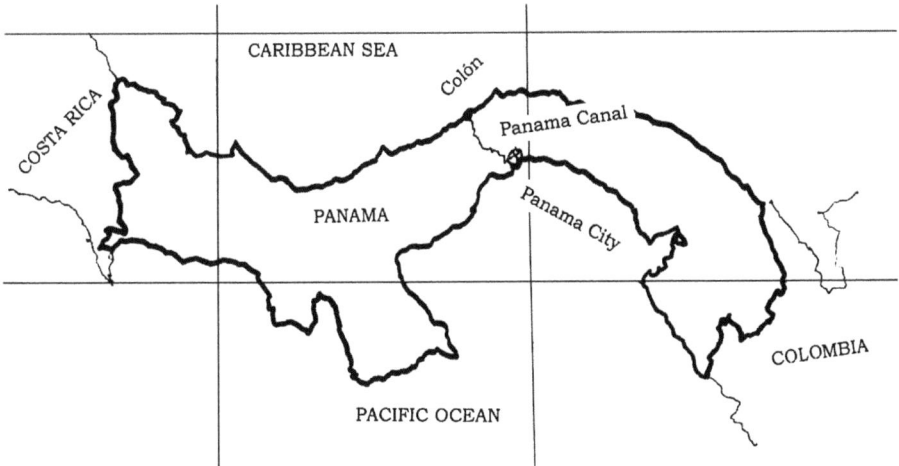

Map of Panama.

into camp and remained there until 16 November. On this date a part of the battalion was withdrawn, and on the 18th the entire force returned aboard the *Panther*.

A treaty, the Hay-Pauncefote, was negotiated and ratified by the United States Senate, 16 December 1901, which gave the United States alone the right to build and control an inter-oceanic canal across the Isthmus of Panama. In January 1903, still another treaty was negotiated, but it was not ratified by the Colombian Congress, possibly because it was hoped that settlement might be delayed until the concession of the company expired, and that then the payment from the United States would come directly to the Colombian government. The Congress, which had been specially called to ratify this treaty, adjourned on October 30, and four days later Panama declared its independence. The uprising to this declaration occurred at 6:00 p.m. on November 3, and the overthrow was accomplished without bloodshed. The organization of a new government was immediately started which was virtually recognized by the United States on the 6th of November.

Rumors of an intended revolution had persisted for some time prior to its actual occurrence, and the United States government had despatched several naval vessels to that locality to observe and report on conditions. The commanders of these vessels had received special instructions as to their actions and duties upon reaching the Isthmus, should an uprising occur or be in progress at the time.

The gunboat *Nashville* under Commander John Hubbard was the first of these vessels to arrive in the area. It reached Colón and came to anchor at

5:30 p.m. on November 2. Shortly before midnight the *Cartagena*, a Colombian troop ship, came in and anchored near the *Nashville*, and about 8:00 a.m. on the 3rd, troops disembarked, which numbered 500, including the general commanding. The destination of these troops was reported to be Panama City, but it was desirable that they not be permitted to proceed there, and the general commanding them was finally persuaded to that effect.

While these Colombian troops remained on shore almost anything could have happened. Quite a number of American citizens were in the city, an American consulate was located there, and it was a terminus for the American owned Panama railroad. As Commander Hubbard's instructions were to protect all American lives and interests, he landed the Marines from the *Nashville* shortly after noon of the 4th, under the command of Lieutenant Commander Horace M. Witzel, and they took up a position in the railroad office. This landing party returned aboard at about 7:00 p.m., but were landed again the following morning, the 5th.

On the evening of the 5th, the *Dixie*, under Commander Francis H. Delano, the second American ship to arrive at Colón, came in and anchored in the harbor. Shortly after its arrival, the Colombian troops sailed from Colón on the Royal Mail steamer *Orinoco*. Commander Hubbard and Commander Delano conferred relative to conditions on shore and as to future action on their part, and decided that a larger landing force was required for the protection of American interests. Accordingly, two companies of Marines, under command of Major John A. Lejeune (see Appendix A), were landed about 1955 on the 5th, relieving those from the *Nashville*. The latter force returned to its ship shortly after noon on the 6th.

At 2035 on the 6th, the *Nashville* left Colón for Porte Belle, arriving the following day. The *Dixie* remained at Colón. On the 15th a small detachment of Marines were sent ashore due to a slight disturbance on the Hamburg dock, but were withdrawn the following morning after a conference between the five Colombian commissioners, who had arrived earlier, and Rear Admiral Coghlan, on the *Mayflower*. However, the same evening (16th), Marines were again landed to act as a signal squad during the night, and continued this duty until the 8th of December. On this date Captain Norman G. Burton, Wirt McCreary and Second Lieutenant Fred A. Ramsey, USMC, and a part of Company B, Marine Battalion on the *Dixie*, were landed and proceeded to Empire (about 30 miles from Colón on the Panama Railroad), to establish a camp.[13] The same afternoon the remainder of the company was also landed, and on the 16th, the entire battalion under Major John A. Lejeune went into camp at Empire.

In the meantime other Marine organizations were being assembled at

Philadelphia, Pennsylvania, and other places for service in Panama. The *Prairie*, under Commander Albion V. Wadhams, sailed from Guantanamo Bay, Cuba, for Colón, on 11 December with a battalion of Marines under Major Lewis C. Lucas to augment the force already there, and arrived on the 13th.[14] The battalion was landed on the 24th and went into camp. The *Dixie* left Colón on 17 December for Philadelphia, where it embarked a regiment under Brigadier General Commandant George F. Elliott and sailed for Colón on the 28th.

The *Dixie* arrived at Colón the first part of January 1904, and on the 7th landed both battalions—the from the First Battalion, Second Regiment, under Major James E. Mahoney (see Appendix A), proceeding to Bas Obispo, and the Second Battalion, First Regiment, under Major Eli K. Cole, to Empire, Panama. The battalion which landed from the Prairie on December 24, was re-embarked on February 15, and returned to Guantanamo Bay, Cuba.[15]

From the time of the first landing on November 4, 1903, until January 21, 1914, with the exceptions previously noted, United States Marines were stationed on the Isthmus of Panama to guard the interests of the American government. On the latter date, all Marines were withdrawn.

4

CUBA

The United States, after considering its options, decided to intervene militarily into the ongoing Cuban rebellion against their Spanish overlords. This rebellion had been in progress for many years and now, in 1898, because it was Spain's last holding in the western world, they pulled out all the stops and were fighting with modern equipment against a badly armed populace.

The United States had a small army, a fair sized navy, and a citizenry overly anxious to prove that the nation was very important and to be taken seriously by the various nations of Europe. Spain was a pushover, especially its navy, which the U.S. Navy quickly disposed of both off Cuba and in Manila Bay in the far away Philippine Islands. The army's fight was a bit more difficult. The Spaniards were better armed than the U.S. Army. But somehow, the inconstant U.S. volunteers, though untrained, managed to defeat the Spanish regulars, whose navy was no longer in position to provide them with substantive support from Spain.

The Marines were a part of the action from the very beginning. When the battleship *Maine* was blown up on 15 February 1898 in the harbor of Havana, 28 members of the Marine detachment lost their lives. Private William Anthony, captain's orderly, was given credit for saving the captain's life.

The U.S. declared war and on 22 April 1898 the 1st Marine Expeditionary Battalion, commanded by Lt. Col. Robert W. Huntington[1] with 24 officers and 623 enlisted men, left New York aboard the USS *Panther* headed for Key West, Florida, and eventually Cuba. His forced was literally "dumped" and though marooned in a Florida swamp, Huntington set them to learning the tricks of their trade. On 4 May a naval appropriation act made available funds for 473 men to bring the corps' strength up to an approved 3,073 officers and men. A week later, on the 11th, Marines and seamen aboard the USS *Marblehead* cut the transoceanic cable off Cienfuegos, Cuba. The next day, Marines served the secondary batteries aboard U.S. warships during the bombardment of San Juan de Puerto Rico. On 31 May they were with Adm William T. Sampson's fleet when it bombarded the Spanish fortress, Morro Castle, at Santiago de Cuba.[2] Huntington and his men aboard the *Panther*, together with the Marine detachment from the USS *Oregon*, landed at Guantanamo on 10 June. Two days later, the 12th, the Marines from the USS *Texas* joined them.

Huntington formed his command into six companies, five of infantry and one equipped with 3-inch landing guns they had brought with them from the Brooklyn Navy Yard. They were the first troops to land on Cuba and would become an early target of the numerous Spanish army forces gathered about them. Because of some supreme stupidity by the captain of the *Panther*, Commander George C. Reiter, the man who dropped them off in the swamp, the Marines had great difficulty unloading their supplies. It should have been the responsibility of the ship's crew to do the unloading while the Marines were facing the enemy. In fact, because Reiter wasn't satisfied that his ship was riding the way he thought it should, he refused to allow them to unload their small arms ammunition, which he was using as ballast. When Bowman McCalla, the *Marblehead*'s captain learned this, he raised hell. McCalla and the Marines had been a close team in the Panama landing so many years before, and in China would be again. McCalla addressed Reiter: "Sir, Break out immediately and land with the crew of the *Panther*, 50,000 rounds of 6-mm. ammunition. In future, do not require Colonel Huntington to break out or land his stores with members of his command. Use your own officers and men for this purpose, and supply the Commanding Officer of Marines promptly with anything he may desire."[3]

Soon after, Huntington named his bivouac Camp McCalla. During the following four days and nights the Spaniards sniped and harassed the Marines. The Americans were also felled by the unbearable heat, which none were accustomed to. Two of the sniper's casualties, both dead, were the battalion's surgeon and its sergeant major, Henry Good. Huntington decided to end this by cutting off the enemy's water source at Cuzco Valley, about two miles from his position. With that, he selected a future commandant, Captain George F. Elliott, and gave him two rifle companies, C and D, and about 50 Cuban rebels led by Colonel Tomas, to do the job. Importantly, the nearby U.S. gunboat *Dolphin* was to supply gunfire support when and if called upon.

On 14 June, Elliott, with support from Company C's First Lieutenant Lewis C. Lucas, pushed the enemy back from the well. A high hill between the two opposing forces was the main object dominating the Spaniards' position and Elliott and his men took it. Several small groups of Marines, one led by First Lieutenant Lewis J. Magill and another by First Lieutenant James E. Mahoney, began gathering back with the main body on that hill.

Elliott sent a message to the *Dolphin* to begin shelling the enemy's positions, but evidently the ship never received that message. Private John FitzGerald, a native of Ireland, was called upon to signal the ship, which he did. As the *Dolphin* was preparing to send the shells, another Marine, Sergeant John H. Quick, was ordered to send a message, which he did. As he was signaling, they began to shell the Spaniards' positions.[4] By 2:00 p.m. the Spaniards' had their fill of those Marines and evacuated that position. A platoon from Company B advanced and occupied the position and captured an officer and 17 privates. They set to work at once to destroy the Cuzco Well. Spanish losses were about five, according to Elliott, though various other estimates went as high as 60 killed and 150 wounded. The Spanish reported that they had been attacked by 10,000 Americans. That was about the end of any further action in the Guantanamo area.

Huntington's Battalion abandoned its camp and boarded the USS *Resolute* on 5 August, and four days later set sail for the Isle of Pines. But as the unit was passing the port of Manzanilla, Captain Caspar F. Goodrich, senior officers present, decided the Marines would land and capture the port. On 13 August, as the Marines prepared to land, they were called off—an armistice had been proclaimed and that was the end of the war for Huntington and his men, who were shipped to Portsmouth, New Hampshire, arriving on 26 August 1898. Though each U.S. Navy warship had a detachment of Marines, their unit was the only Marine expeditionary force used during that war.[5]

On 26 July 1898, Spain, through the good offices of France, asked for conditions of peace. President William McKinley instituted the following terms:

1. Relinquishment by Spain of all claim of sovereignty over or title to Cuba.

2. In lieu of indemnity, cession to the United States by Spain of Puerto Rico and other islands in the West Indies, and cession of the island of Guam.

3. Retention of the city of Manila by the United States until the disposition of the Philippines should be determined in the peace treaty.

Largely, Spain agreed to those terms, and for the sum of 20 million dollars it relinquished the Philippines, Guam and Puerto Rico plus several smaller islands in the Caribbean. The treaty was proclaimed on 11 April 1899 and Cuba was formally transferred to the possession of the United States on 1 January 1899.

Within three months it was necessary to land Marines once again. Major William S. Muse with five officers and 75 Marines landed from the *Resolute* at Havana to guard the naval base during another disturbance.

Military Government Under General Leonard Wood, U.S.A.

From the close of 1898 to the spring of 1902, the independence of Cuba was postponed, and the country was under a military government of the United States. During most of 1899 General John R. Brooke was in command, but in December of that year he was succeeded by General Leonard Wood, with ultimate direction from Elihu Root, secretary of war, in Washington. Brooke relieved suffering, disbanded the Cuban army, provided revenue by reorganizing the customs service, took a census, pacified the island, and in general did the preliminary for General Wood, whose main task was to prepare Cuba for self-government.

In his message to Congress of 11 April 1898, McKinley made no reference to a Cuban "government," but spoke of the war between "Spain and the Cuban people," for the insurrectionists had not as yet been recognized even as belligerents. Naturally this attitude was not received with enthusiasm by the Cubans in the field; they had endured terrible hardships on behalf of independence, and saw no reason why they should not have it at once. They were suspicious of American intentions, despite the promise contained in the Joint Resolution of 20 April 1898, and it was clear that steps would have to be taken promptly to allay these suspicions. A law of elections must be promulgated. General Wood called an informal meeting of leading Cubans, at the same time submitting a plan prepared by Cuban officials under his direction. A majority of the notables favored a sweeping democratic suffrage, but the governor adopted the opinions of the minority which accorded with his own. His plan provided that all native-born Cuban men at least 21 years old might vote, if they could read and write, or had $250 worth of property, or had served in the Cuban army during the war. The secret ballot and other familiar American features were also called for in the new law.

The first, a municipal, election under this law met with fair success. General Wood then announced a fresh step in the direction of independence. Acting on orders from Washington, he issued an order, 25 July 1900, for the election of a convention "to frame and adopt a constitution for the people of Cuba, and, as a part thereof, to provide for and agree with the government of the United States upon the relations to exist between that government and the government of Cuba."

The requirement for determining the nature of relations with the United States "as a part" of their own constitution did not escape the notice of the Cuban politicians, but on assurances that the terms of the order would be modified, they elected delegates. The convention met at Havana on 5 November

1900, when General Wood read an order setting forth that the first duty of the delegates was to "frame and adopt a constitution," and then "formulate what, in your opinion, ought to be the relations between Cuba and the United States." Afterward, "the government of the United States will doubtless take such action on its part as shall lead to a final and authoritative agreement between the people of the two countries to the promotion of their common interests." So the delegates prepared a constitution and signed it on 21 February 1901.

Root's Proposals.

Although the new constitution paid slight attention to relations with the United States, Elihu Root posed no objection to it. In his annual report for 1901 he remarked:

> I do not fully agree with the wisdom of some of the provisions of this constitution; but it provides for a republican form of government; it was adopted after long and patient consideration and discussion; it represents the views of the delegates elected by the people of Cuba; and it contains no features which would justify the assertion that a government organized under it will not be one to which the United States may properly transfer the obligations for the protection of life and property under international law, assumed in the Treaty of Paris.

But strong as was his desire to prepare Cuba for self-government, Root was equally anxious to see Cuban-American relations formalized.[6]

As part of the Treaty of Paris, signed by the U.S. and Spain at the conclusion of what has become known as the Spanish-Cuban-American War, the U.S. agreed to occupy and help the Cubans develop a republican form of government. As part of that obligation, the first leaders of that group, including Brooke and later Wood, were anxious to succeed, as was the Congress of the U.S.

To follow Root's suggestions an amendment to the annual army appropriation bill, named after Connecticut Senator Orville H. Platt, basically limited the Cuban government to enter into no foreign agreements contrary to the interests of the U.S., and to grant to the U.S. the right to intervene in Cuban affairs if necessary to keep order. The actual eight amendments follow. They have been the cause of many years of unpleasant relations between the two nations.

The Platt Amendment

I. That the government of Cuba shall never enter into any treaty or other compact with any foreign power or powers which will impair or tend to impair the independence of Cuba, nor in any manner authorize or permit any foreign power or powers to obtain by colonization or for military or naval purposes or otherwise, lodgment in or control over any portion of said island.

II. That said government shall not assume or contract any public debt, to pay the interest upon which, and to make reasonable sinking fund provision for the ultimate discharge of which the ordinary revenues of the island, after defraying the current expenses of government, shall be inadequate.

III. That the government of Cuba consents that the United States may exercise the right to intervene for the preservation of Cuban independence, the maintenance of a government adequate for the protection of life, property, and individual liberty, and for discharging the obligations with respect to Cuba imposed by the Treaty of Paris on the United States, now to be assumed and undertaken by the government of Cuba.[7]

IV. That all acts of the United States in Cuba during its military occupancy thereof are ratified and validated, and all lawful rights acquired thereunder shall be maintained and protected.

V. That the government of Cuba will execute, and, as far as necessary extend, the plans already devised or other plans to be mutually agreed upon, for the sanitation of the cities of the island, to the end that a recurrence of epidemic and infectious diseases may be prevented, thereby assuring protection to the people and commerce of Cuba, as well as to the commerce of the southern ports of the United States and the people residing therein.

VI. That the Isle of Pines shall be omitted from the proposed constitutional boundaries of Cuba, the title thereto being left to future adjustment by treaty.

VII. That to enable the United States to maintain the independence of Cuba, and to protect the people thereof, as well as for its own defense, the government of Cuba will sell or lease to the United States lands necessary for coaling or naval stations at certain specified points, to be agreed upon with the president of the United States.

VIII. That by way of further assurance the government of Cuba will embody the foregoing provisions in a permanent treaty with the United States.

In Cuba only the most conservative elements accepted the amendment. Cubans in general complained bitterly that it allowed them less than independence and was therefore a violation of the promise contained in the Teller Amendment to the Joint Resolution.

This reaction would contain the seeds of numerous interventions in the years to come by the United States into the affairs of that island nation.

Before the little island republic of Cuba was ten years old, a revolution of considerable proportions was well underway. By the middle of the year 1906 its affairs were in a chaotic condition. The political parties, as usual, were the "ins" and the "outs," and the latter always were making efforts to be "in." At this time, the Moderates were in. They listed a registry of 432,313 voters, of whom 150,000 represented fraudulent names. Because of this, the Liberals refused to vote and instead turned to revolution to obtain their rights.

U.S. Consul-General Frank M. Steinhart, who was in charge during the absence of the U.S. minister, telegraphed to the State Department: "At the request of President Palma, send two ships, one to Havana, other to Cienfuegos: Government forces unable to quell rebellion, etc."

Though President Theodore Roosevelt authorized sending the ships, he believed "actual, immediate intervention to be out of the question." In fact Roosevelt was angry that the Cubans didn't seem able to control their own affairs and continued looking to Uncle Sam for assistance. More requests for aid included one from Palma asking for rapidly sending 2,000 to 3,000 men.

Palma went so far as to advise the State Department, through Steinhart, that unless the U.S. responded he would throw up his presidency and "deliver the island to the Americans." Finally, officials of the United States felt that there was a poor outlook for a change for the better, and that intervention was necessary to bring about order, protection to foreigners and the establishment of a stable regime to administer properly the affairs of government.

Although no special move had been made to intervene militarily, orders had been issued for the Marines to prepare, and in June 1906, a battalion had been placed aboard the USS *Dixie* for service in Caribbean waters. It was augmented in July and again in early September with an additional two officers and 110 enlisted Marines. Meanwhile, on the 13th of that month, the Palma government, panic-stricken, begged the American chargé d'affaires Sleeper to have Marines landed. Sleeper apparently was not aware of President Roosevelt's intentions, because he directed the captain of the USS *Denver* to have troops landed. A detachment of Marines and seamen, including six officers and 124 enlisted, were landed under the command of Lieutenant Commander Marcus L. Miller and hoisted the American flag over the fortress La Fuerza. A few hours later, when the U.S. State Department got wind of what happened, Miller and his command were ordered to withdraw, which they did the following morning. No matter that the landing was contrary to Roosevelt's desires, the rebels ceased hostilities and offered to disband all their soldiers.[8]

However, detachments of Marines and sailors from the USS *Dixie* and *Marietta* landed at Cienfuegos on 14 September to protect American-owned plantations during that period of political unrest. The situation was considered very bad at that town and the following day 35 sailors led by Lieutenant John V. Klemann landed from the *Marietta*.[9] Four days later, Major Albertus W. Catlin with a Marine battalion landed at that same place for the same reasons.[10]

All preliminary steps having been completed, the U.S. Marine Headquarters was directed, on September 14, to assemble three battalions of Marines for duty in the troubled area and, on the 25th of the same month, two additional battalions. The first three battalions sailed on the *Tacoma*, *Newark*, and

Minneapolis on September 16th, 17th, and 18th respectively. The additional two battalions sailed on the *Prairie*, *Texas*, and *Brooklyn* on October 1st and 2d respectively. The *Dixie* transported one company of four officers and 123 men from San Juan to Havana to complete the quota of the battalions. On the 18th, First Lieutenant William E. Parker led a group of 50 Marines from the *Dixie* ashore at Cienfuegos to guard the Constancia sugar plantation. Another 25 Marines under the command of Second Lieutenant Ralph L. Shepard landed from the *Dixie* to guard the Soledad plantation. Major Albertus Catlin, in command of the *Dixie* Marines, transferred his headquarters, four officers and 125 Marines to the Hormiguero sugar plantation.

The 25 remaining Marines aboard the *Dixie* were then transferred to the USS *Marietta* for temporary duty. On the 21st, Lieutenant John V. Klemann led 32 Marines and sailors ashore to protect the railroad at Sagua la Grande. This same group moved aboard the *Marietta* to Cienfuegos and on the 25th went ashore to protect the railroad at Palmira, still led by Klemann with 22 Marines and 64 sailors. They were later relieved by two officers and 51 Marines from Catlin's battalion.

While this movement was in process, the Atlantic Fleet assembled its Marine guards (804 officers and men) aboard the *Kentucky* and *Indiana* on September 24 and despatched them to Havana. This latter force, together with the five battalions mentioned before, gave a total strength of 97 officers and 2,795 men, which was organized into the First Provisional Brigade with Colonel Littleton W. T. Waller (see Appendix A), commanding. This unit functioned under naval jurisdiction until 1 November 1906. Prior to this date many of the Marine guards had been returned to their respective ships or sent to stations in the United States.[11]

Meanwhile, President Palma refused to cooperate with anything suggested by the American representative, Howard Taft, and resigned his position effective on September 28. The Cuban Congress was ineffective and no official action was taken. That left the U.S. without a central government to deal with and Roosevelt ordered Taft to land American forces and establish a provisional government. Before Palma resigned he asked that Americans place a guard over the Cuban treasury. Second Lieutenant Gerard M. Kincaid and 30 Marines were sent ashore for that purpose on September 28.

The two battalions of Marines from Philadelphia and Norfolk, still aboard ships in Havana Harbor, had been organized as the First Regiment of Marines, about 500 men, under the command of Lieutenant Colonel George Barnett (see Appendix A). They were now under orders to prepare to land. About 2,000 Marines landed at Havana; some went to Camp Colombia, about seven miles away, while Barnett's men went to Cienfuegos on the 30th. Barnett was in command of all naval forces in the community. On the 1st he sent one officer and 50 Marines to relieve the detachment at Constancia, two officers and 75 Marines to Soledad, and company to occupy Santa Clara. A few days later he dispersed an officer and 25 Marines each to occupy Arriete, Santo Domingo, and Esperanza. Detachments of 11 Marines were sent to both San Marcos and Caunao. Their orders were general: to protect the railroads. They were to live in some buildings nearby or railway cars, or in tents. Later small detachments were sent to Ranchuelo, Manicaragua, Cruces, and Trinidad.

The arrival of Marines at Santa Clara was just in time to prevent serious disturbances by several thousand rebels in that province. Conditions everywhere were soon returning to normal under the protection of the Marines.

Meanwhile, on September 30, a detachment of five officers and 151 Marines under the command of Captain William C. Harllee was sent by naval vessel to Neuvitas, where it arrived and on October 4 disembarked.[12] That night they camped on the beach and the following day two officers and 102 Marines went by rail to Camaguey to occupy that town. Second Lieutenant Robert L. Denig with the remainder of the detachment remained at Neuvitas.[13]

Colonel Waller was designated by the commandant to command all Marines in Cuba and to organize them into a provisional brigade. He arrived at Havana on October 1 and established his headquarters at Camp Colombia. There, he organized the brigade with the following units and commanders:

First Regiment: Lieutenant Colonel George Barnett
    First Battalion of 4 companies, Major Theodore P. Kane
    Second Battalion of 4 companies, Major Dion Williams
    Third Battalion of 3 companies, Major Edward R. Lowndes
    Fourth (separate) Battalion of 3 companies, Major Albertus W. Catlin

Second Regiment: Lieutenant Colonel Franklin J. Moses
    First Battalion of 6 companies, Major Wendell C. Neville (see Appendix A)
    Second Battalion of 3 companies, Captain William N. McKelvey
    Third Battalion of 4 companies, Captain Phillip M. Bannon

Conditions in Pinar del Rio and Havana Provinces continued to cause considerable concern. On 3 October, Taft, greatly concerned, ordered a detachment of 4 officers and 207 Marines sent to occupy that town. Captain Logan Feland (see Appendix A) led the company to Guines. A battalion which had sailed on the *Prairie* arrived at Havana on October 6 and was added to the brigade reserve at Camp Colombia. Major Lowndes Third Battalion arrived at Havana on October 8 and was added to the Camp Colombia reserve.

Two officers and 50 Marines landed October 11 at Baracoa and established a regular rail station. Captain Harold C. Reisinger landed at Santiago with his detachment and on October 23 went by rail to Guantanamo City to protect Americans in that vicinity. The village of Bejucal was occupied by a detachment, and 50 Marines on 19 October and one officer with 25 Marines was sent to Nueva Gerona on the Isle of Pines on October 22. Several naval ship detachments were landed and Major Wendell C. Neville formed them into a reserve force at Havana. By the 27th the Marine brigade reached its maximum strength with 100 officers and 2,800 Marines. On that date the distribution was as follows[14]:

Station	Officers	Enlisted Men
Camp Colombia	50	1133
Pinar del Rio	5	207
Bejucal	2	50
Guines	3	103
Santo Domingo	5	105
Sagua la Grande	1	50
Santa Clara	3	87
Ranchuelo	4	101
Cruces	1	50
Hormiguero	6	182
Arrite	1	25
Palmira	2	78
Constancia	3	50
Cienfuegos	13	267
Caunao	0	11
Soledad	1	51
Casilda	1	25
Sancti Spiritus	3	98
Camaguey	3	110
Neuvitas	2	48
Guantanamo	2	47
Baracoa	3	31
Nueva Gerona	1	25
Manicaragua	1	25

Most of the trouble from the insurrectionists, especially in Santa Clara Province, settled down with a Marine regiment in residence. A few drunken rebels terrorized Camaguey but the Marines under Captain Harllee soon quieted them down and sent them on their way. At Palmira, Barnett and Steinhart became involved when rebels uninstalled government officials and installed their own selection. That was soon turned completely around. Rebels gave up their weapons in Guines, but wouldn't disperse. The problem was the local police, so Captain Feland disarmed them and the rebels dispersed. Feland was so well-liked by the local officials that when he was going to be removed, they made a special request that he remain, and he did.

United States Army units from Newport News began arriving on October 10. The secretary of war commented in his annual report dated 1906: "The Army landed without opposition." The Navy ships landed Marines about a month prior to the U.S. Army's arrival, so no opponents were there.

At the urgent request of the commandant, Marines on duty in Cuba were transferred back to their ships or returned to the United States as rapidly as their duties could be assumed by the U.S. Army. Nearly 600 Marines, officers and men were returned to the United States on or about October 22. On November 1, Col. Waller was returned to the States and Lt. Col. Franklin J. Moses was his replacement. On 1 December 1906, the First Provisional Regiment of Marines occupied stations as follows[15]:

Station	*Unit*	*Commanding*	*Strength*	
			Off.	*Enl.*
Camp Colombia	HQDS	Col. F. J. Moses	22	287
Manzanillo	1/1 & Co. B	Maj. T. P. Kane	5	74
Santo Domingo	3/1 & Co. I	Maj. A. W. Catlin	3	54
Guines	Detch. Co. H	Capt. L. Feland	3	33
Neuvitas	Co. H	Capt. George C. Thorpe	3	77
Sancti Spiritus	Co. D	Capt. Wirt McCreary	3	93
Palmira	Co. E	Capt. David D. Porter	4	44
Hormiguero	Detch. Co. E	2d Lt. Henry S. Green	1	21
Isle of Pines	Detch. Co. H	2d Lt. Robert Tittoni	1	25
San Marcos	Detch. Co. I	Sgt. B. E. Stingle	0	8
Trinidad	Co. K	Capt. Philip S. Brown	3	91
Lajas	Co. L	Capt. Charles S. Hill	4	101
Baracoa	Co. M	Capt Henry C. Davis	3	52

As late as 1 October 1907, 39 Marine officers and 891 enlisted Marines still remained in Cuba.[16]

On 1 November 1906, the First Provisional Brigade was disbanded, the First Provisional Regiment formed therefrom, and led by future commandant Lt. Col. George Barnett, was detached for duty with the Army of Cuban Pacification under Army jurisdiction. It remained on such duty until 23 January 1909, when the regiment returned to the United States.

Meanwhile, as the army was organizing itself for a protracted occupation, the Marines were busy disarming the rebels. It was a less than pleasant job. According to a letter from First Lieutenant William P. Upshur to his father: "We went to the station to receive the rebels who came in to surrender ... we have the dirty rabble of Negroes armed with every type of antiquated weapon. We are living on hardtack, coffee, and canned beef (Armour's) and I think the food is excellent, the people are harmless, and you wouldn't give them another thought. If you could only see these 'spiketys,' our detachment could clear the island of them in a jiffy."[17]

In another scene, Major Albertus Catlin described what he witnessed while in the capital of the eastern province, Camagüey. There, as the Marines were processing the disarming of rebels:

> A rebel column of 3,000 men was coming through. Twenty-five Marines had the job of collecting their weapons and several hundred insurgents were disarmed. A villainous-looking negro captain came riding up on horseback, at the head of a bunch of ruffians. The sergeant in command stepped up and ordered him to dismount and disarm. By way of reply, the captain drew and cocked his revolver. The sergeant promptly clubbed his rifle and smashed the stock over the rebel's hard head, and the party threw down their arms.

Though the rebels came in, surrendered, and seemed to be returned to peaceable tasks, roughly only 700 ancient rusted pieces were accumulated, and that included machetes. Weapons would be needed once again when another revolution would happen. William Howard Taft, soon to be president, was relieved as provisional governor and returned to the United States. He was replaced on October 12 by Charles Magoon.

The years of Magoon's governorship were a massive mistake. He allowed many individuals to make a mockery of the settlement, though he personally probably was reasonably honest. In fact, Frank Steinhart, soon to be very close to Magoon, became the director of Havana Electric, a company which in short order earned the hatred of most Cubans. Several army officers had been appointed by Roosevelt to assist Magoon, and each was soon sadly disgusted. One, Robert L. Bullard, later to become a most famous general, was appointed as an aide to Magoon. As soon as he was able, he managed a transfer and announced that the U.S. military would have to return to Cuba soon enough.

President Theodore (Teddy) Roosevelt, in his message to Congress on 3 December 1906, wrote: "It was owing in large part to the General Board that the Navy was able at the outset to meet the Cuban crisis with such instant efficiency; ship after ship appearing on the shortest notice at any threatened point, while the Marine Corps in particular performed indispensable service."

American troops remained in Cuba until 1909 but they would return, sooner than expected.[18]

After the withdrawal of the Army of Cuban Pacification in 1909, economic considerations became the important part of the policy of the U.S. State Department. United States citizens had much money invested in Cuban plantations. That led to a more careful observation of ongoing situations in that island nation. Indeed, the political machinations in Cuba brought about unbelievable depths of inefficiency and corruption, especially the latter. Veterans of the late Spanish war were pushed out of government and by 1912 most were ready to rebel against the debauched Magoon leadership.

The Second Regiment, commanded by Colonel Franklin J. Moses, was formed at Philadelphia on 9 March 1911 as part of the 1st Provisional Brigade.[19] It was designed for duty in Cuba because of internal disorder which threatened U.S. interests. They immediately board the USS *Dixie* and sailed for Guantanamo, arriving on the 15th. Within three months order was restored on the island and in June the regiment returned to the U.S. where it was disbanded on 14 June.[20]

The following year, 1912, another serious problem arose in the eastern Oriente Province. Demands from Negroes by their leader, Evaristo Estenoz, for an independent party along their racial lines were thwarted by the politicians in Havana. The party in power, the Liberals, needed the vote of the Negroes to stay in power, consequently they weren't about to allow a separate party for Negroes; even the Negro Liberals voted against that idea. Thirty percent of the province was composed of Negroes and they had been the mainstays of the fight for independence from Spain, so they weren't going to take this lying down. In May 1912, armed Negroes rose in Havana, Santa Clara, and Oriente Provinces, and serious outbreaks of violence occurred in the vicinity of Guantanamo and Santiago. The government was able to resist most of the problems. However, the most serious problem was that Estenoz wanted the U.S. to physically intervene, and he ordered the destruction of American owned property. If that wasn't sufficient to impress the U.S., his rebels were to then begin killing white people.[21]

The American minister to Cuba, Mr. Beaupré, recommended that a U.S. battleship force with a large contingent of Marines be posted in Cuban waters. That force was the Second Provisional Regiment commanded by Colonel James E. Mahoney, had 40 officers and 1,252 enlisted Marines aboard nine warships, and was headed for Guantanamo on May 25. On June 2, the town of La Maya with 4,000 inhabitants was burnt to the ground. American owned corporations began howling for protection. In the meantime, the USS *Prairie* with the First Provisional Regiment of Marines aboard, commanded by Colonel Lincoln Karmany, was on its way to Cuba on May 28. The regiment had 32 officers and 777 enlisted Marines. It was composed of a cadre from the Advanced Base Battalion at Philadelphia on May 23.[22]

The first landing was by Company A of Karmany's command, landing from the *Paducah* on June 7 at Santiago to protect American owned mines in that vicinity. Their ultimate stop was at El Cobre, Puerto Sal, and Hermantanas essentially to protect the Daiquiri Mines near Siboney. That company wasn't strong enough for the task at hand and on June 8, 125 more Marines arrived in that vicinity. On the night of June 9–10 a detachment of Marines at El Cuero was attacked by the rebels, without a loss to either side. On June 10,

Lieutenant Colonel John A. Lejeune was sent to Santiago to assume command of all Marines in that district.[23]

Another company was sent to Manzanillo where conditions were reported to be very threatening. The Central Teresa Sugar Company, American owned, requested protection, and Company H, led by Captain Frederick L. Bradman, was assigned there. The balance of the regiment was landed at Guantanamo. From there, after June 5 it was moved into the inland areas. Three companies commanded by Lieutenant Colonel Lewis C. Lucas went to the general vicinity of Guantanamo City but were split up and sent around the immediate neighborhood. In the meantime, Mahoney's 1st Battalion was sent to Guantanamo, and the 2d Battalion to Havana, arriving on the 10th of June.

By this time some sailors from the USS *Nashville* were landed at Nipe Bay and provided protection to the Spanish-American Iron Company. A few days later a Marine detachment from the USS *Ohio* was sent to relieve them. Early in July, Company E of the 2d Regiment relieved them. All trains running in the eastern part of Cuba were protected by Marine guards. In the meantime, various other foreign nationals requested and were provided protection by American Marines. Most were British, Brazilian or French nationals.

The Cuban government offered the rebels an amnesty if they surrendered by June 22d. Though many turned themselves in, Estenoz with a large group continued to annoy the vicinity of Soledad and San José. Estenoz was killed on June 26, and soon afterward the rest of the holdouts turned themselves in.

Colonel Mahoney's Companies B, D, and E helped quell the revolt. Within two months peace on the island was restored and the Negro Rebellion of 1912 was over. On 1 August the 2d Provisional Regiment was deactivated and its personnel transferred to the 1st Provisional Regiment or returned to the United States. Meanwhile, the Marines were turning over their duties to Cubans, and on 1 August the 1st Provisional Regiment departed Camp Meyer, Guantanamo Bay, and proceeded to Philadelphia aboard the USS *Prairie*, arriving by 5 August, and that regiment was deactivated. Incidentally, the *Ferrocarril Nacional de Cuba*, the national railroad company, sent the U.S. a bill for tickets for each and every Marine guard who rode the rails. No evidence surfaced whether it was paid.

The next time the U.S. militarily intervened in Cuba was when the Liberal Party revolted in the fall of 1916, and the rebels began destroying American property, especially on the sugar plantations. That product, now that the U.S. was also nearly involved in the war, was of greatest importance, so the U.S. responded in February 1917 by sending warships to Guantanamo Bay. This became known as the Sugar Intervention, 1917–1922. According to U.S. Navy reports, by January, 300 Marines were in Cuba and another 100 were on the

The 7th Marine Regiment fighting in a Cuban jungle in October 1917.

way. On 12 January the 55th Company of Marines arrived at Guacanayabo Bay aboard the USS *Maine*, prepared to land to protect American interests at any given moment.

The battleships of Division Five—*Connecticut*, *Michigan*, and *South Carolina*—dropped anchor early that month. But it wasn't until the 25th that 80 Marines led by Major Charles H. Lyman, as part of a naval landing force from those ships, moved into Guantanamo City.[24] From there they marched inland about a dozen miles to protect the sugar companies' mills and plantation. Also on that date, a detachment of 220 Marines, which included the 24th Company from the USS *Montana* led by Captain Harry Schmidt, also moved into that city to join the other group.[25] On March 1st two more warships, the *New York* and the *Machias*, arrived and added their landing forces to those already on the ground. Two days later, Marines from the *New York* and the *South Carolina* moved into the interior of Oriente Province to suppress rebel activity. On that date, the 3d, another detachment was sent inland to guard the Rio Cauto Estate, 20 miles northeast on Manzanillo, where serious losses had been reported. A week later the 55th Company, also just in from Haiti, took over that job, relieving the smaller unit to return to their ship. From this time forward, the month of March saw an enormous number of Americans arriving

Top: Marines posing for a photograph in Cuba in 1912. *Bottom:* Marines on patrol in Cuba, c. 1917.

and landing in Cuba. The Marines' main task would be to preserve American lives and property while the Cuban army chased the rebels.

From Haiti, where many Marines had been engaged since 1915, the 7th, 17th and 20th Companies embarked aboard the USS *Hancock* for service in Cuba. A few days later the Marine detachments aboard the USS *Texas* and those from the *South Carolina* landed at Rio Canto to protect American owned sugar plantations. This was followed the next day when eight officers and 144 enlisted Marines landed from the USS *Olympia* at Santiago to protect the El Cobre mines; then on the 9th, at Santiago, the 49th and 51st Companies landed from the USS *Jupiter* to protect American lives and properties, followed that same day when 11 officers and 111 Marines and sailors from the *Montana* landed at Guantanamo City for the same reason. More Marines from the 43d Company landed at Santiago on the 10th; more on the 12th from the *Machias* to San Geronimo, Banes, and Boqueron for the same reason. A week went by before a group of seven officers and 92 Marines and sailors landed from the *Olympia* to help out at Guantanamo City. Then the following day, the 20th of March, the 43d Company disembarked from the USS *Ontario* at Daiquiri. This continued on the 22d when the 55th Company landed at Guantanamo Bay.

On the 20th of March a large group of insurgents was reported in the vicinity of the El Cobre mines and to meet the situation, the 43d Company was sent to Daiquiri to guard the Spanish-American iron mines and the La Playa ore docks. At this same time, the insurgents were in strength around Nipe and Nuevitas Bays, where there still were valuable American properties. Around Nipe rebels were holding up trains, robbing stores, and attacking the town of Nipe Bay. The few Marines and sailors from the *Machias* had real trouble trying to handle the situation, and on the 31st the 55th Company was transferred to their aid. That unit established posts all about that territory. The *Machias* group was withdrawn back to its ship on the 11th of April. The 55th would remain there only until it was withdrawn on 25 May for service with the 5th Regiment in France.[26] It was one of the last Marine units to leave Cuba. This was all the activity for the Marines and seamen in Cuba until August. So successful had been the Marines, and now so many were needed for the brigade in France, most of them were withdrawn from Cuba.

In July 1917, the situation in Cuba was again considered serious because of reports that German agents were fermenting trouble. This was after the 5th Regiment had sailed for France and several other Marine units had landed at St. Croix, the Virgin Islands, which the U.S. had just purchased from Denmark. The corps' personnel demands were making life miserable for the leadership. Developing enough Marines, in fact, finding enough Marines to occupy every billet necessary was becoming a major burden. There were Marines in "every clime and place," including those in China, and at other various embassies throughout the civilized (and not so civilized) world. Every capital ship in the U.S. Navy had Marine detachments, as did most every naval base on the American continent. This was in addition to the enormous needs of the 4th Marine Brigade in France, which was engaged in a variety of conditions.

It was soon confirmed that there truly were German agents in that country backing the rebels in sabotaging sugar-producing installations. The first decision was to send a U.S. Army unit of cavalry down there for anti-guerrilla operations. That was soon a non-actionable decision when the Army, unable to supply the troops, backed off. It was decided that a regiment of Marines would instead be sent. On 21 August, Colonel Melville Shaw and his newly created 7th Marine Regiment embarked aboard the *Prairie* at Philadelphia bound for service in Cuba.[27]

That regiment was encamped at Guantanamo Bay, where they underwent a two month training period. Late in October several of the companies were sent to occupy important centers in the sugar-growing areas. The 37th and 72d Companies, under the command of Major Frank Halford, were stationed at Camaguey.[28] The 59th and 86th Companies went into camp at the famous San Juan Hill which lay just outside Santiago. The Regimental Headquarters also moved to that district in November. The 90th Company was sent to Engenio Confluente, which lays near Guantanamo City, the 93d Company to Central la Union and San Luis. Two more companies arrived from Quantico in November, of which the 94th Company was sent to Bayamo on 11 December.

It was decided that more Marines were needed in Cuba. On 25 December the newly created 9th Marine Regiment arrived at Guantanamo Bay aboard the USS *Von Steuben*. With the addition of a headquarters, it was designated the 3d Brigade and commanded by Colonel James E. Mahoney, who arrived on the 24th of December.

Somehow, the corps managed to produce another two regiments, the 8th and 9th, both of which would remain within the American world. One of them, the 9th, would also appear at Guantanamo Bay on 25 December 1917. Lieutenant Colonel Frederick L. Bradman commanded the 9th Marines.[29] The brigade headquarters and the 9th Marine Regiment would remain at Guantanamo Bay until 31 July 1918 when, except for two companies, it was transferred to Galveston, Texas, for duty with the 8th Regiment. The brigade was resumed when Colonel Thomas C. Treadwell with the 1st Regiment of Marines arrived aboard the USS *Hancock* at Guantanamo Bay on 8 November 1918 and was designated the 6th Brigade.[30] The brigade was joined on 26 January 1919 by a hero of the 4th Brigade, Major Julian C. Smith, and the Second

Machine Gun Battalion. Four companies of the 7th Regiment were transferred to Haiti on 25 March 1919 to aid in suppressing "bandits" in their own country.

Treadwell and the 6th Brigade began a rotation back to the U.S. in May 1919, which was followed by Smith and the 2d Machine Gun Battalion in June. The 6th Brigade and 1st Marine Regiment were disbanded. However, the 7th Regiment remained in Cuba until August 1919, when it was reduced to a two battalion unit. Those two battalions were returned to the U.S. on 6 February 1922. Marines then in Cuba totaled 350, and the initial excuse that they were there to protect Cuba from German intervention was rather slender by that date. On 6 February 1922 the last Marines withdrew to their base at Guantanamo Bay.

Once again the U.S. government considered interference in Cuban affairs in the year 1933. President Gerado Machado was deposed and had to leave the country. However, the new U.S. administration decided to maintain "Hands Off."

The final interference in Cuba by the United States happened in 1961. That was when President Eisenhower, supported by his successor, President Kennedy, decided to upset the recent revolution in Cuba. That was when a far left group under the command of Fidel Castro, eventually to proclaim a communist government, took control. The U.S. Marines were only concerned when the U.S. government made decisions, to invade, and to not invade. They did not make those decisions.

5

HAITI

The earliest record I have of a U.S. intervention in Haiti occurred on 2 June 1891 when the Marine detachment led by First Lieutenant George T. Bates aboard the USS *Kearsarge* landed on Navassa Island, located just west of Haiti between it and the island of Jamaica. An American company engaged in removing guano was having difficulties with its Negro laborers; in fact the local Americans were seriously threatened. The Marines remained ashore until the 20th, when the difficulties terminated.[1]

Secretary of State William Jennings Bryan and his aides had made several efforts to put Haiti directly under U.S. control in 1914. The governors of that small island republic repeatedly avoided making any commitments that would allow the giant from the north any more domination than currently existed over their affairs. Several times during the period, British, French, and German vessels had landed their Marines and seamen to protect their own citizens in Haiti. This was contrary to the Roosevelt Corollary to the Monroe Doctrine, and with trouble brewing loudly in Europe, the U.S. agents were anxious to end any further European interference.[2]

Haiti, like Santo Domingo, was constantly in debt, and both had fallen behind in payment of their debt to various nations. The newly formed 5th Regiment of Marines was, at this time, sailing off the coast of Santo Domingo and when several actions by rebels constituted problems, they were landed at Port-au-Prince on 31 October 1914. In a few weeks the situation cleared up considerably, and on 23 November the regiment embarked and went back to sailing in various Caribbean waters.[3]

Continued efforts by Bryan to take control of Haiti's finances fell on deaf ears. Various loans extended by British, French, and German bankers had prompted their forming the Banque Nationale to act as the government treasury. Their task was to receive and have custody over all government funds.

The bank, in hopes of forcing the government to allow the Americans to

A detachment of the 3d Signal Company of Marines on duty at Port-au-Prince, Haiti, in October 1914.

take charge of finances, refused to make further advances for any purpose. Rumors reaching the bank that the government was going to seize the gold reserves prompted the National City Bank of New York to ask the U.S. government to intercede. And soon arrangements were made to transfer the gold to New York. Major Charles B. Hatch and 65 Marines aboard the USS *Machias* landed at Port-au-Prince on 17 December 1914. They then proceeded to the bank and secretly took a half million dollars in gold aboard the *Machias*, which then sailed for New York. It wasn't long before those in charge discovered the looting of the bank.[4]

In fact, who was in charge of Haiti? It was a nation which had almost as many presidents as years of existence. Every ruler from 1886 until 1915 had been killed during a bloody revolution. In the previous seven years there had been seven presidents. Revolutions came as repeatedly as the rain, and usually oftener. A revolution to overthrow the Joseph Theodore presidency began in north Haiti early in 1915 under the leadership of Vilbrun Guillaume Sam. In a few weeks he and his followers, almost all Cacos, had control of the entire country and on 4 March he was proclaimed the new president.[5] Almost immediately Dr. Rosalvo Bobo hired a bunch of Cacos and started another revolution. Thereupon Sam had 200 of Haiti's leading citizen's thrown in the hoosegow. He easily assured himself that they were in a conspiracy with Bobo, an unproven allegation.

5. Haiti

The 2d Marine Regiment newly landed in Haiti, July 1915.

When a bloody revolt broke out in Port-au-Prince, Sam made the jailer, Gen. Charles Oscar Ettienne, promise to execute the 200 prisoners should he be overthrown. He was driven out and took shelter in the French Legation. The obedient Oscar did as he was told. That outraged the mob, and on 27 July they dragged him from his hiding place in the Dominican Legation out into the streets, where they beat him to death. Then on to the French Legation. On the following day, 28 July, Sam was also dragged out into the streets and he too was taken apart. All this while the legation personnel were hiding for their lives. Haitians took their politics seriously.[6]

Meanwhile, on 9 July 1915, a detachment of Marines from the USS *Washington* had landed at Cape Haitien to protect and guard a radio station. Protecting American lives and property from revolutionary elements was *de rigueur* for Marines in most of the landings. At times like these it was very important that bluejackets and Marines be sent ashore because practically every citizen of Haiti was a revolutionary element. Rear Admiral William B. Caperton, USN, who commanded the U.S. Cruiser Force in Haitian waters, arrived on the scene aboard his flagship, the USS *Washington*, under the command of Capt. Edward L. Beach. In order to provide the civilians, American and foreigners some strong evidence that the U.S. was going to do something, a detachment of Marines, including the 12th Company, plus some bluejackets from Beach's ship, landed at Port-au-Prince to reinforce Marines already

A U.S. Navy barge in Haitian waters, c. 1914.

ashore. Captain George Van Orden, USMC, was placed in command of the combined force where they landed at Bizotan, a few miles south of Port-au-Prince.[7] As they marched toward the city a gathering crowd of very unpleasant and unhappy Haitians began to form along their route. Van Orden and his men forced their way through the crowd threatening to block their advance. Indeed, several times shots were fired over the marching Americans' heads as a sort of warning. For some reason, which would later be learned, no one was hurt in the exchanges.[8] By midnight Van Orden and his men had occupied the most important places in the city and encountered no resistance except for minor sniping, which soon settled down.

On 29 July the 24th Company (2d Marine Regiment) arrived at Port-au-Prince from Guantánamo aboard the USS *Jason* as reinforcements for Marines already ashore. But it was on the following day that the first serious clash between the Americans and the locals took place in the city. Several U.S. sailors were killed, as were six attacking Haitians.[9] That same day, 30 July, a captain of the French warship *Descartes*, then off-shore, insisted upon sending in some French Marines to protect his consulate.

In the meantime, on 29 July, Caperton requested assistance. His words were, "Men have little rest and much exposed to extreme heat ... earnestly request marine regiment be sent Port au Prince."[10] Another request later in

5. Haiti 57

The 2d Marine Regiment landing at Port-au-Prince, Haiti, in July 1915.

the day delineated that the city had 60,000 people and 400 Marines were just not enough. His unwelcome reply was simply that he would get two gunboats, the *Castine* and the *Newark*, but no more Marines. "Nevertheless he should retain possession of the town until further orders." Though the naval officers aboard the *Washington* were less than enthusiastic about the response, just a few hours later they were informed that 500 additional Marines would set forth from Philadelphia aboard the USS *Connecticut*. Following this, Colonel Littleton Waller Tazwell Waller, who, regardless of his moniker, was a real grunt Marine, began the formation of the First Brigade of Marines with its base being the 1st Regiment of Marines.[11]

In the meantime, on 4 August, five companies from the 2d Marine Regiment arrived at Port-au-Prince aboard the USS *Connecticut* and immediately went ashore to assist those already landed. Apparently it had an effect upon Bobo and his followers. This greatly eased a threatening situation when his troops assumed a more peaceful attitude and promised to disarm. Caperton, not knowing what was really going on between the various factions in the city, ordered that vigorous action be taken the following day. The Marines occupied Fort National in Port-au-Prince on 5 August and all Haitian soldiers not residents of the city were ordered out. Some hesitated and were arrested, a few resisted and two were killed.[12]

Caperton realized that there could be no peace in Port-au-Prince as long as the Cacos remained in power. The U.S. government agreed and Caperton was directed to advise the Haitian people that he was going to establish a firm and stable government, whether they liked it or not. After making this clear he advised the Haitians that the U.S. presence in Haiti would cease as soon as those tenets took effect. On the following day, 6 August, the Cacos were being gotten rid of. They were ordered off the streets by 11:00 p.m. Failure to comply meant arrest. Some were, and there was some upset. A Marine patrol bringing a number of Cacos to the Custom House for confinement was fired upon. But that ceased almost as soon as it began. Most of the citizens realized these actions were for their own good and peace and order was soon restored.[13]

In the north at Cape Haitien, 2,000 of Bobo's Cacos were refused entrance to that city by a citizen's group unless they forfeited their weapons. Bobo appeared to be trying to get along with the Americans and ordered his followers to surrender their arms. But, as was to be the case in most instances, few weapons were. One company of Marines from the 2d Regiment was landed at Cape Haitien on 6 August to lend support to those attempting to bring order into the chaotic situation there. Bobo's influence in the north made a satisfactory solution to the chaos impossible. So, on 12 August, Admiral Harry S. Knapp established a military government in Cape Haitien.[14]

On 15 August, the 1st Marine Regiment (minus the 2d Company, still training in Philadelphia) but including the 4th, 6th, 22d Companies, and Headquarters of the 1st Marine Brigade, arrived at Port-au-Prince.[15] Beginning a week earlier, since the 8th of August, Col. Theodore P. Kane commanded, but this same day, the 15th, Col. Eli K. Cole assumed command. Captain Frederick "Fritz" Wise (see Appendix A) was with the 1st Marine Regiment and commanded the 6th Company. The balance of the regiment—the 5th, 11th, 13th, 19th, and 23d Companies—went ashore at Cape Haitien. The regiment went ashore in lighters to a wharf jutting out into the roadstead. Disembarking, the regiment set out directly to the center of the town. There they took up residence in a brand new caserne (barracks), previously unoccupied. That last factor must have been very important to the Marines who knew not what could have been left behind had there been previous occupants.[16]

The First Regiment was designated an advanced base force regiment and its commander, Cole, was a product of the training at Philadelphia where planning had brought about increased firepower and technological sophistication. Consequently, certainly not entirely due exclusively to his input, the regiment landed with what Smedley Butler (see Appendix A) called "an avalanche of 400 tons of material representing some misconceptions of what is actually required for Marines in the field." Butler, like the brigade commander, Waller, and a few other Marines, were the doers, and most of that was in jungle country. They were the knock-down fighters of the corps and slowly were being circumvented by the "intellectuals" who were planning for more expansive land combat. Both had their place, but the Waller-Butler faction were correct at this moment in time and location.

Cole would tend to be the more careful type of warrior. He would be severely criticized during this early part of the intervention for timidity, of which, it is obvious, he was guilty. Waller was sending critical letters back to John A. Lejeune, assistant commandant, which really castigated Cole. Supposedly Barnett knew nothing about this. He had made it clear that only the commandant should ever receive letters critical of individual officers. But Lejeune showed Barnett all the letters and Waller knew it—and naturally so would Butler. One letter Waller wrote a week after the landing stated that "Cole is very nervous." At another time, when Cole requested more Marine reinforcements, Waller took men away from him. Instead of pressing forward into the wilds after the Cacos, Cole remained in Cape Haitien under the guns of American warships until he was pushed out by Waller.[17]

Butler later wrote a critical letter to his father, Congressman Thomas Butler, which says it all about his feelings toward the "educated" and the "warrior types" like himself:

> Now this sort of warfare [negotiating with the enemy] will pass and gain you much credit and high marks in a million dollar war college.... Colonel Waller has never been to a war college and does not, therefore, grasp the full scope of such warfare, is of the old fashioned school that believes the way to end a row with a savage monkey is to first to go into the region ... occupied by that monkey and find out how savage he is. If the monkey attacks you, return the compliment.[18]

The task assigned to the brigade was greatly enlarged on 18 August when the State Department ordered the Marines to take over 10 custom houses in parts of the nation. Funds collected would go toward supporting the U.S. client government. Those included the formation and maintenance of a constabulary, relieve unemployment, and initiating a program of public works, which was badly needed throughout the country. Beginning on 25 August the 7th Company occupied Gonaives, the 12th Company Petit-Goave, and Miragoane and the 19th Company occupied Port-de-Paix. A couple of weeks later, the 4th Company occupied the large town of Cayes, and the day following, 16 September, the 17th Company, Jacmel. Essentially, most of the Marines were spread around and there were few companies available for quick dispersal, should that be required.[19]

At the end of August a three battery battalion of U.S. Marine artillery arrived to reinforce Waller's brigade. Waller kept two in Port-au-Prince and sent the third up to Cape Haitien. At that point the 1st Brigade had a strength of 88 officers and 1,941 enlisted Marines in Haiti.[20]

At any rate, martial law was in effect and the Haitians were not allowed to pack weapons. The Marines called for all weapons to be brought to the Marines, who would confiscate them. Taking or even collecting weapons, especially rifles, was a difficult undertaking in a country like Haiti. Every man, practically, owned a gun. It was sometimes, most times, the only protection one had in a nation which had many thousands of laws but most of them unenforceable. The police were generally worse than the Cacos. A rifle or gun was a high holy thing in Haiti; it automatically meant self-protection in a nation in which hardly anyone obeyed laws. Disarming the general public was a major undertaking.

Meanwhile, Marine squads patrolled the streets to successfully prevent further disorder. Additionally, the regiment provided patrols for the interior in which an estimated 50,000 Cacos lived in the rugged mountains. The term *Cacos* was derived from a Haiti bird of prey and those "birds" (revolutionaries) certainly were well named. They were inclined to be in bands with their own leaders. The leaders were hired by revolutionary leaders and so their followers could be quickly formed into armed bands at the drop of a hat, or rather a few shekels. This had been going on for many years, almost since the French were driven from the island over a hundred years before, even though Americans were on the island the Bobo revolution continued.

There were at least two likely candidates for the presidential throne: Bobo, who had the backing of most of the Cacos, and Philippe Sudre Dartiguenave, a member of the Haitian senate. Caperton let the senate know that only a government headed by a strongman who could control the situation, especially the finances, would be recognized by the U.S. government. Dartiguenave let Caperton know that he and his followers would be glad to have the U.S. intervene and allow them to control the nation's finances. Dartiguenave let Bobo know that if he were elected president, he, Dartiguenave, would support him. Bobo replied that he wouldn't support Daritguenave under any circumstances.[21]

Bobo's men continued creating disturbances in the north and actively opposed the restoration of peace. They had refused any entreaties by Caperton to relinquish their weapons and were assembling in Port-au-Prince. It was their declared aim to come out in action when the senate voted for a new president unless it was Bobo. They controlled a revolutionary committee in the city which anticipated the outcome of an election by declaring the senate dissolved. They had already decided to oppose anyone besides Bobo who was elected. Caperton then dissolved that committee and stated that he would consider anyone acting against his policies as an enemy of the United States. Understandably, Dartiguenave was elected president. Bobo's men immediately went into action and ordered the congress to be dissolved, but they were prevented by Marines from sealing the doors. To back up his proclamation, Caperton had the *Castine* and the *Eagle* pulled up to the wharves, and both Marine detachments unloaded to back up those already ashore.

On 16 September the United States and the government of Haiti signed an agreement which contained a proviso for the creation of a constabulary of native Haitians under Marine supervision. This was worded so that the organization would take the place of a standing army or separate police force anywhere in Haiti. The new creation was initially named the *Gendarmerie d'Haiti*.[22]

There were many articles in the treaty but essentially, it was for ten years and would make the Haitian government a client of the United States. Although there were numerous attempts by members of the Haitian senate to modify the various articles, mostly it was face-saving. For the most part the words were mangled but the intent was still very clear.[23]

Meanwhile Marine companies were being dispersed throughout much of the countryside. Their job was to collect weapons and send the Cacos back home unarmed. Sometime during September "Fritz" Wise and his company were ordered out of Port-au-Prince to Jérémie, a small town out on the southwest point of land. They went there on the gunboat *Marietta*, landed on the

The 6th Company of Marines in camp, Haiti, 1915.

wharf and marched to the center of the town of about 5,000. Wise added: "We found Jérémie garrisoned by about a hundred native Haitian soldiers. They were barefoot, clad in ragged shirts and cotton trousers, but the carried excellent rifles. It was my job to get those rifles. I knew if I demanded the immediate surrender of those guns, I'd never get all of them. I knew they'd disappear."

Wise described how he managed to obtain the rifles, which took several days. He cajoled the Haitian captain by telling him how great his soldiers looked. The man responded by offering Wise a review, which the latter hastily accepted. He appeared alone and began his inspection. He had already ordered his second in command, 1st Lt. Randolph Coyle, to wait until the inspection began before venturing forth. Wise realized that any early appearance of Marines might have warned off the Haitian soldiers. As he was going through the exercise, Coyle came forward with a squad of eight Marines. The Haitian captain was told he wanted the guns and was willing to pay for them. A deal was struck and Wise agreed to shell out 30 gourdes—the equal of six American dollars—for each. After the collection, he, unfortunately, then refused to honor the agreement, which created a less than desirable climate in that town. Most likely that was an example of how the process worked, each with his own little gimmick, but mostly the turned-in rifles were duly paid for.[24]

At any event, Wise and his navy opposite, Lt. Manning H. Philbrick, a U.S. Navy paymaster, ran into passive resistance. The natives refused to play the game and they had trouble getting some of them to work for the occupiers. Wise lamented that he didn't have a provost court there "and could have handed out punishments that I wished." He admits that he let the town run itself and soon the natives were cooperating.[25]

"Don't shoot first"[26]

Orders were officially issued that Marines were never to shoot first but to respond only if they were fired upon. Waller went to Caperton at Port-au-Prince to discuss the new directive. He then wrote Lejeune, "When I told Caperton the instructions I had given Butler he nearly had a fit but, when he learned of the success of the work he rejoiced."[27]

On 18 September the first clash between Cacos and a Marine patrol occurred at Gonaives. Shots were exchanged between a Marine patrol and a band of approximately 75 Cacos. A few days later Maj. Smedley D. Butler took command of that Marine post and immediately initiated one of his spirited operations. He began by establishing a communication with the local Caco chief, Pierre Benoit Rameau. But in the meantime, he went forward with a progressive program. He opened the railroad lines and connections and reestablished water flow and food supplies into the town. He himself went out on patrols, as well as sending other patrols to nearby locals. Rameau soon got the word that times had changed. In a meeting between Butler and Rameau he pulled the latter from his horse, which caused Rameau to lose face. Later Admiral Caperton referred to this instance in his memoirs: "I could not but commend Butler's success and often wondered at his methods. Unarmed, in Nicaragua, three years previously, he had done the same thing, in even a more telling manner."[28]

This new *chef*, Butler, was going to make life miserable for Rameau and his men. After several clashes Rameau proposed to withdraw his forces from the area, forthwith. Continued efforts by the Marines produced more weapons, but few from Rameau and his band. Butler was still working on the railroad. Guarded trains were now working and conditions were almost back to normal in that locale. Things did get worse in the north.

In early September the Cacos had begun to impede the flow of supplies into Cape Haitien. Colonel Cole was less than active and did nothing, at least temporarily.[29] By 18 September rail traffic was freed up and communications reestablished with Grande Riviere du Nord. This certainly upset the local Caco chiefs. Although Cole, in meetings with the chiefs, attempted to have them turn in their arms, nothing came of it.

Cole took another tack. He began regular Marine patrols in the vicinity and almost immediately there was confrontation. One patrol leader had an argument with a Caco outpost leader but the latter allowed the patrol to complete its assigned task without further disruption. The outpost commander's chief was annoyed, and the miscreant was soon minus his head from a machete molestation.

The next day Capt. Frederick A. Barker and his patrol of five Marine squads were fired upon as they attempted to pass a Caco line.[30] Another patrol of six squads from the 13th Company under Capt. Chandler Campbell was nearby and came running to Barker's aid while another hurriedly started out from Cape Haitien towards the firing.[31] Campbell's group was caught in a trap before they got to Barker and two Marines were wounded. As soon as they arrived the two patrols units were surrounded by wildly yelling Cacos. Soon another four Marines were wounded. Cole, hearing the firing, had a Marine detachment from the *Connecticut* take over the town while he and his men raced from the town to help the surrounded Marines.

There was a helluva fight; the Cacos, showing unusual bravery but little skill, had caught the Marines' attention. The word would soon spread that

The 2d Marine Regiment boarding the USS *Connecticut* at League Island, California, in July 1915, bound for Haiti.

U.S. Marine headquarters at Port-au-Prince, Haiti, in 1916.

these fellows weren't going to be an easy mark, after all. The Cacos seemed not to understand the danger they were in and repeatedly showed themselves. That was grievous. Marine marksmen took every advantage of their training and shooting skills. The Cacos lost about 40 men, all of them dead and left behind. The Caco wounded disappeared but that segment must also have been heavy.

On 27 September five Marine companies, commanded by Col. Eli K. Cole himself, marched out early that morning aiming to drive the Cacos from their main headquarters at Quartier Morin. After a short skirmish they overwhelmed the site and captured it rather easily. On the following day Cole and detachments of his group circled the countryside, and they soon broke up the slowdown of supplies into Cape Haitien.

Although the rebel activity was slowing down some, one Marine mounted patrol from St. Marc ran into difficulty at Pointe Riviere de l'Artibonite. This one-half a company had gone to that town to protect it from a raid by Cacos. It was to be the site of the first death of a Marine in Haiti—Sgt. John Platt. That plus the other troubles in the north distressed Waller. He liked things to be nice and quiet and the north of Haiti was anything but. He determined to take personal charge of events in the north and proceeded there with the 11th Company. Having obtained written promises from several Caco leaders to surrender, he managed to assemble some hard cash with which he intended to purchase weapons. When he arrived at Quartier Morin he learned that the leaders were willing but the followers weren't. At any rate, several hundred rifles were turned in, so it was partial success.

That wasn't the end of Waller's adventures in Haiti. He proceeded by the USS *Nashville* to Fort Liberte, also on the north coast. There he left some of his men and proceeded to Ouanaminthe on the Haiti-Dominican border. This was where most of the Haitian revolutions had started and Waller was determined to make sure no more began there. The Haitian "army," about 400 strong (and that is the wrong word to use), were thrilled to get out of their hell-hole. It probably wasn't quite that bad but close to it. They wore ragged clothes and were half starved from lack of supplies. They were all delighted to receive food, clothes and transportation to their homes plus a little money for their troubles. Payment to each was in the amount of 30 gourdes, which unit was equal to about 20 cents U.S. Six dollars didn't seem like much even in the States, but it was a huge largess in 1915 Haiti.

The reconnaissances in force were for the most part successful. But the need for finalization was soon perceived and the Marines began to get tough. In order to build up strength in the north, the 13th Company, commanded by Capt. Campbell, was reassigned to Grande Riviere du Nord; Capt. William

P. (Deacon) Upshur's 15th Company was sent to Fort Liberte and the 11th was sent to Ouanaminthe. They didn't just sit at those places. A detachment from the 13th, under 1st Lt. Thomas E. Thrasher, Jr., was shoved deep into bandit country to Bahon and soon after was joined by the balance of the 13th Company.³² Cole was soon joined by Butler and their headquarters moved to replace Campbell at Grande Riviere du Nord. Patrols were continued with a potency the native Haitians hadn't seen before. There were many and they took their trips through the Caco country looking for victims and their strongholds.

Butler with several other officers led a mounted patrol of 40 Marines on a six-day reconnaissance covering about 120 miles. On 24 October the patrol was ambushed by Caco rebels, but the Cacos were successfully routed in the Battle of Grosse Roche. Butler described it as follows:

> After dark on the evening of twenty-fourth [October] while ... crossing river in deep ravine suddenly fired upon from three sides by about 400 Cacos in bushes about 100 yards from fort [Dipitie]. One horse killed, fought our way forward to good positions and remained there for the night surrounded by Cacos who kept up continuous but poorly aimed fire{ellip}. At daybreak three squads in charge of Captain Upshur, [1st Lt.] Lieutenant [Edward A.] Ostermann and Sergeant [Daniel J.] Daly advanced in three different directions, surprising and chasing the Cacos in all directions. Eight Cacos killed and ten wounded ... Upshur and Ostermann advancing from two directions captured Fort Dipitie with a total of 13 marines.... Demolished and burned fort. Captain William P. Upshur, First Lieutenant Edward A. Ostermann and Gunnery Sergeant Dan Daly were awarded Congressional Medals of Honor for their part in this engagement.³³

What Butler didn't mention in his report was how Daly should have been cited for his second Medal of Honor. His citation was for the same service as Ostermann and Upshur. But what it should have been for was something he did that, while entirely brilliant, was uncalled for and above and beyond the call of duty, and it was spectacular.³⁴ It was another example of how one individual, acting as an individual, could alter events.

Dan Daly earned his first Medal of Honor in 1900 by staving off countless nighttime Boxer attacks on a section of the city walls at Peking. Not only did he stave off all attacks, but he did it all by himself, all night long. When daylight returned the "rescuers" found Private Daly safe but a huge number of "unsafe" Chinese corpses' before his position. Daly may not have been a one-man Marine Corps but he came damn close to it.³⁵ As one young Marine was quoted as saying when he was assigned to Daly's 73d Machine Company at Quantico in 1917, "you mean he's real? I thought he was somebody the Marine Corps made up, sort of like Paul Bunyan."

When Butler and his command reached high ground he immediately turned to his right arm and said, "Better set up the machine gun, Daly." "It was lost in the river, sir." "Well, we'll do the best we can without it," Butler replied. Daly didn't respond. He had already disappeared into the brush. In a period of time described as an hour Daly was back and told Butler, "I've set up the machine gun, Major." He had retired at least a mile downhill, dove into the water, found the mule the gun was strapped to and removed it. Bringing the gun to the land, he then went for the ammo and accouterments and left them by the gun. Satisfied that he had everything he needed, he then hauled everything up the hill and, as he later said, set it up. This was all while the Cacos were firing at anything that moved. They still had soldiers covering the river crossing looking for retreating Marines. That was wasted effort on their part. The machine gun made a great difference and helped keep the wolves from the door that night. It undoubtedly saved many Marines' lives. The Cacos were not too fond of the "sprinkling gun."[36]

Butler later described their approach with the Cacos: "Just go for those devils as soon as it's light. Move straight forward and shoot everyone you see." So much for directions from the top. The ambush had frightened them, and everyone was madder than hell as soon as daylight allowed them to see who had been shooting at them all night. Even Cole was satisfied with Butler's performance: "Butler, I am glad to say, as he is a very good officer, particularly in the kind of work we have to do in the mountains, takes my view, and that is that the only way to do the job is by systematic cleaning up of a place."[37]

The Cacos were slowly being forced to recognize that their days of running wild and generating revolutions was being brought to a close by the U.S. Marines. Regardless, there were a few more times when the Marines would have their chances to "shoot second." In early November, Butler, now with 700 Marines and bluejackets, went back to clear out an area measuring 20 by 30 miles of mountainous terrain. "I know that the experts of the brain trust will say that we are violating all the rules, but I am sure that if they were here they would not move out of the towns."

As the patrol moved forward it was under constant attack by snipers. At a base camp named Le Trou it was forced to beat off a dawn attack by at least 100 Cacos coming from all directions. On 5 November the unit fought the Cacos at what later became known as the Battle of Fort Capois. Capois was just a gathering of huts connected with a stone wall and lay atop a 3,500 foot mountain. It was a killing affair and perhaps 150 of the Cacos managed to elude the bloodbath by escaping in the fog. Butler and his avengers continued on their prowl, burning anything that looked as though it were giving shelter to their enemy, the Cacos. On 8 November, Maj. Smedley D. Butler with a detachment of Marines successfully fought off Cacos in the vicinities of both Forts Selon and Berthol.[38]

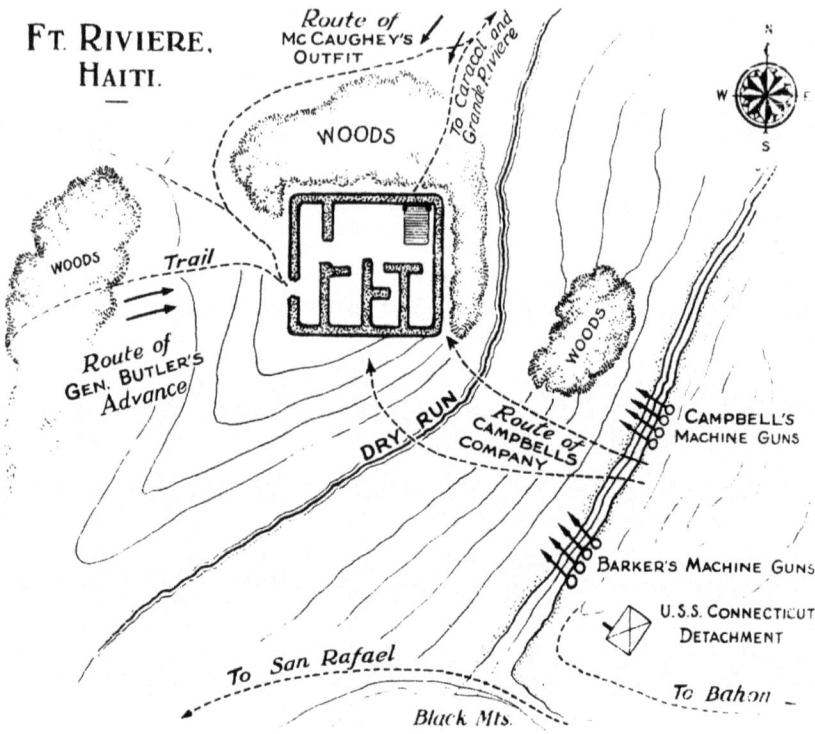

Fort Rivière in Haiti, showing the attack plan by Major S.D. Butler's force in November 1915.

Their next engagement with Cacos was the crowning blow and nearly finished off the rebels' future activities against the Marines. It was possibly the most widely mentioned fight and, as usual, Maj. Smedley D. Butler was in the middle of it. Actually he was in the forefront. It was at the most inaccessible site in which the Cacos continued to maintain a presence. It was called Fort Rivière and it was built over 100 years before by the French atop 4,000 foot Montagne Noire. It was Black Mountain, all right, and its was loaded with fighting blacks just waiting to take on the white devils. They honestly feared white domination because they were positive that whites would bring back slavery, which they had eliminated when they drove the French out. The natives were well aware that in Norte America, but a short time before, slavery of blacks was a common situation.[39]

On 17 November Butler and his Marines fought rebels at Fort Rivière. His own official report of the affair follows because it is the best description of one of the major actions during the period of intervention.

5. *Haiti* 69

A prison camp in Haiti, c. 1916.

Official Report on action at Fort Riviere
Port-au-Prince
December 7, 1915
NOVEMBER 17th: at 4.00 a.m. left St. Raphael with Capt. [William W.] Low, Lieut. [1st Lt. John] Marston (see Appendix A), Asst. Surgeon [Robert A.] Torrance, Lieut. [2d Lt. George A.] Stowell, and four squads 5th Company, two automatic guns.[40] Climbed Montagne Noire going towards Fort Riviere. At 7.40 a.m., reached a position about 800 yards southwest of fort. Communicated with Captain Chandler Campbell's column of the 13th Company and the Marine Detachment of the U.S.S. *Connecticut*, under Capt. F.A. Barker, found they were in position as planned on the hill, about 800 yards south of east of the fort. Moved towards fort with Low's company, being fired on at 7.45 a.m. Placed automatic guns under Lieutenant Marston in position about 500 yards from fort to cover the advance and commenced the assault from the south, crossing the open plain without cover and slightly rising toward fort. Fire from the garrison was heavy, but inaccurate, and we had no casualties. Riviere on the top of Montagne Noire, about 4,000 feet above the sea, was an old French Bastion Fort, about 200 feet on a side with thick walls [c. 100'] of brick and stone, loop holed and ranging from 15 to 25 feet high. The original entrance had been on the northern side, but had been blocked, a small breach in the southern wall being used in its stead. This breach in the wall being its only entrance was naturally covered by the defenders on the inside making passage through it into the fort a very dangerous feat for at least the first man. Not-withstanding the fact that the fire of the

Map of Haiti.

defenders was constantly passing through this hole in the wall, Sgt. Ross L. Iams of the 5th Company unhesitatingly jumped through, closely followed by Private Samuel Gross, of the 23d Company,[41] and the remainder of the 5th Company in single file; the breach being too small to admit more than one man at a time. A melee then ensued inside the fort for about ten minutes, the Cacos fighting desperately with rifles, clubs, stones, etc., during which several jumped from the walls in an effort to escape, but were shot by the automatic guns of the 5th Company and by the 13th Company advancing to the attack. After about ten minutes of this close fighting the fort was in our hands and the 13th Company climbed into the fort, followed in about ten minutes by Lieutenant [Lt. j.g. Scott D.] McCaughey with the U.S.S. *Connecticut* sailors, they having advanced on the fort from the north. The plans for the capture of the fort worked without a hitch, the automatic guns of all companies, particularly those of the 5th Company doing splendid work in covering the advance of their company, and I believe making possible this assault without casualty. Immediately after its capture, having determined to blow up the fort to forever eliminate it as a stronghold for the sheltering of bandits, I with Lt. [j.g. Homer C.] Wicks, USN, of the *Connecticut*, took the blasting squad of the 5th Company and proceeded down the mountains to Grand[e] Riviere to secure a ton of dynamite. Before leaving I sent Capt. Low with the remainder of his company back to San Raphael. Capt. Barker with his detachment to Bahon and Lieut. McCaughey with his sailors to Dondon, leaving Captain Campbell and his company in charge of the fort. We reached Grande Riviere at 3.45 p.m. Lieut Wicks with the dynamite squad going on in a hand car to Cape Haitien for the explosives.

Sgt. Ross L. Iams, 5th Company, M.C. and Private Samuel Gross, 23d Company, M.C., I recommend for the Medals of Honor. The action of these two men in entering the breach in the wall of Fort Riviere, I have already described. The amount of courage required to do as they did is fully appreciated by the undersigned, who was close by at the time and I unhesitatingly recommend them for this distinction.[42]

In 1921 at Senate Hearings, General Barnett, recently "retired" as commandant, was being questioned about offensive operations against the Cacos:

> GENERAL BARNETT: One particular one was the capture of Fort Rivière. That was really quite an affair.
>
> QUESTION: That was the affair when there were 51 Haitians killed but no casualties on our side?
>
> GENERAL BARNETT: It was quite an affair. The Haitians were not well armed, but they stood up and fought to the best of their ability. [Continues, reading the field commander's report of the engagement.] All companies were in their position at the time specified and Butler and Low's companies made the assault, supported by five other companies. Hand-to-hand conflict in the fort lasted ten minutes. Twenty-nine killed and 22 jumped parapet, but all were killed by fire from the automatics, all avenues of escape being blocked.
>
> QUESTION: Was that operation fairly characteristic of the operations in general conducted by our forces against the natives?
>
> GENERAL BARNETT: I should say that was a sample. They had a little better protection there than they would have ordinarily, it being an old fort on a high mountain.[43]

No prisoners were taken. One Marine officer who took part in the engagement, recalling that the only American casualty was a man who was struck in the face with a rock and lost two teeth, remarked, "We were fighting a people who did not know what sights were for, and in a tight spot they threw away their rifles and reached for rocks."

Caco attacks and ambushes against Marine patrols were generally unsuccessful, although they provided some tense moments in the early days of campaigning. Major Smedley Butler's group of 27 Marines, trapped in a nighttime ambush, was terrified by surrounding cacos who blew incessantly on their conch shells, but in daylight the Haitians were no match against superior Marine firepower. Butler recalled that his men "went wild after their devilish night and hunted the Cacos like pigs," killing about 75 of them on the day following the ambush. Marine casualties in this campaign were characteristically light, with Butler's group suffering only one man wounded. Butler's field commander, Colonel Eli K. Cole, had ordered vigorous pursuit of the guerrillas and was pleased with Butler's performance.

This battle at the fort was bloody. It later came out that at least 77 Cacos were killed in the fort or attempting to escape. No Marines were even seriously wounded, much less killed. When Secretary Josephus Daniels, a pacifist, learned of the massacre, he sent out instructions that operations had to be carried out with less bloodshed. Consequently, except for self-protection or that of peaceful natives, all operations by Marines were discontinued. This was, in effect, the end of the First Caco War. From this time forward, until some serious mistakes were made by the Americans, the only activity would include the formation and training of the *Gendarmiere d'Haiti* and the occupation of numerous towns and cities. The 1st Marine Brigade was gradually reduced to 100 officers and 1,667 enlisted men by the end of 1915.[44]

Developing the Gendarmerie d'Haiti

As a temporary expedient, the Marines scattered about the nation were acting provost marshals and as such were to maintain the peace. As one Marine officer reported: "Coming as they did, fresh from spotless marine camps ... immaculate marine compartments aboard men of war, the sanitary conditions of the Haitian police stations was an abomination." The same report described the "police" as filthy. Searches for brooms and swabs were usually fruitless—they were not standard equipment for the police stations. Worse, evidently the occupants didn't want to even know why those tools were to be used. The caste system in Haiti was as rigid as that in India. One did not do women's nor slaves' work. Needless to state, the Marines soon had things working the way they intended that they should work. The barracks and offices were soon spick and span and the police stations were objects of beauty in an otherwise squalid environment.

In 1916 all that was well and good. Now the Marines had to learn where the police were to patrol. No one seemed to have any idea that was their responsibility. The native occupants of the stations, for the most part, had no idea where their limits lay. No maps of the cities or towns existed nor were the walking beats laid out anywhere. Within a short period the Marines had it all worked out and established rules and regulations to go with the new efficiency.

Of course this success was actually a makeshift affair for the organization that was being created.

There was a feeble attempt to start another revolution early in January 1916. Again it was in the capital, Port-au-Prince. Barracks occupied by Marines was fired upon, but the return fire forced the rebels to quickly run for cover. Otherwise, mostly, the land was peaceful, by comparison to the usual circumstance. On 3 December 1915, Butler, now a Marine lieutenant colonel, was returned to Port-au-Prince to assume command of the newly formed *Gendarmerie d'Haiti*. His rank as head of that formation was to be major general and his pay would be an additional $250 per month, in addition to his base U.S. Marine salary. Prior to Butler, Waller had briefly been responsible for the initial laying out of the organization, but his many other duties with the brigade soon made continuation of that role impossible.[45]

Other Marines were "hired" on by the Haitian government, many enlisted Marines but all as Haitian officers. Usually, but not always, a first sergeant down to sergeant would be hired as a captain; corporals as 1st or 2d lieutenants, and occasionally, privates as second lieutenants. They received substantial pay from the Haitian government as well as their regular Marine salary. Additionally, they received 45 days' leave per year outside Haiti. They worked hard and long hours but many enjoyed this time as officers and superiors to those they commanded. The fact that they were able to manage their own organizations with little outside interference also helped.[46] As Butler phrased it when speaking of the Marine's responsibilities in Haiti: "We were all embued [*sic*] with the fact that we were trustees of a huge estate that belonged to minors."

Initially, and for some time to come, the Marines were really running Haiti, and, for the most part, things were going smoothly. That is, until the Haitian politicians managed to regain some of their former control. That would be especially the case after the U.S. entered the European war and was forced to temporarily reduce the number of Marines in Haiti. One civilian who went to Haiti in 1917 came back with the statement that "the running of the government comes pretty near being vested in General Butler and his young colonels and majors."[47]

The majority of the former members of the dissolved Haitian army would, or would try to, enlist in this new constabulary formation. At one time that army had the following paper composition: 38 regiments of the line; four regiments of artillery; four regiments of the Presidential Guard, and a *gendarmerie* of 43 companies. It included over 300 generals and at least 50 colonels. Those figures, it is important to realize, far exceeded the era's U.S. Army by a landslide. That monumental Haitian army was disbanded shortly after the Marines first landed.[48]

Enlistment for the *gendarmerie* took place at 10 ports in which the Marines were based. The total initial formation was not to exceed 336 men, including non-commissioned officers. At first recruitment was slow. The main problem was that those who had previously served in any federal job were hardly ever paid. When the new recruits were actually paid as promised at the end of the first month, recruits began flowing in. It was especially enlightening for the Haitian trainees, who earned the equivalent of $10 per month for privates, when they learned that they weren't required to share their income with their Marine officers. Would wonders never cease. Not only were they paid, but they received fine new clothes. That was something that hardly any native had ever had before. The clothing was bought from Marine stocks and each man received much the same as would a Marine recruit. Weapons issued were those taken from the disbanded army. Old rifles without ammunition. Not because they weren't trusted but because the ammunition wasn't available. Besides, all the Marines could do at this early stage was teach the recruits how to hold and handle their weapons. Shooting would come later when new weapons and ammunition became available.[49]

Regardless of how many of these recruits had served previously, the applicants were mainly "warped, corrupted, and extremely ignorant material." The assigned task of the *Gendarmerie d'Haiti* was the protection of lives and property of the 2,500,000 citizens of the land. Since most of the Haitians had little if any regard for life, limb or property of others, it would be an uphill job turning them around. Language would certainly be a major problem for all concerned. The vernacular of the inhabitants was a bastard French with words from African dialects, some Spanish, some English. The Marines, few of whom could speak any of the languages mentioned except English, would have their hands full. But, they set to their task, as always, full of vim and vigor and eventually, succeeded far beyond anyone else's dreams. Including the top-dogs of Haiti, the French educated elite.

Training the recruits was relatively easy after the Marines began using English and showing exactly what each word meant, by example. "Right face" would be best described by a Marine doing exactly that as another Marine called out the words. Discipline was created as was a schedule of confinement for each major infraction of the rules. It wasn't long before the Haitian members of the *gendarmerie* were making the decisions for punishments after court trials. This sort of treatment wasn't normal, but the natives soon grasped the pleasantness of deciding their own fate based upon a system which was just.[50]

The recruits' physical condition was terrible. Most had been the victims' of numerous generations of syphilitic breeding. Almost everyone had hookworm, the climate being especially conducive in its continual development.[51]

In plain terms, most were in a weakened state with minimal strength for active duty. Consequently, remaining awake after strenuous activity was nearly impossible for most of the recruits. At least in the beginning, few were entrusted with standing guard over important positions. Even though the doctors that were hired were usually well trained in French medical schools, most often the superstitious recruits from the lowest orders went to voodoo priests instead. Injections of medicine made tremendous inroads. Within a year many of the gendarmes could stand watches of up to three hours before falling asleep from exhaustion.

One of the most important inroads made by the Marines was the complete overhaul of the frightful sanitary conditions then in existence in Haiti. Upon arrival, the Marines found themselves desperately working to eradicate the persistent filthy conditions prevalent everywhere. If the Marines accomplished anything during their sojourn in Haiti, they were somewhat successful in making the country almost habitable. Their success was great but covering it in detail exceeds the space available. Suffice to state, they turned the nation and its people 180 degrees.

In February 1916 the new *Gendarmerie d'Haiti* assumed its duties in all 13 *arronidissement* (after the French fashion) or counties. Butler and his men had done their jobs extremely well. Butler acknowledged that his old friend Waller "with his usual generosity" had provided Butler with the pick of the Marines then on duty. That helped, but he also made it clear that the natives chosen were the pick of the crop. If only they could be made to keep "shoes on their big feet." The so-called political "elite" weren't all that happy with the new formation. Their usual graft connections were quickly terminated, therefore they were instantly against the *gendarmerie*. The president, Dartiguenave, tried to stall implementation of the force. However, Butler had gone forward with Article X, even before the treaty was formally approved, and its provisions left many of the elite up in the air. They didn't like it, and they tried everything possible to get the president to drastically change it or disapprove it. He knew what side his bread was buttered on and, after a very difficult time, finally approved the United States plan.[52]

One event cast a shadow upon the *gendarmerie* during 1916. During the absence of the Marine officer commanding the national penitentiary at Port-au-Prince, 500 prisoners managed to overwhelm their guards and escape custody. This was on 30 May 1916. The prisoners had taken possession of many of the stacked Krag rifles and some of the guards had shown cowardice by not making any attempt to stop them. Nine were court-martialed for cowardice and desertion and were sentenced to five to ten years' confinement.

The *gendarmerie* attached to the Port-au-Prince police greatly assisted

Marines escorting Haitian civilian prisoners at Port-au-Prince, c. 1916.

the Marines in rounding up the prisoners. But some 50 managed to steal horses and escaped toward the Haitian-Dominican border. They only managed to get to mountains just outside the city, where they were caught by Marines and a *gendarmerie* patrol. They are said to have resisted and all were killed in the ensuing clash. Within a few days most of the rest were rounded up within the city and returned to the prison, except for two. It was believed that those two possibly drowned while hiding in the city sewers.

Corvée

The nation completely lacked even a modest network of roads. A person could not travel between the north and the south by road. The two major cities, Port-au-Prince in the south and its sister in the north, Cape Haitien, could be reached only via horseback. There had once been a French built road that had disintegrated from lack of care and maintenance and in places was almost invisible. The American command made an early decision that in order to bring the country under lawful control, a system of roads had to be created. The *gendarmerie* had to be able to move about freely and relatively easily. Money was the original stumbling block. But the commandant of the *gendarmerie*, Major General Smedley Darlington Butler, discovered a law on the books since the time of the French occupation. It was derived from a French law that had a part in initiating the French Revolution. It was called the *corvée* and after its appearance on Haitian books in 1864, it had never been repealed, and it eventually caused the same situation in Haiti as in France—revolution. Haitian peasants inherently resented the unpaid work—they feared that white men were trying to return them to slavery.[53]

Actually, the law wasn't all that bad; neither was it in practice. The problem wasn't the *corvée* or the Marines who invoked it, the problem was with the Haitian civil servants and their part in it. It was supposed to work as follows: local mayors would assign people to work on the road being developed or repaired within a limited range from their own homes. They were to be fed and housed and would donate a certain amount of labor to the cause.

After gaining approval, various *gendarmerie* commanders (Marines) began to improve roads in their own districts and for two years there was a continual improvement. In the beginning the workers were very satisfied with the conditions they worked under and most were reluctant to return to their homes after their part was completed. They actually hung around for over a month, extending the housing and food which they continued to receive.

Work was rushed on the 63-mile stretch of road between Cape Haitien and Gonaives, alternately draining swamps and climbing mountains as much as 2,500 feet in height. In little more than a month they accomplished this engineering feat and an automobile actually covered the stretch for the first time on 11 December 1917. Prior to this it was only manageable on horseback and then with great difficulty. While the system was in place and working reasonably well, many miles of road were built, including that 170 mile stretch between Port-au-Prince and Cape Haitien. In the hearings on the occupation of both Haiti and Santo Domingo, by the 67th U.S. Congress, Butler was asked what amount of new roads were built during the initial occupation. He said there were three miles of usable roads when the Marines landed, between Port-au-Prince and a village named Mardissant. He stated that in the two years the system was in place that 470 miles of road had been completed.[54]

The fact that they were under constant guard, and the local *gendarmerie* were none too gentle with those they guarded, began the extreme resentment felt by the laborers. Oftentimes when not working they were tied together to prevent their disappearance. But worse was to come. The local politicians who assigned the locals to the *corvée* found a way to make the work pay—for them. They established rates of payment, to them by those assigned, to be let off the *corvée*. Those that couldn't pay were assigned, those that could pay were let off. When the peasant's time for release came, unless he could pay, he was put back on the *corvée* in place of those who could pay. Additionally, if the local chief liked someone, they were excused from duty; if they didn't like someone, he was on for good. Later reports indicated that even individual Marines were occasionally harsh and sometimes beat the natives on the gangs if they weren't satisfied with their effort.[55]

Not only were the local politicians on the take, but even the more dishonest *gendarme* managed to get into the act. Frequently they collected bribes from the workers for favors, and may have delivered on promises made but more likely didn't. They also embezzled part or all the money provided to them for food or even entertainment. Sometimes the workers were manacled and taken as much as several days from their homes to work and frequently no shelter was provided. The Marines provided money for food, which was given to the *gendarmes* but often they managed to grab a portion, with a consequent reduction of edibles.

Butler received congratulations from Washington but he knew that trouble was brewing and sent a note to Assistant Secretary of the Navy Franklin D. Roosevelt, "It would not do to ask too many questions as to how we accomplish this work." He was right. Trouble was really stirring and the *corvée* was officially abolished in August 1918. But the damage had already been done. The abuse, mainly physical, had been sufficient to generate a resurgence of the Cacos. There was now a relatively new generation of rebels who were prepared for and committed to destruction of the in-place political systems and individuals. And the U.S. Marines were high up on their "A" list.

Unfortunately, the new brigade commander, Col. John Russell, decided that certain roads had to be complete.[56] So the *corvée* was continued in certain districts until October 1918. The hated system continued to be imposed on the less powerful, who were also those who would rise in rebellion. But despite the "official" cessation, Maj. Clarke H. Wells, a district commander, who denied its continuance in his reports to headquarters, continued it. There is little question that his area needed roads for military purposes more than any of the others. His district, in the mountainous Hinche area near the border, was the source of continual bandit activity, and the *corvée* made it worse. Consequently, that district became the center for the forthcoming uprising of 1918–1919.[57]

There were other matters generating unrest in Haiti. As usual, the educated continued their machinations toward keeping the uneducated under their thumbs. In late 1916, the president, by decree, reduced the number of deputies from 102 to 36. Elections were to be held on 10 January 1917, and since most of the Haitians couldn't read or write, their votes were cast for those whom they were told to vote. In fact, their voting registration cards were purchased from them by the upper class politicians and held until election time. Then henchmen of the candidate would fill in the names "properly." Even one secret service man of the Port-au-Prince police bought blank cards

5. Haiti

Marines capturing smugglers along the Haitian border with Santo Domingo, c. 1915.

at 4 cents each and sold them to candidates for 10 cents each. On 29 November 1916 the 51st Company of Marines arrived at Port-au-Prince aboard the USS *Vermont*. It would be a few short months later when that company, plus many more, would be sent back to the United States to form the 5th Marine Regiment for service in France.[58]

In Haiti in 1917, according to an American civilian, Dr. S. G. Inman,

> The marine who becomes an officer in the gendarmerie finds himself clothed with practically unlimited power, in the district where he serves. He is the judge of practically all civil and criminal cases, settling everything from a family fight to murder. He is the paymaster for all funds expended by the national government, he is ex-officio director of schools, inasmuch as he pays the teachers. He controls the mayor and city council, since they can spend no funds without his o.k. As collector of taxes he exercises a strong influence on all individuals in the community.[59]

The voting in January went quietly, though several repeat voters were arrested. During a victory ball days later, there was a Caco attack on a town where 2,000,000 gourdes (Haitian money) was supposedly located on a train. But it was a halfhearted attempt and no one was hurt, nor was any money lost. Trouble was again brewing in Cuba, so on 4 March 7, 17, and 20, companies of the 7th Marine Regiment boarded the USS *Hancock* at Port-au-Prince bound for Cuba to protect American interests during the period of a revolution in that island nation. Marines had been shipped back and forth between Haiti and Santo Domingo since the previous year when trouble started in the other part of Hispaniola. Before long the 7th Marines would return.

But it wasn't until 4 April 1917 that the peace was seriously broken in Haiti with the death of a Marine corporal, a second lieutenant in the *gendarmerie*, Grover T. McNabb. He had been unsuccessfully attempting to arrest a civilian. His murderer managed to escape to Santo Domingo. This was the first Marine officer casualty of the *gendarmerie*.

Meanwhile, American women, mostly wives of Marines and some civilians, began to arrive in Haiti. That is when the most serious trouble between whites and blacks began. Almost immediately the American style of racial separation, known as "Jim Crow," took effect in Haiti. Black Haitians had not known racial separation before, especially in their own black nation. As one American civilian testified before the House hearings in 1922:

> Up to that time the American officers had free and complete intercourse with the Haitians, both in their families and in their clubs.... With the coming of the women of the occupation this peaceful state of affairs was completely upset, the women [American] having a natural aversion, due to their former training and method of thinking, to dancing and general social intercourse with the Haitians, men or women; the husbands of these women also strongly objecting for the same reason.[60]

Segregation was justified by the Americans, that with the arrival of women, the Americans were now "socially self-sufficient and that segregation did not indicate 'snobbishness.'" Of course, the Haitian elite, most of whom were well educated in France, were well aware of what the Americans were doing and resented it. In France and in other Caucasian societies they had been welcomed as equals. Now, they weren't, and in their own country. Racial hostility was manifested passionately and exceedingly by the elite rulers of Haiti, who formerly welcomed the Americans. Hotels used by the occupation force adopted "Jim Crow" and even Catholic churches began having separate masses for whites.

In later years there were incidents, one of which was considered explosive at the time in 1930. A Haitian man grabbed the arm of a young white female who was the daughter of a Marine sergeant. A Marine corporal in turn manhandled him. The matter was immediately hushed up by the American authorities, who considered it a serious threat to the safety and morale of the occupation force. Apparently the abuse to the Haitian was not taken into consideration, seriously. There were instances of drunken Marines wandering about in towns muttering about "niggers" and "gooks" and otherwise making themselves offensive. Haitian pride could bear just so much. After the initial occupation, when the Haitians accepted their fate with at least a little grace, the Americans began turning the situation around. Rebellion, always close to the surface, began again in late October 1917.

On 11 October 1917 at 3:00 a.m. about 60 Cacos attacked the home of Marine Captain John L. Doxey located in Hinche.[61] He, the local commander of the *gendarmerie*, had the previous day just brought the equivalent of about $12,000 to his home. It was to pay salaries and local expenses for the operations and maintenance of his command.

The attack was beaten off and two Cacos were killed in the process. The band then withdrew without collecting anything for their pains other than enough lead to satisfy any bandit. Doxey immediately set out with his force to capture the fleeing Cacos. They managed to kill the leader and captured his second in command, one March Ducheine. The latter, the band's unofficial executioner, was well known in the northern district. He wasn't long in hand before he blew the trumpet loudly and three additional Cacos were implicated. They were the three brothers Peralte—Charlemagne, Saul and St. Remy. The first two were apprehended and on 4 January 1918 they were tried before a U.S. Marine provost court at Ouanaminthe. Saul was acquitted but Charlemagne was sentenced to five years' confinement at hard labor. The Marines didn't know it at the time but they had a tiger by the tail and in few short years he would make life very difficult for the occupation forces.

The streets of Cape Haitien needed sweeping, and the *gendarmerie* had a new sweeper. For the several months following, Peralte was kept busy in plain view of the citizens of that town. Needless to say, with a population so dedicated to keeping "face" at all costs, this caused this very proud man to hate everyone involved, especially the Marines who were in charge of the *gendarmerie*.

Charlemagne never submitted and was always planning. He talked his *gendarme* guard sentry into deserting and on 3 September 1918, he took his rifle and ammo and they both headed for the nearby hills. It wasn't long after that this firebrand convinced numerous Cacos to join him in his fight to drive the invaders out of Haiti. Most of those men who had been with him in the attack upon Hinche and many others who had been angered about the *corvée* were soon part of his growing band. It wasn't long before an estimated 5,000 men were with him. Another 15,000 rebels, in various districts, could also be counted upon when Charlemagne was in need of their services in their own areas. These latter and their wives, in markets, while washing and when in churches, functioned as his intelligence gatherers.

Weapons consisted of a few antiquated rifles but primarily machetes and sharpened bamboo stakes. The latter were exchanged when serviceable weapons were confiscated. Initially they gathered together as many modern weapons as possible before taking chances on serious altercations with the *gen-*

darmerie or U.S. Marines. They knew the country, operated in small bands and gave the *gendarmerie* little chance to interfere with their depredations. Within a few months of "collections" Peralte finally decided he and his force were ready. This time for the big one. He would go for Hinche, which, if he could hold it for even a few days, would strengthen his hand and reputation.

On 17 October 1918, under the leadership of someone other than Charlemagne, at approximately 10:00 p.m. 100 Cacos assaulted the town. At their great surprise, 1st Lt. Patrick Kelly, and Lt. Lang, with their now well-trained *gendarmeries*, met them with a very "warm reception." Within a half hour the Cacos had received their taste of what to expect from future encounters.

Kelly had been a gendarme officer since the time when Smedley Butler was running the *gendarmerie*. He was described by Capt John H. Craige as "a tall, handsome son of Erin, with jet black hair and eyes cut from blue rock-crystal [and] had the manners of a Chesterfield." (Whatever that meant; quoted in *Black Baghdad*.) For his success at Hinche, Kelly was promoted to captain of the *gendarmerie* and awarded the Haitian *Medaille Militaire*. The contact lasted about a half hour and failed.

Thirty-five of the Cacos lay dead as the balance fled in disorder. The *gendarmes* followed and managed to pick off more of the Cacos. This was just a taste of what the future held for them. Saul Peralte, Charlemagne's brother, was killed in one encounter and the deserter who aided Charlemagne was captured, tried and executed.

But was Charlemagne discouraged? He was not. Not quite one month later he led an attack upon the *gendarmerie* barracks at the small town of Maissade early on the morning of 10 November 1918. The Marine lieutenant in charge was away and his Haitian sergeant who was left in charge managed to hold the ten members of the guard together to fight off that attack. Though the barracks and a number of houses in the town were destroyed by fire, no fatalities resulted on either side.

Caco bands in Haiti were extremely active in 1919 all throughout the countryside, mainly in the north and along the eastern border.

On 3 February 1919 a patrol under Lt. Williams of the *gendarmerie* nailed about 200 bandits near Mirebalaise and captured 12 rifles and about 40 machetes. The next day 1st Lt. Kelly and his men were attacked at Cerca-la-Source by at least 100 Cacos. Captain John Craige continued writing about Patrick Kelly: "In the early 1920s [*sic*] he was in command of a wild, mountainous district, the lone Marine among thousands of native Haitians." Craige added, "He had been the hero of more desperate enterprises than there were hairs on his head. The Haitians had songs about his exploits."

The Kelly group had been on patrol when they made their encounter on

4 February 1919 at the town of Cerca-la-Source. The 100 or so "bandits" attacked that town, and as later written by Col. Robert Debs Heinl, "The unquestioned hero of the fight was Lieutenant [actually First Sergeant] Patrick Francis Kelly, one of the most popular NCOs in the Corps." Then Craige wrote, "Even in a service where courage was taken for granted, his iron nerve and ice cold daring marked him among his fellows," as quoted in *Black Bagdad*. Kelly survived because one of his *gendarmes* dived between a Caco and Kelly as a shot was fired. The man received five wounds, resulting in the loss of a leg and arm.[62]

Shortly after the war in Europe terminated, early in 1919, a wounded colonel of Marines, Albertus Catlin, became the new brigade commander. He personally investigated rumors that the *corvée* was then in use in the Hinche area. He found that to be true and the countryside depopulated. Because of brutality, Catlin ordered all patrolling by *gendarmes* to cease and desist. His second in command, Lt. Col. Richard S. Hooker, was directed to investigate whether the outlawed *corvée* was the reason that the Cacos continued their reign of terror in the interior.[63]

His report signified that to be true, and he got the impression "that the officers higher up were approving these methods." He added, "The situation in that whole district is, to say the least, out of hand." Catlin then relieved the Marine district commander. The *gendarmerie* commander, Lt. Col. Alexander S. Williams, under questioning a few years later, made the comment, "Every offense is followed by an order forbidding everyone else to do the same."[64]

On 25 March four companies of the 7th Marine Regiment were transferred from Guantanamo Bay, Cuba, to Port-au-Prince to reinforce Marine units fighting Cacos in the country. A few days later, on 31 March, Capt. Harvey B. Mims, leading 1st Division, Squadron E (4th), Marine Corps aviation, landed at Port-au-Prince to join forces already ashore in fighting Cacos.[65] The equipment included seven HS-2 seaplanes and six Jenny land-planes. Marine air would continue to operate in Haiti for the next 15 years. During this period, 1st Lt. Lawson H.M. Sanderson found that he could hit his target more often by pointing his plane toward his target and releasing his bomb from a makeshift rack after diving to about 250 feet. The attack at an angle of 45 degrees later became known as "glide bombing."[66] Other nations observed and utilized this skill, notably Germany. In July, Marine air operated against the Cacos near the village of Mata de la Palma. And their attacks would continue, much to the distress of the Haitian villagers.

Meanwhile, the Caco movement was spreading rapidly and they were getting bolder. During February and March there were numerous encounters between *gendarmes* patrols and the Cacos. In fact the movement was assuming alarming proportions. Marine units took the field in the center and in the north and combined units were kept in the field constantly. Charlemagne and his crowd were the recipients of new weapons, food, and even money from Germans and rich Haitians in Port-au-Prince. One such supporter was described in various letters and messages as the "Englishman," but who that person was has never been determined. These were people who expected to be well rewarded when the Americans were driven out. There were fewer attacks upon settled areas, but those that happened were getting more vicious.

As an act of revenge for a *gendarmerie* attack upon his camp on 8 October, Charlemagne Peralte and over 300 of his followers attacked Marines and *gendarmes* on 7 October in the Battle of Port-au-Prince. They murdered three engineers working for the Department of Public Works. That brought demands that troops be assigned to protect the capital. Later that month Charlemagne would pay the ultimate price for his continued resistance to the presence of the American Marines.

Charlemagne's prestige had so grown during the time he was in the field that even before he attacked Port-au-Prince, *gendarmerie* Capt. Herman H. Hanneken (see Appendix A), a first sergeant of Marines, was in command of the District of Grande Riviere Nord and had begun to lay plans to capture or kill Charlemagne. During the month of August 1919, Hanneken arranged with a Haitian civilian named Jean B. Conze to aid him. Conze, a well-to-do citizen of Grande Riviere du Nord, left his interests in that town and publicly declared his antipathy for the occupation. In the company of Cherubin Blot, another civilian, and Private Edmond Francois, a private of Hanneken's company, who pretended to desert, he established himself as a Caco chief at Capois, five hours distant from Grande Riviere du Nord. As Conze remained for some time unmolested, his small band was soon augmented by the arrival of numerous thieves and chiefs until a fairly large force was gathered.

On the suggestion of Hanneken, Conze began at once to make overtures to Charlemagne through the medium of the lesser chiefs who had joined him, with a view to inducing Charlemagne to come to Fort Capois. Conze's overtures had good effect, even though suspicion was rife that Conze was not what he pretended to be. Charlemagne sent Papillon, one of his higher commanders, with 200 men to interview Conze. Conze used such good argument and diplomacy that Papillon returned and reported himself satisfied with Conze's devotion to Charlemagne's cause. During the two and one-half months Conze was at Grande Riviere du Nord, he received various delegations from Charlemagne and many of the lesser chiefs came in person and joined the bandits at Fort Capois.

All this time Conze and his assistants ran the risk of lingering torture and brutal death should the slightest error be made. There was grave risk not only from the bandits but danger of death at the hands of the *gendarmes* or Marines, none of whom knew the true situation. Yet in spite of this, Conze slipped into Grande Riviere du Nord weekly, or if necessary more often, to make a complete report on what was going on to Captain Hanneken. He gave information that was of great value at the time and received Hanneken's orders as to future procedure. During the time Conze was at Fort Capois, there was no pillaging or disorder committed by his men, as Hanneken gave money from his personal funds with which Conze furnished his men food, drink, and amusement.

The fact that Conze was established at Fort Capois became widely known. Hanneken, in order to show that no alliance existed between him and Conze, simulated an attack on the fort and after much wild firing retired with his men. He appeared on the streets of Grande Riviere du Nord shortly afterwards with his arm bandaged as a result of a wound supposedly received in the attack on Conze's command. Hanneken transferred some of his gendarmes to Cape Haitien and then went about the town of Grande Riviere du Nord openly expressing his fear that, being wounded and his command depleted by transfers, the town would fall an easy prey to a bandit attack.

This fear was transmitted to Charlemagne Peralte by bandit sympathizers from Grande Riviere du Nord and by Conze. Conze counseled an attack on the town, the capture of which, even if it could not be held, would greatly heighten the fame of Charlemagne, and he swallowed the bait. With his brother St. Remy Peralte, Ademar Francismar, Ectravil, Papilion, many other chiefs and about 1,000 bandits, he arrived at Fort Capois on Sunday, 26 October 1919, to make plans for the capture of Grande Riviere du Nord.

Conze took part in the preparation for the attack. The plan was for the main body to attack the town; Charlemagne was to wait at Mazare, about a half hour from Grande Riviere du Nord, for news of the victory after which he would make a triumphal entry into the captured town. Conze relayed this information to Hanneken with the news that this attack was to take place on the night of Friday, 31 October.

The preceding night under the cover of darkness, the garrison was reinforced by additional *gendarmes* under Colonel (Marine Major) James J. Meade, department commander of the Cape. Hanneken, with First Lieutenant (Marine Corporal) William R. Button, both with faces blackened, and 18 *gendarmes*, all dressed as civilians in old dirty clothes, well-armed and with one machine gun, took up position at Mazare where Charlemagne was to await news of the attack on Grande Riviere du Nord.

At about 10:00 p.m. on the night of the attack, some 700 bandits passed

Mazare en route to Grande Riviere du Nord. Charlemagne did not appear. Finally the *gendarme* assistant to Conze, Private Jean Edmond Francois, reported to Hanneken that Charlemagne had changed his mind and that he would remain up in the mountains between Grande Riviere du Nord and Fort Capois on top of a high hill to await news of the capture of the town. Conze, now a bandit "general," was to lead the attack on Grande Riviere du Nord, and when successful was to send a detachment with countersign "General Jean" to notify Charlemagne of the capture of the town, whereupon Charlemagne would come down to Grande Riviere du Nord.

Hanneken's original preparation then being of no use, it was decided that he, Button and their *gendarmes* would be the detachment bringing news of the victory. With Private Francois leading, the party proceeded for three hours through difficult mountains before arriving at the first outpost of Charlemagne's band. When they were halted by a sentry, the countersign was given by Private Francois, who was well-known to the bandits as the secretary of Conze. The party was permitted to pass.

Private Francois then went directly to Charlemagne and told him that Grande Riviere du Nord had been captured and that the detachment sent by Conze had arrived at the first outpost. Charlemagne immediately directed Francois to have the detachment report to him. Francois returned to Hanneken's party and repeated Charlemagne's orders, adding that the procedure would be dangerous, as there were six additional outposts between Hanneken's party and Charlemagne. Hanneken and his men did not hesitate but immediately went forward.

Francois took the lead, followed by Hanneken, armed with a .45-caliber automatic and a .38-caliber Colt revolver. Button, armed with the machine gun, brought up the rear, accompanied by the *gendarmes*, who were armed with carbines, ammunition for which was carried in native-made straw sacks slung over their shoulders.

The party easily passed the first outpost, which consisted of about 20 men armed mostly with machetes. After walking about five minutes, they reached the second outpost. The bandits scrutinized the party very closely. Hanneken and his men acted as if they were nearing exhaustion. This ruse was successful and the party continued. The next two outposts permitted them to pass without question, merely making commonplace remarks which the *gendarmes* answered satisfactorily.

But at the fifth outpost, it appeared that Hanneken and his men would have to go into action. Revolver in hand, the chief of this outpost stood before the party, partly blocking the trail. Hanneken, by appearing greatly exhausted and winded, slipped by, but the bandit grabbed Button's arm and said, "Where did you get such a fine looking rifle?" referring to the light machine gun Button carried.

By then Hanneken had got about eight paces ahead. Button snapped, "Let me go, don't you see my chief is getting out of sight?" meanwhile jerking his arm from the grasp of the Caco, barely escaping detection, for it is seldom a foreign speaking Creole could deceive a Haitian.

The next outpost was the immediate guard over Charlemagne, located about 30 feet from the bandit chief. Private Francois slipped behind Hanneken after the party passed. Hanneken and Button advanced to within 15 feet of Charlemagne, who was standing over a fire speaking to his woman.

Hanneken said to Button, "All right," raised his .45-caliber automatic, took deliberate aim, and dropped Charlemagne with two bullets in his heart.

Button immediately opened fire with the machine gun and cleared the camp. The *gendarmes* were placed in position to beat off counterattacks. A search was made of the area for the dead. Charlemagne's body and the bodies of nine others were found. St. Remy Peralte, brother of the bandit chief, though wounded, escaped. Also taken were nine serviceable rifles, three revolvers, 200 rounds of ammunition, seven swords, 15 animals and a large amount of correspondence.

Hanneken and his party remained at the camp until daybreak, when they left to return to Grande Riviere du Nord, taking Charlemagne's body with them and fighting off halfhearted bandit onslaughts along the way. They arrived in Grande Riviere du Nord at 9:00 a.m. on 1 November 1919 and delivered the body of Charlemagne to the *gendarmerie* authorities.

No study of the *gendarmerie* that accompanied Hanneken would be complete without including in it the names of the party who made possible the death of Charlemagne[67]:

Captain Hermann H. Hanneken
1st Lt. William R. Button
Mr. Jean-Baptiste Conze
Cpl. Clomence Eugene
Mr. Cherubin Blot
1st Sgt. Demetrius Meompromier
Sgt. Leon Michel
Pvt. Andre Bogage
Cpl. Darius Fenclon
Cpl. Maro Destin
Cpl. Saul Lamour

Cpl. Supplice Vincent
Pvt. Justin Achille
Pvt. Albert Augustin
Pvt. Leon Belizaire
Pvt. Ernest Charles
Pvt. Zamor Desistorie
Pvt. Neite Eugene
Pvt. Jean Edmond Francois
Pvt. Morilus Moise
Pvt. Norville Pierre

Conze threw off the cloak of a bandit leader and returned to Gande Riviere du Nord. Colonel Meade and his men easily repulsed the attack on the town, but some bandits still remained at Fort Capois. In order to eliminate them, plans were made for Captain Hanneken and his men to attack the north and south sides of the fort at daybreak on 2 November, and for the Marines to assault the other sides of the fort at the same time.

Hanneken and his men were in position at 4:45 p.m. on that date. While waiting for the detachment of Marines to attack the other sides of the fort, he and his men crawled to within 150 yards of the first bandit outpost. The *gendarmes* remained here until long after daybreak and still the Marines did not attack. Suddenly being sighted by the outpost of six bandits, who opened fire, Hanneken and his men were forced to advance upon the fort through the outposts. These fired and retreated into the fort. When the party came within 300 yards the fort, they were subjected to heavy cannon and rifle fire from behind the walls. These walls were 14 feet high by three feet thick. Crawling on their stomachs, and with no concealment, these men advanced under cover of their own fire to within 150 yards. The bandits then fled. Although one Marine detachment had meanwhile arrived and covered one side of the fort, the bandits escaped from the uncovered sides. All outposts and huts were burned before the Marine and *gendarme* detachments retired at 9:00 a.m.

Banditry in the North was generally crushed by this and other concurrent operations. An unbroken line of Marines and *gendarmes* on all trails prevented the escape of Charlemagne's men to the command of his chief lieutenant, Benoit Batraville, operating in the central area. Many refugee bandits were captured by the trail-guarding Marines and *gendarmes*, and others, realizing the end of Cacoism in the north, gave themselves up. Over 300 bandits surrendered to Hanneken at Grande Riviere du Nord within a week after Charlemagne's death.[68]

For the first time in many months, northern Haiti was at peace due to the work of Hanneken, who had spent more than $800 of his personal funds to bring about the downfall of Charlemagne. Conze received the standing reward for the capture of Charlemagne, the money Hanneken spent was refunded him, and he and Button received the highest decorations the United States and Haiti had to offer in recognition of their bravery, the United States Medal of Honor and the Haitian *Medaille Militaire*. Private Francois was promoted to sergeant and given a money reward. Cherubin Blot also received a money reward.

The death of Charlemagne brought widespread rejoicing among Marines, *gendarmes*, government officials and citizens throughout the country. The Haitian government, though professing great satisfaction at his death, as attested by the congratulatory letter addressed to the chief of the *gendarmerie* by the president, nevertheless attempted to conciliate certain friends of Charlemagne, the hero, by failing to pay the reward offered for him. The chief of the *gendarmerie* paid the reward from the *gendarmerie* operating funds, thus forcing the government to make good its promise.

The Marine Corps subsequently awarded Hanneken an officer's commission. He went on to achieve a fine record in Nicaragua and World War II and to retire a brigadier general. Before Button could be similarly rewarded, he fell victim to malaria and died at Cap-Haitien in 1920. In recognition of his services, the *gendarmerie* named its caserne at Cap-Haitien "Caserne William R. Button." However, in later years, an American *gendarmerie* commander changed the name of the caserne to "Caserne Dessalines."

The morale of the *gendarmes*, heightened immensely by the removal of Charlemagne Peralte, received a severe blow six nights later when, near Hinche, a Marine patrol came upon a mixed patrol of *gendarmes* and local vigilantes, but the darkness of the night precluded each from recognizing the other. The Marines opened fire and the *gendarmes* responded. The Marine officer fired his Thompson and the others recognized that it must be Marines. They called out and each side ceased the firing. Unfortunately, a *gendarme* was killed, two vigilantes were wounded and a prisoner was also killed.

On 17 December 1919 the 8th Marine Regiment was reactivated from the 3d Battalion, 2d Marine Regiment, and ordered to Haiti under the command of Lt. Col. Louis McCarty Little. Half the unit was located in Port-au-Prince and would withstand an attack launched by Benoit Batraville. The 8th Regiment would serve for the next five and one half years but with no true battalion structure being created. It was a formation of Marine companies for the entire period.[69]

With the death of Charlemagne, his lieutenant, Benoit Batraville, still in the field with about 2,500 men in 1920, was the going concern for Cacos. In his first show of strength, he attacked the town of La Chapelle with 600 of his troop. The *gendarmerie* garrison killed 25 Cacos and captured a dozen rifles, revolvers, and machetes. In reply, Col. John H. Russell, the Marine brigade commander, as a result of Batraville's actions, began an intensive campaign that was shortly to result in the Cacos' complete rout. All *gendarmerie* and Marine commanders spared no effort to track down every Caco band no matter how small.

Batraville, needing a success, sent 300 men to attack Port-au-Prince. Led by some locals, they entered the capital at 4:00 a.m. on 15 January 1920 and began destroying, of all things, the shacks of the poor. Before they had finished, they burned down a city block. They were caught by the Marines and *gendarmerie* and in a short period at least 50 percent that entered the city were dead, wounded, or captured. Several Marines were wounded and one man was killed. Those Cacos that remained fled to nearby Plaine du Cul de Sac where they were surrounded. For days after, small groups would attempt to escape, and before they could, they were at the mercy of the Marine or *gendarmerie* patrols on constant duty. Colonel Little was acknowledged as the main reason for the success of that operation.[70]

Minor skirmishes continued for several months, but no major clash with Batraville took place until 4 April 1920. At 7:00 a.m. a small patrol of Marines and *gendarmes* led by 2d Lt. (Marine sergeant) Laurence Muth spotted a group of Cacos on the summit of Mount Michel. Muth instantly ordered his men to open fire. Unexpectedly, heavy return fire came from another group of Cacos that had taken up ambush positions in a different direction. Muth was killed in the first volley, and in the ensuing battle ten Cacos were killed but they still were in overwhelming numbers and the patrol withdrew, without Muth.

Twenty-one patrols went out upon learning of this disaster with Lt. Col. Little's own patrol first in the area. They managed to catch a load of Cacos off guard and quickly killed 25 of the enemy. After this victory the patrol began a search for Muth and after a while found his badly handled body minus his head and heart, which according to the story the latter had been eaten by the Cacos.

On 19 May Captain Jesse L. Perkins of the 8th Marines led a patrol of 11 men in the area around Marche Canard which located the Cacos' main encampment. They made a march of five hours to the site where a band of about 200 natives were billeted. They ran into a five-man guard post at about 6:00 a.m. The natives got off one round and ran. Perkins sent 2d Lt. Edgar G. Kirkpatrick with seven Marines to find and eliminate them before they managed to get word to the main body.[71]

Then, Perkins with Sergeants William F. Passmore and Albert A. Taubert, and Private Emery L. Entrekin headed for the native camp. Although far outnumbered, Perkins gambled on rushing the camp with his three compatriots to seize Batraville by surprise. Hoping not to arouse suspicion, the four men silently crept forward through the underbrush to get as close as possible to the camp before they made their rush. Some of the Cacos, alerted by the shot that had been fired, caught sight of the Americans making their way towards them. Instantly, 12 Caco rifles opened fire on the approaching Marines. Having been found out, Perkins was undismayed by the new turn of events. He jumped up and ordered his three men to make a dash for the camp. Despite the enemy fusillade, the four Marines ran forward, firing as they came. The fire from the rifles and automatic weapons of the charging Marines momentarily stunned the rebels. Benoit Batraville then appeared and took command of the Haitians in an effort to halt the chaos that was spreading through the encampment. It was too late, for the Americans burst into the cantonment and continued to pour fire into the disorganized defenders. Batraville, unlike some of his men, held his ground and fired at the Marines from 10 feet away. Sergeant Passmore wheeled around and recognized the bandit chieftain. Firing his Browning Automatic Rifle (BAR) from the hip, Passmore cut him down with a burst of fire.

Seeing Batraville fall, the remaining rebels withdrew to some large boulders on the perimeter of the camp and from there resumed the fight. Lieutenant Kirkpatrick, hearing the gunfire, abandoned his chase of outpost guards and made his way to the scene of the battle. Kirkpatrick's group entered the camp and joined in the fight, which lasted for another 15 minutes. The rebels, having lost heart for further fighting, scattered into the bush, leaving their wounded comrades to fend for themselves. As the Marines approached the prone body of Batraville, the still-alive bandit leader rose and attempted to reach for his revolver. Sergeant Taubert finished him off by a single shot from his rifle. The infamous career of one of the last major Caco chiefs was thus brought to a close. The weapon that Batraville had tried to draw was the Colt revolver that belonged to Sergeant Muth before he was killed.

Besides Batraville, the Marine patrol killed 10 other bandits. The number of wounded sustained by the Haitians could not be determined. Captain Perkins, Sergeants Passmore and Taubert, and Private Entrekin received the Navy Cross for the gallantry and conspicuous bravery they displayed during attack on the bandit camp. Taubert actually received a Gold Star in lieu of this being his second Navy Cross, the first being awarded at the Battle for Soissons in France on 19 July 1918.

Active patrolling continued after the death of Batraville to prevent those Cacos that still remained at large from reorganizing and regrouping under a new leader. The 8th Regiment at times sent out patrols mounted on horses and mules in order to increase its mobility, for these animals were excellent as a means of transportation over rough terrain. The life of the individual Marine in his pursuit of Cacos was far from pleasurable. His job was both tedious and difficult. General Gerald C. Thomas, in retirement, offered an apt description of his career as a bandit chaser in Haiti:

> I stayed on at Port-au-Prince until April 1920. I was ordered to the hills, and there I stayed for the next six months. I made one brief trip back into town. My life was like the others.' It was just a life of drudgery, chasing Cacos over the mountains.... Sometimes we would be gone two weeks. We'd corner the Cacos and have a fight with them. Sometimes we would be out two weeks and we

Top: Marines guarding Haitian prisoners in their huts, c. 1927. *Bottom:* Mounted Marines on patrol in the Haitian jungle, c. 1918.

wouldn't see anybody. They hid out in the daytime and traveled at night so we did the same thing. We would hide out in the jungle all day long; and then we would get on the trail at night, watching for fires where they might be gathered around. We'd try to find them. Sometimes we would and we'd have a fight and it would be all over and passing. But we gradually whittled them down and killed enough of them off.

In the meantime, along with our patrolling and fighting against the bandits, there was a pacification program going on; trying to induce them to come in and pick up what they called bon habitant passes, good inhabitants passes, and go back to their gardens where they lived. They were natives who had lived in these areas; and, because of corvée [labor exacted in lieu of taxes by public authorities], a lot of them had taken to the mountains and joined the bandits.[72]

He continued: "McCarty Little drove officers and men at a furious pace. We got little rest but more importantly neither did the cacos." He also mentioned that a member of the *gendarmerie*, a Marine lieutenant by the name of Louis Cukela, a hero from back at Soissons with a Medal of Honor, at one point shot a prisoner in cold blood. He got away with it, because that medal was significant enough to allow it.

General Alexander Vandegrift (see Appendix A), later to be commandant of the Marine Corps, wrote in his memoir:

> I think most of us profited from our long years in Haiti. Whether in the Gendarmerie or the brigade, Marines learned valuable lessons in jungle and guerrilla warfare. We learned many cunning and wily tricks the hard way, but we invented many ourselves. Survival in the field often depended upon quick thinking, always on self reliance. I think it was more than an accident that many of our future generals campaigned in Haiti, among them myself, Roy Geiger, Hal Turnage, Deacon Upshur, John Marston, Jerry Thomas and Lewis Puller.[73]

The death of Batraville put an end the Caco revolt, although sporadic outbreaks of violence and lawlessness lasted for some time. For instance, attacks on women bringing their wares to village markets endured despite efforts to thwart the robbers. Lieutenant Colonel Little decided to eliminate this type of crime by dressing some of his men as women and then sending the disguised Marines shuffling along trails leading to various villages. When the Cacos swooped down on the "women," the leathernecks dropped their market baskets and grabbed their weapons to meet the astonished marauders. After a few such episodes, market women were no longer molested.

The 16th Provisional Regiment was organized in Philadelphia on 11 May 1920 to assist in settling conditions in Haiti and Santo Domingo. Two days later they sailed aboard the USS *Henderson* for the West Indies. Upon arrival they were partly sent to Santo Domingo where, on 7 July 1920, they deactivated.

In the closing weeks of the U.S. national election in November 1920, the Marine commandant, Maj. Gen. George Barnett, released a report alluding to the "indiscriminate killing of natives" which the newspapers quickly picked up. One of the more sensational stories appeared in the *New York Times* two days after Barnett's statement:

> How American marines, largely made up of and officered [sic] by Southerners, opened fire with machine guns from airplanes upon defenseless Haitian villages, killing men, women, and children in the open market places; how natives were slain for "sport" by a hoodlum element among those same Southerners; and how the ancient corvee system of enforced labor was revived and ruthlessly executed, increasing, through retaliation, the banditry in Haiti and Santo Domingo, which was told yesterday by Henry A. Franck, the noted traveler and authority on the West Indies.[74]

Meanwhile, politics being what it is, the Republicans campaigning to defeat the Democrats in 1920 used the occupation of Haiti and now Santo Domingo as a major portion of their platform. As usual, the Republicans claimed that the nation was going to the dogs under the Democrats. Interestingly, the Democrats were making the same charge against the Republicans.

In the meantime, the nearly complete destruction of organized banditry in Haiti during this year allowed the peaceful natives an opportunity to go back to work in their fields and to begin once again to produce food for their families and those who lived in settled communities like Port-au-Prince.

In 1921, the natives of Haiti in revolt had grown quiet and returned to their usual domestic affairs. The problems were developing in the U.S., mostly in government circles. Republican charges had grown, with their election victories, into a full-scale Senate inquiry. The inquiry would be the most important happening during this and the following years.

In a letter to Secretary of the Navy Josephus Daniels previously, Maj. Gen. Commandant Barnett referred to "indiscriminate killings" of Haitians. For some reason the Navy Department published the letter and later a congressional committee, with a political agenda, decided to have hearings. This was titled "Inquiry into Occupation and Administration of Haiti and Santo Domingo" and many people—Haitian, Dominicans, and Americans, civilians and military—were called to testify, including Marines Barnett, Butler, Catlin, Cole, Russell, Waller, and notably Clarke H. Wells and Alexander Williams. Also interviewed were members of both political parties and members of various societies, like representatives from the Haiti–Santo Domingo Independence Society.

The questions were of a varied kind. Our interest will be in those interviews with Marines. Maj. Gen. Commandant George Barnett appears to have been the first, on 24 October 1921. His questions and answers were largely about the harsh treatment of the natives in Haiti and Santo Domingo. The statements were mainly about two enlisted Marines who had been charged with killing civilians and were already tried before a court-martial. Barnett acknowledged that he had read the trial, as a commandant was required to do. He said that the two claimed to have received orders from a Lieutenant Brokaw to execute the prisoners before their opened graves. Barnett told the inquiry that Brokaw had been committed to an insane asylum. He added that this was at a time when Col. A. S. Williams was in command of the *gendarmerie*.

Other interviewees included Maj. Thomas C. Turner, in charge of Marine Aviation, Headquarters, USMC, who had been brigade adjutant and acting chief of staff to Col. John H. Russell, commanding the Marine brigade in Haiti. He mentioned a sergeant of Marines named Lavoie who had machine gunned 15 to 19 prisoners. He was never punished because he left the corps before charges were brought.

Others interviewed included Col. Albertus W. Catlin, Capt. John L. Doxey, Maj. Clarke H. Wells, and at long last, Lt. Col. Alexander S. Williams. He was told of his right to decline to answer any incriminating questions. He admitted that the killing of prisoners was never discussed between he and his subordinate, Maj. Wells. He also told the court that though he had been told of the corvée and saw several gangs working on roads, he believed it wasn't against regulations, at that time.

Sergeant Dorcas L. Williams was also told of his rights. He explained that he commanded a road crew under the direction of "Captain Ernest Lavoie" and that as far as he knew the natives were paid extremely well for their work on the roads. He also was unaware that any prisoners were ever executed.

Brigadier General Smedley D. Butler was questioned on 27 October. He described how he organized the *gendarmerie* of Haiti. As part of his testimony, he was asked, "What about the public there? How could you describe those, General, the Haitians?" Butler replied it was a primary cause of him not being selected to head up the Haitian government and Col. John Russell being chosen instead.

> The Haitian people are divided into two classes; one class wears shoes and the other does not. The class that wears shoes is about 1 percent. I should say that not more than one-fifth of 1 percent of the population of Haiti can read and write. Many of those that wear shoes cannot read or write. In fact many of the teachers cannot read or write. I remember in one instance in sending money to certain district, money to pay a school teacher who had a claim against the government. The gendarmerie officer took the money to the school teacher, and he said "I can not sign that receipt; I can not sign my name." He said, "You are a

teacher aren't you not?" He said "Yes: I am a teacher of reading but not of writing."

Ninety-nine percent of the people of Haiti are the most kindly, generous, hospitable, pleasure-loving people I have ever known. They would not hurt anybody. They are most gentle when in their natural state. When the other one percent that wears vici kid shoes with long pointed toes and celluloid collars, stirs them up and incites them with liquor and voodoo stuff, they are capable of the most horrible atrocities; they are cannibals. They ate the liver of one marine. But in their natural state they are the most docile, harmless people in the world.[75]

Butler's testimony was lengthy and as usual, concise in each answer. A little later, on 8 November, recently retired Maj. Gen. Littleton W. T. Waller was interviewed and mainly told about the early days of the intervention. He was followed the following day by Col. Catlin, then Brig. Gen. Eli K. Cole. Mainly they were questioned about the corvée system. These were followed by various civilians who worked for corporations operating in either nation and those of Haiti and Santo Domingo. The inquiry continued into the early months of 1922 and some changes in the method of government of both nations occurred.

The result of the hearings was what usually came out of congressional hearings. Nothing of consequence and only small-fry potentially guilty of mis-, mal-, or nonfeasance. In fact several native prisoners were killed upon orders issued by Wells and the war hero Louis Cukela, whom no one wanted to touch. They shipped each officer back to the States without further action. Alex Williams was also mixed up in the matter but he was a survivor of the Samar tragedy which seemed to save his hide several times.[76]

On 11 February 1922, Brig. Gen. John H. Russell was appointed American high commissioner of Haiti and personal representative of the U.S. president to the government of Haiti. He would continue to hold this position until 12 November 1930.[77]

Marines would continue to serve in Haiti for an additional dozen years. Colonel Julius S. Turrill would be the commandant of the *gendarmerie* during Russell's early years.[78] During this period of occupation, numerous changes were instituted within the Haitian government that were conducive to the well-being of the U.S. banks and companies investing in Haiti.

Good relations between the U.S. governing body and the Haitian government began especially when, on 10 April 1922, Louis Borno was elected president of Haiti. The cordial relationships between he and Russell were of the highest and this was a four year period of relative peace and harmony. The *gendarmerie* was constantly improving and natives were being promoted within as officers. Mostly, what transpired was improvements in the well-being of the Haitian populace. On 1 November the name of the *Gendarmerie d'Haiti* was changed to the new and more descriptive title *Garde d'Haiti*. By this time 46 percent of the officers were native Haitians and the total enlisted personnel of the force was 2,622. It was now the entire police and military force in the nation.

By 1929 President Borno had been in office a total of eight years and the opposition party had been demanding elections. Borno, however, like many Haitian leaders, past, present, and future, didn't believe the people were ready for regular suffrage. In October 1929, Borno announced that there would be no popular elections in 1930, and consequently the Council of State would elect a president.

Student walk-outs and riots began in late October 1929 and quickly spread over the nation. The cause was the reduction in incentive scholarships for city students at the *Service Technique* central agricultural college at Damien. Students in the medical and law colleges joined in sympathy and other public and private school students soon joined their ranks.

Borno decided against seeking a third term; the *Garde d'Haiti*'s rank and file tended to sympathize with the rebels, making enforcement of security difficult; the high commissioner, Brig. Gen. John Russell, USMC, decided to call in more U.S. Marines to support the government and the 1st Provisional Battalion of Marines was despatched from Hampton Roads, Virginia, on 7 December. They came, but never landed, because the situation was by then considered "well-in-hand."

At Les Cayes on the southern edge of the far western tip of Haiti, 1,500 angry peasants, armed with stones, machetes, and clubs, surrounded a detachment of 20 Marines on 6 December. The Marines had gone out to meet the advancing mob who were bent upon releasing a number of prisoners arrested the previous day. Marine planes had dropped bombs in the harbor of Les Cayes hoping to scare off the mob, but without success. In fact, it appeared to further increase the mob's volatile temperament.

A Haitian, according to two Marine participants, instigated a scuffle. Private Gillaspey hit the man with the stock of his Browning Automatic sending the man to the ground, where he grabbed the Marine's leg and bit it. Private First Class William T. Meyers bayoneted the man, forcing him to release Gillaspey's leg. The natives, now infuriated, attacked the Marines.

The Marines fired point-blank on the on-rushing mob, killing 12 and wounding 23 natives. This number was confirmed later. This was almost instantly labeled the "Cayes Massacre." The following January the Haitian press insisted the loss was 24 dead and 51 wounded. There was the usual "blame the Marines" outcry in the U.S. press, and even in the State Department, where Undersecretary Joseph P. Cotten referred to the Marine Detachment as a "firing squad." The Navy Department, however, later awarded the Navy Cross to the Marine detachment commander, Capt. Hal N. Potter.[79]

Members of the Forbes Commission, sent to Haiti in February 1930 to try to re-establish control of the country. Pictured (left to right): W. Cameron Forbes, Henry P. Fletcher, Elie Vezina, James Kerney, and William Allen White.

In the meantime, in the U.S. government there had been serious efforts to plan an exit strategy. Native Haitians were developing a serious hatred for the continued U.S. occupation. The so-called elite, those Haitians who, according to Smedley Butler, wore shoes, had become very anti–American. But, so far little had come from the various study groups. The latest, as part of a campaign promise, in 1930 U.S. President Herbert Hoover had gathered together a five-man commission for the study and review of conditions in Haiti. Hoover was also annoyed (angry) at the lengthy intervention in Nicaragua which was by now almost five years old.

On 28 March 1931 Hoover announced that he had accepted the commission's recommendations as American policy toward Haiti. The one-sided report and accompanying U.S. press coverage was decidedly against the rule of John Russell and he resented it. His approved rebuttal to the commission was virtually ignored and not allowed to be provided to the news media. In other words, the U.S. participation in Haiti was all wrong and could be attributed to the U.S. Marines. The United States government hadn't had anything to do with initiating it.

Haiti was in an uproar; many of its citizens, rightly, were demanding that the American occupation end. On 5 July 1934 the new American president, Franklin D. Roosevelt, journeyed to Haiti to visit its president. The main result of that meeting was that the U.S. Marines would be out of Haiti by 15 August 1934. By 1 August the Marines' families set sail aboard the USS *Chateau Thierry* and Lt. Col. (Maj. Gen. of the *Garde*) Clayton B. Vogel handed the command of the *Garde d'Haiti* to Col. Demosthenes Calixte. On 14 August the Marine Guard at Brigade Headquarters removed the Stars and Stripes from the flagpole and the Haitian standard ascended the pole in its stead. On 15 August the last elements of the 1st Marine Brigade withdrew from the Republic of Haiti, after nearly 20 years of occupation.

USMC Units That Served in Haiti

The occupation of Haiti was continuous from 28 January 1914 to 15 August 1934, a total of 20 years. Following are the various Marine organizations that participated.

First Brigade: Brigade headquarters, constabulary detachment, brigade depot detachment, brigade signal company, brigade motor transport company.

Second Regiment: Headquarters Company; Thirty-sixth Company; Fifty-third Company (machine gun); Fifty-fourth Company; Sixty-fourth Company; Second Battalion, Headquarters detachment, Sixty-third Company; Observation Squadron 9, M. Headquarters Company; Division 1.

First Battalion, Eleventh Regiment, composed of: Headquarters Company,

Second Company, Fourteenth Company, Forty-sixth Company (joined 31 August 1927, from Nicaragua and was disbanded 6 September 1927).[80]

6

HONDURAS

On 26 October 1838, Honduras declared its complete independence from Spain, and maintained this status until 1847, when it joined Nicaragua and Salvador in a loose confederation which lasted until 1863. In that year Honduras separated from this confederation and became an independent republic. This latter status continued 40 years, notwithstanding the fact that it has been the scene of frequent revolutions alternating with corrupt dictator ships. Relatively weak, this republic has suffered the frequent interference of neighboring countries in its domestic affairs which, added to its own internal turmoil, has kept it in an almost continual state of unrest.

In the year 1903, Manuel Bonilla gained the presidency of Honduras and seemed likely to repeat the success of Marco Aurelio Soto in maintaining order. However, as his term of office drew to a close and his-reelection appeared certain, the supporters of rival candidates and some of his own disaffected adherents intrigued to secure the cooperation of Nicaragua for his overthrow. Bonilla welcomed the opportunity which a successful campaign would assure for consolidating his own position. Jose Santos Zelaya, president of Nicaragua, was equally anxious, and several alleged violations of territory had embittered popular feeling on both sides.[1] The United States and Mexican governments endeavored to secure a peaceful settlement without intervention, but failed.

During this period of revolutionary intrigue, the United States had several naval vessels in Honduran waters to look after American interests. These vessels were the *Marietta*, Lieutenant-Commander Samuel W. B. Diehl, *Olympia* (flagship of Rear Admiral Joseph B. Coghlan), Commander John C. Wilson; *Raleigh*, Commander Arthur P. Nazro; and the *San Francisco*, Captain Asa Walker. On March 15 this squadron sailed from Culebra, West Indies, and arrived off Puerto Cortez about the 21st. Different ships of the squadron then visited the ports of La Ceiba, Trujillo, Tela, and Puerto Sierra. In a letter home, Capt. Butler told his mother about a "battleship" of the Honduras navy lying off shore at Puerto Cortes. He told about his warship firing a friendly salute to which the Honduran responded with their lone gun. Afterward their Marines met Butler's Marines, at which time the USMC laughed out loud, embarrassing on-looking Americans. Otherwise conditions at all of these ports, with the exception of Puerto Cortes, were quiet.[2]

At the latter port conditions were quite serious and at the request of the American consul, William J. Alger, a guard of 13 Marines from the *Marietta* was landed on the 23rd of March for the protection of the consulate. This guard, which included Smedley Butler, remained until the 30th or 31st, when it was withdrawn.

In a letter dated 26 March, he said he and his command marched to the town of Trujillo, "about 53 miles," which was in the hands of the revolutionists, with the regulars holding the fort. They remained in the town observing events until the morning of the 25th, when they returned to Puerto Cortes.

On the 24th of March the flagship *Olympia* landed a detachment of 30 Marines under the command of Captain Henry W. Carpenter and Midshipman Kintner to guard the steamship wharf at Puerto Cortes. They returned to the ship on the 26th.[3]

In February of 1907 a new outbreak of hostilities occurred between Honduras and Nicaragua. The Honduran forces were commanded by Bonilla in person and, by General Sotero Barahona, his minister of war. One of their chief subordinates was Lee Christmas, an adventurer from Memphis, Tennessee, who had previously been a locomotive engineer. Honduras received active support from its ally, Salvador, and was favored by public opinion throughout Central America. But from the outset the Nicaraguans proved victorious, largely owing to their mobility. Their superior naval force enabled them to capture Puerto Cortez and La Ceiba, and to threaten other cities on the Caribbean Coast; on land they were aided by a body of Honduran rebels, who also established a provisional government. Zelaya captured Tegucigalpa after severe fighting, and besieged Bonilla in Amapala. Lee Christmas was killed.

The Marine Guard aboard the *Marietta* landed at Truxillo on the 18th of March to protect the American consulate during this period of political disturbances. The surrender of Amapala on the 11th of April practically ended the war, and Bonilla took refuge on board the United States cruiser *Chicago*. A noteworthy feature of the war was the attitude of the American naval officers, who landed Marines, arranged the surrender of Amapala, and prevented Nicaragua from prolonging hostilities. Honduras was now evacuated by the Nicaraguans and its provisional government was recognized by Zelaya.

Commander Albert G. Winterhalter, in the *Paducah*, was looking after

American interests in the vicinity of Puerto Cortez. Due to the serious state of affairs around Laguna and Choloma (on the Chamelicon River), he deemed it necessary to land his Marine Guard for their protection. Accordingly, the entire guard of 12 Marines, under the command of Ensign Lawrence P. Treadwell, were landed at Laguna on the 28th of April and remained there until the 23rd of May. On this date they were transferred to Choloma, where they guarded American interests until the 8th of June.

7

Mexico

The history of Mexico and the United States has been clouded with troubles, particularly since the Mexican state of Texas decided to withdraw from that nation in 1835–1836. Texans under Gen. Sam Houston defeated the army of Santa Ana and within ten years applied to be annexed to the United States. Thereupon war with Mexico was a certainty. That war was not an intervention so is not described here. But there was one indiscretion which will be described here.

On 21 October 1842, USN Commodore Thomas A.C. Jones had mistakenly learned that war had broken out between the U.S. and Mexico and took it upon himself to land Marines and seamen from the *United States* and *Cyane* at Monterey, California. They seized the town but when they found out they were in error, they withdrew and apologized for their embarrassment.[1]

The merchant ship *Forward*, formerly a British gunboat, was ostensibly employed in the fishing trade on the coast of Mexico in the latter part of May 1870. It was seized by an armed party acting supposedly under orders of Pacido Vega, a former governor of Sinaloa. They raised the Salvadoran flag and, on the night of 27 May, made a raid upon Guaymas, took possession of and robbed the custom-house, and then forced the foreign merchants to contribute a large sum of funds, and, finally, compelled the United States consul, over his protest, to supply coal for the vessel.

Commander William W. Low, USN, with the USS *Mohican*, was in the vicinity, and a few days after the *Forward* was seized, paid a visit to the neighboring port of Mazatlan.

While at this port on 6 June, the American consul, Isaac Sisson, acquainted Low with the facts of the seizure and subsequent actions of the pirate crew of the *Forward*. It was rumored that it was still in the gulf, so Commander Low decided to locate it if possible and exact proper redress for the outrage at Guaymas. He sailed and proceeded along the coast for several days without learning of its whereabouts. On the morning of the 16th he reached San Blas and despatched an officer ashore for information that might lead to the *Forward*'s location. The officer returned and reported that the *Forward* had gone to Boca Teacapan for the purpose of disposing of its plunder.

Commander Low decided to proceed immediately in pursuit. The next morning, on the 17th, the *Mohican* arrived off Boca Teacapan, and Low ordered a landing force of Marines and sailors under Lieutenant Willard H. Brownson, USN, embarked in six boats, and despatched them up the river with instructions to find the piratical steamer and bring it out. The landing party saw nothing of the steamer, nor did they hear of it, until they had proceeded up the river about 25 miles, when they fell in with a fisherman who informed them that the *Forward* was aground some 15 miles farther up the stream. They pushed on as rapidly as possible and at 7:45 p.m. sighted their quest about 206 yards off, aground, and headed inshore.

Lieutenant Brownson and his party pulled alongside, gained the decks without opposition, took possession of the vessel, and made prisoners of the six men who were on board. As the American landing party was approaching the ship, a boat was seen leaving the port bow. Ensign Jonathon M. Wainwright, being under orders to intercept and cut it off, if possible, captured its occupants and brought them aboard the vessel. He then ordered a shot fired to stop the escaping boat when, almost immediately, a volley of musketry, canister and grape was fired from shore, which raked the docks and sides of the steamer and the boat in which he was pursuing the fugitives. This volley was so severe that he had to fall back to the steamer for protection, with casualties of one killed; Assistant Engineer Frederick W. Townrow, two men, and himself wounded. One of the two men wounded was Private James Higgins of the Marines.

The pirates had landed most of their crew, about 170 men. Their shore battery of four 12-pounders had flanked these by riflemen and placed the whole in such a position as to bring a cross and raking fire upon the sides and decks of the grounded ship. Lieutenant Brownson, after holding the vessel for about an hour, decided that it was impossible to get it out and down the river because of the falling tide and the manner in which it was grounded, so he then made preparations to destroy it. Placing his dead and wounded, the prisoners and most of its men in the boats, he with the few remaining set fire to the vessel in the coal-bunker and several places aft. As the party shoved off, they gave a parting shot of shrapnel to insure its complete destruction.

The landing party pulled down the river and regained their own ship early in the afternoon of the 18th, after having been absent about 32 hours.

Lieutenant Brownson commended the officers and men of his party for their coolness and courage under most trying circumstances, and picked several for special consideration, among whom were two Marines—First Sergeant Philip Moore and Corporal F. Moulton.[2]

A short time after the *Forward* had been destroyed, Rear Admiral Thomas Turner, commander of the Pacific Fleet, paid his respects to Admiral Farquhar of the British naval forces in the Pacific, and when about to depart from the British flagship, Admiral Farquhar stated, "This is always the way with you American officers; you are ahead of us when a ship of war is required to be on the spot."

A Marine detachment was part of a small force landed from American ships on 16 May 1876. The U.S. consul at Matamoros had made the request when the rebels vacated the city and before the Mexican army arrived. This was to protect American lives and property.

During 1913 considerable fighting between different factions in Mexico was in progress, and American citizens were urged to leave the troubled area and return to the United States. Some had heeded this warning, but others had remained with their property until conditions made it necessary for United States naval forces to proceed there and assist them in making their departure.

On 4 September, Rear Admiral Walter C. Cowles, commander-in-chief of the Pacific Fleet, directed Commander Dewitt Blamer of the *Buffalo*, which was at Guaymas, to proceed to Ciaris Estoro, and there land R.W. Vail, American consular agent at Guaymas, who would proceed to the Richardson Construction Company's headquarters in the Yaqui Valley for the purpose of bringing to the coast all Americans and foreigners who wished to avail themselves of an opportunity to leave the country, and to then sail for San Diego and land the refugees.

The *Buffalo* arrived at Ciaris Estero the following morning, and at 0905 Mr. Vail, First Lieutenant John R. Henley, Ensigns Arthur H. Hawley and John L. Neilson, and Pilot Charles C. Ross landed and proceeded to the Yaqui Valley.[3] This party returned on the 7th, bringing with them 12 American refugees, and 83 others from the Richardson Construction Company, who wished to leave the country. On the 14th, the *Buffalo* proceeded to San Diego, California, where the refugees were landed.[4]

The culmination of indignities upon the United States by General Huerta in 1914 Mexico came in the arrest of the paymaster and boat's crew of the USS *Dolphin* at Tampico on 6 April of that year. This ship carried, both at her bow and stern, the American flag. Admiral Henry T. Mayo, who was at Tampico at the time, regarded this incident as so serious an affront as to warrant the demand that the flag of the United States be saluted with special ceremony by the military commander of the port. Which did not happen. A few days after this incident, an orderly from the USS *Minnesota*, then at Vera Cruz, was arrested while on shore to obtain the ship's mail, and was for a time in the local jail. An official despatch from the American government to its embassy in Mexico City was withheld by the authorities of the telegraphic service until peremptorily demanded by the chargé d' affaires of the United States in person. President Woodrow Wilson said in his special message to Congress on April 20 said he "felt it my duty to sustain Admiral Mayo in the whole of his demand and to insist that the flag of the United States should be saluted in such a way as to indicate a new spirit and attitude on the part of the Huertaistaa. Such a salute General Huerta has refused." The president asked and obtained the approval of Congress to use the armed forces "in such ways and to such extent as may be necessary to obtain from General Huerta and his adherents the fullest recognition of the rights and dignity of the United States."[5]

The Marine Corps was called upon to make a maximum effort with its strength of fewer than 10,000 officers and men. Actually, the First Advanced Base Force had been practically on a war-time basis during the 1913–1914 winter. As anticipated, it had been on extensive maneuvers with the fleet off Culebra Island and was, apparently based upon potential activity, either on board various ships or in camps ashore at gulf ports.

Brigade Headquarters and the First Marine Regiment, composed of 24 officers and 810 enlisted men, under the command of Lieutenant Colonel Charles G. Long (see Appendix A), had been sent from Pensacola to New Orleans to board the USS *Hancock*.[6] Part of the Second Marine Regiment had spent some time aboard the USS *Prairie* off Vera Cruz.[7] The latter named regiment was of a rather complicated background.[8] The remainder of the Second Regiment, then at a camp in Pensacola, went aboard the USS *Mississippi* for transfer to Vera Cruz. On the 21st of April the elements of the 2d Regiment went ashore under the temporary command of Lieutenant Colonel Wendell C. Neville.

While this was going on some U.S. Navy ships were directed to the Pacific waters off the Mexican coast. The Fourth Regiment of Marines, commanded by Colonel Joseph H. Pendleton (see Appendix A), was reactivated at the Navy Barracks, Puget Sound Navy Yard, in Washington State.[9]

Before the fleet under Rear Admiral Charles J. Badger reached the Mexican shores, it became necessary to issue orders to Rear Admiral Frank F. Fletcher to seize the port of Vera Cruz. Accordingly, early in the morning of the 21st of April, Fletcher prepared a landing force of Marines and sailors from his division, constituting approximately 700 of the former and 5000 of the latter, all under the command of Captain William R. Rush, USN, sent them ashore in ship's boats, and the capture of the city was in progress of accomplishment.

Lieutenant Colonel Wendell C. Neville, a Marine who would someday be commandant, led the first detachments ashore on the 21st and occupied the wharf without opposition. That night Lieutenant Colonel Albertus W. Catlin led ashore another large body of Marines culled from the various ship's detachments. That latter unit was assigned the title "The 3d Marine Regiment."

One of the Marine officers landing that day was Captain Frederick M. Wise. He was aboard the *Hancock*, and he and the command landed at Ward Line wharf. Lieutenant Colonel Long allocated one block for each of his companies. Wise found the blocks were

Sailors taking part in the landing at Vera Cruz, Mexico, in April 1914.

A sailor on horseback during the Vera Cruz, Mexico, landing in April 1914.

built solid. "Walls flush with the streets. Patio inside. We started with the first house. The heavy wooden doors were locked and barred. Marines with sledgehammers were ready. We smashed the doors and went in.

"Not a shot was fired at us. We never found an armed Mexican. We did find old rifles and pistols. We picked them up and went along. It took us most of the afternoon."[10]

The Marines took possession of the custom-house under a rain of fire from snipers hidden in every conceivable place, then proceeded in small parties to take other parts of the city, and to "mop up" the hiding places of the troublesome sharpshooters. Most of the Huerta soldiers had left the town, but there were still a few left who, together with numerous sympathizers, continued to fire upon the Americans from ambush, house tops, and particularly from the military academy. To quiet the fire from the academy, it was necessary for the USS *Chester* and *San Francisco* to use their 3 and 5 inch guns, which they did with telling effect.[11]

Additional troops were landed the second day, and the occupation of the city continued. By the third day the entire metropolis and its environs were in the hands of the American Marines and sailors and the city was fairly quiet, with only an occasional shot being fired. At a later date additional Marines were dispatched from the United States under the command of Colonel Littleton W. T. Waller, at which time the Marine detachments as well as the sailors from the fleet were returned to their ships. The Marines left ashore were organized into the First, Second and Third Regiments, and the Artillery Battalion, the whole being designated First Brigade of Marines, with a strength of 84 officers and 2,321 men.

Marines and seamen landed. However, the two fought a different kind of war. The navy, unused to fighting on land, went hell bent for action and suffered higher rates of casualties than did the Marines. The sailors raced up a street and the Mexican snipers and occasional machine gun operators had a field day killing them. The Marines decided on a different course of action. They cleared each street as they went along, using a different method entirely. The buildings were all attached, made of adobe stone, and the Marines went through each building using pickaxes to bludgeon the walls, on into the next building, managing to capture or kill anyone who resisted. Most roof tops were flat, and snipers were working over the sailors. The Marines would take those roofs and snipers in turn. That street taken, they moved onto another and the same pattern.[12]

Captain Hiram Bearss (see Appendix A) led his company shore on the 22d. After passing through most of the other companies, Bearss and his men found themselves being fired upon from a church tower lying just before them.

First they drove out the Mexicans firing from the church, then went after the accurate snipers in that church tower. Hiram directed two of his best shots, McNewland and Trainor, to fire at anyone they saw firing from the tower. It was then he discovered that those snipers firing down at them were bluejackets from the fleet. As he said, like so many other observers of the landing, the U.S. sailors caused more casualties among the Americans than the Mexicans.

Another captain of Marines, William Harllee, with his company aboard the USS *Florida*, landed at 1110 that same morning. Their job was to take and protect the electric plant on the north edge of town. Just after their noon meal, firing became intense and Harllee moved his command to some nearby sandhills. In his biography, the author describes what happened when some U.S. sailors occupied the roof of the power station. They began to fire upon Marines at the railroad station. Harllee went to the roof and forced them to cease firing. He had to "manhandle personally some of them and threaten to put their officer under arrest, but he succeeded."

When Colonel John A. Lejeune arrived on the 22d and assumed command, all Marines were considered as part of his command, the 2d Advanced Base Force. He noted some of the sacrifices made by the U.S. sailors as they tried to fight the war on their terms. Fortunately for them, their ships were alongside and both the *Prairie* and *Chester* opened fire on the buildings which housed the Mexican Naval School in which the cadets bravely tried to hold for the city. The fire was accurate and the cadets hastily withdrew.

Lejeune was ordered by Adm. Badger to report to Adm. Fletcher, aboard the *Prairie*, who was in command of the shore forces. After his brief interview with Fletcher, Lejeune noted in his memoir that he fell between the *Prairie* and the seawall and had a difficult time returning to the surface.[13] After his recovery he assumed from Neville overall command of all Marine forces ashore.

In the meantime small groups of Marines scattered about the fleet were assembled under the command of Major Albertus W. Catlin. Included in that body, labeled the 3d Regiment, was a unit from Panama under the command of Major Smedley D. Butler, a Marine who had been making a name for himself since he joined the corps in 1899.

Butler had already been in Mexico, back in March, when he took a train ride to Mexico City in a spying mission. That was a program thought up by Adm. Fletcher and Butler. It was further evidence that the U.S. government, under President Wilson, was looking to make trouble for the Mexico of Huerta. Actually, the mission had little to do with the landing in April.

The landing of Butler's Marine detachment aboard the USS *Chester*, which included a young man named Alexander Archer Vandegrift, was described in his autobiography. They arrived late at night on the 23d and immediately landed and went into position for the morning assault. Vandergrift's platoon was on the right. They went on the attack early until caught by some of the Navy's 5-inch shells, though they suffered no casualties and were part of the force that secured the town that day.[14]

Butler ordered him and his platoon to establish an outpost line of trenches in the sand dunes west of the city. They had to tear down a house blocking their view and when a citizen saw what they were doing, he demanded compensation. It amounted to 5,000 pesos. When Vandegrift was later questioned as to what right he had to sign such a letter, he went to Lejeune, who told him, "I ordered you, so let them question me." He further stated that Butler was a great leader and fighting man, as so many other people have been quoted.[15]

The Mexican civil officials of the city quit their offices as soon as the American force made its appearance and refused to resume their duties. Consequently, it became necessary for Adm. Fletcher to appoint Marine and Naval officers to those administrative offices in order to reestablish a regular civil government for the town. By the 27th of April, conditions were tranquil; shops and stores were opened for regular business and, from outward appearances, it was difficult to believe that the city was in the hands of an occupying force from a foreign power.

Meanwhile, the Americans had been extremely active. The First Regiment was soon located in a large flour mill while the Second Regiment was quartered in the train yard.

One interesting situation occurred in the command of Major John H. Russell, Jr., a later commandant. He was, with his battalion, on the outskirts of Ver Cruz defending the water works at El Tejar, when they were approached by a lone Mexican cavalryman. The latter, according to several reports, demanded that Russell surrender his command because they were supposedly surrounded. Russell, was said to have gone slightly berserk and called Lejeune asking what he should do, to which Lejeune responded in a negative manner. Later, during the confirmation hearings for Russell's promotion to commandant, this matter came up but was pooh pood by Russell and some of his friends.[16]

On the 28th, the 1st day of his arrival, General Frederick Funston, U.S. Army, with several army units, took over the command of all land operations and the Navy withdrew. The balance of his force arrived by the 30th of April. The Marine brigade was detached from naval jurisdiction, and reported to General Funston, remaining on such duty until the city was evacuated on November 23rd, when they returned to the United States and to naval control.

"Fritz" Wise tells us in his memoir of the other, most of them later famous, Marines who were with this brigade which remained in Vera Curz under the army's control. Such names as Hiram Bearss, Logan Feland, "Jumbo" Hill, Smedley Butler and Robert H. Dunlap, and of course, John Lejeune, who commanded the Marines but was replaced by Col. Paul Mahoney.

During this operation the Marines suffered casualties of three killed in action, 11 wounded in action, and one accidentally wounded. The Navy's loss was 18 killed in action and about 58 wounded.[17]

This was the last overt action by the United States Marines with Mexico. However, because a Mexican rebel, General Pancho Villa, raided a few settlements in Texas killing some Americans, a fairly large movement of U.S. Army troops led by Brig. Gen. John J. Pershing invaded Mexico in 1916. Additionally, a large force of U.S. Army National Guard troops were called up and stationed on that border for a period during World War One. Later, but during that war, several Marine regiments, the 8th and 9th, were created and wound up in Texas, near the Mexican border, "just in case."

8

NICARAGUA

The United States Navy landed Marines in Nicaragua several times during the 19th century. Most of those occasions—in 1853, 1854, 1894, 1896, 1898, and 1899—were of a one day intervene with no lasting results.

On 11 March 1853 a Marine detachment commanded by Marine Orderly Sergeant James E. Thompson was landed at Greytown (aka San Juan del Sur), Nicaragua, from the sloop *Cyane* for the protection of the American Steamship Company's property (the railroad) and remained until 13 March.[1] Later that year the American minister to Nicaragua, Mr. Borland, while in Greytown, was assaulted and kept a prisoner for 24 hours. A U.S. naval party landed and demanded and received an apology for that offense.

The following year on 12 July the sloop *Cyane* sent a small naval force ashore at Greytown to protect Americans with Sergeant Thompson once again leading the Marines. They captured and destroyed three field pieces and numerous muskets and then returned to the *Cyane*. The following morning Captain George N. Hollins had his ship open fire on the town at 8:00 a.m. The firing ceased at 3:00 p.m. and the small landing force went ashore once again. They destroyed what remained of the town and were back aboard at 7:30 p.m.[2]

During the early part of the period the Navy undertook a series of surveys to determine the best location for an inter-oceanic canal. A number of routes across the Isthmus of Panama were examined and also the route which has been more seriously considered in recent years across Nicaragua. A detachment of three officers and 60 Marines assisted in the survey of the Darien route in 1870.

One of the periodic revolutions of that turbulent republic was in full swing during the summer of 1894. The *Colombia* and *Marblehead* were kept stationed in the waters of the east coast of that country to look after American interests.

At the request of the American consul at Bluefields, the Marine detachment of the *Marblehead*, commanded by First Lieutenant Franklin J. Moses, and a company of sailors landed on 6 July and provided protection for about one month. The force was approximately doubled on 31 July by the addition of the Marine guard and a company of seamen from the *Colombia*. The combined landing forces withdrew one week later. A small landing force was sent ashore from the *Alert* at Bluefields in May 1896 under similar conditions. The *Alert* remained in the vicinity for some time and had occasion to send a landing force ashore to protect the American consular agent at San Juan del Sur about two years later.[3]

The Reyes Insurrection was the cause of disturbances in the first part of 1899. The cause of the insurrectionists appeared hopeless, but the attending circumstances caused great excitement, and disorders were imminent.

The United States was represented by Commander Frederick M. Symonds, in the *Marietta*. The British government was also represented by the HMS *Intrepid*. These two vessels were at anchor at Bluefields about the middle of February, when the foreign merchants of the city petitioned their commanding officers to despatch a landing party ashore to protect the lives and property of foreigners. The American vice-consul from Greytown, F. Percy Scott, was aboard the *Marietta*, and he together with Commander Symonds went ashore on the morning of 13 February to obtain firsthand information relative to conditions. No landing was made, however, until late in the evening of the 24th, when Lieutenant Frederic B. Bassett, Jr., USN, a detachment of Marines and sailors, numbering about 13 men, and a Colt automatic gun, together with a like force from the British ship, were sent ashore to guard foreign interests. The American force returned to the *Marietta* about 7:00 p.m. on the 28th.[4]

A conference had been held in Washington in 1907 by which the Central American Republics agreed to avoid war and revolutionary disturbances. President José Santos Zelaya of Nicaragua had consistently violated these conventions, and the governments of Costa Rica, Salvador, and Guatemala protested to the United States against Zelaya's continual disregard of the general treaty and other agreements which had been signed.

To make matters still worse, Zelaya sanctioned the execution of two Americans in November 1909. These Americans, Lee Roy Cannon and Leonard Groce, had served with the revolutionary forces under General Juan J. Estrada, but were later captured by the Zelayaistas, summarily tried and executed. Upon Zelaya's acknowledgment of responsibility for this last crime against American citizens, Secretary of State Philander Knox informed the Nicaraguan chargè d'affaires that President Zelaya had notoriously kept Central America in turmoil since the Washington Convention of 1907, as opposed to the patient efforts of neighboring states to support the conventionists. He further pointed out that under Zelaya's regime republican institutions had ceased to exist except in name; that public opinion and the press had been throttled; and that any tendency to real patriotism had been rewarded by incarceration.[5]

The Nicaraguan chargè d'affaires was handed his passport, whereupon President Zelaya attempted a reconciliation, but without success, and then resigned in favor of Dr. Jose Madriz. This maneuver failed, and Madriz then launched an offensive against the Conservatives and tried to recapture Bluefields.[6]

The U.S. State Department decided that action was "illegal" and determined to intervene in Nicaragua. In view of these conditions, several vessels of the Navy were despatched to Nicaraguan waters to protect American interests, and in late 1909 several Marine Corps units were likewise despatched, but no landings were made until early in the following year.

A regiment of Marines was embarked aboard the *Buffalo*, under the command of Colonel James E. Mahoney, and on the 22d of February the vessel was at anchor at Corinto, when Commander Guy N. Brown ordered Captain John A. Hughes,[7] with a detachment of Marines to proceed ashore to gain

Marines of Captain John A. Hughes' company patrolling the western beach in Nicaragua in 1910.

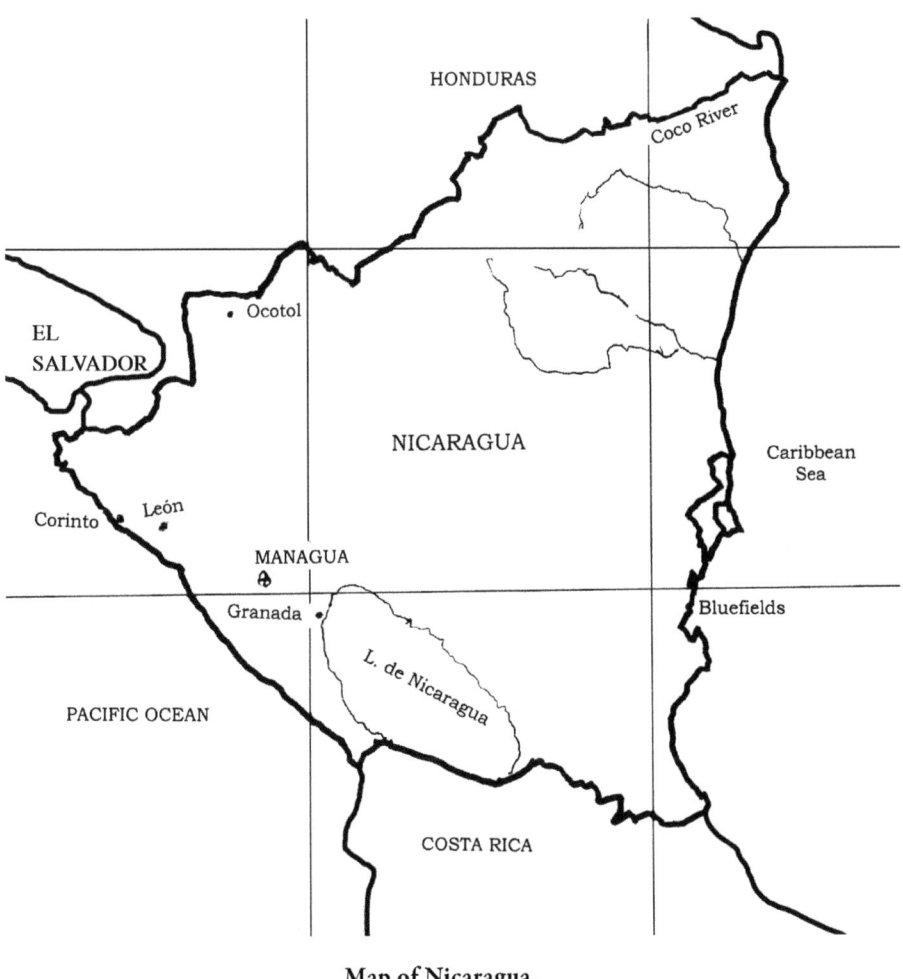

Map of Nicaragua.

information. Captain Hughes landed about 8:00 p.m. and returned aboard just before midnight, having completed his mission.

In the early part of April the *Dubuque*, under Commander Harold K. Hines, and the *Paducah*, under Commander William W. Gilmer, were looking after American interests at Bluefields where General Larra was conducting operations. Both of these vessels sent a landing force ashore on the 19th of May under Commander Hines. These two detachments not being considered sufficient to adequately protect American interests, the *Dubuque* sailed for Colón, Panama, on the 27th of May, to transport a force of Marines from that place. It arrived at Colón, embarked a force of 6 officers and 200 enlisted Marines, under the command of Major Smedley D. Butler, then returned to

Bluefields and, on the 30th, sent half of the battalion on board the *Paducah*. On the following day, Major Butler and the remainder of the battalion was landed in Bluefields, as was also those on the *Paducah*. On the 5th of June the bluejacket landing forces returned to their respective ships. Major Butler proceeded to Colón, Panama, on the 9th of August, secured the Marine band of 29 pieces, and returned with them to Bluefields. This battalion remained on shore at Bluefields until the 4th of September, when it was withdrawn and returned to Panama via the *Tacoma*.

Colonel James E. Mahoney and larger group of Marines landed in May 1910 at Corinto. Another major disturbance ashore was the reason. It was a largely a clash between those out of government who wanted more participation in Nicaraguan affairs by the United States. And of course, they were opposed by the Zelayan government, which, as always, wanted less or preferably no involvement by the U.S.

Butler was very anxious to land and do something but was, through the good offices of Secretary of State Philander Knox restrained aboard ship.

The U.S. government was anxious to separate Zelaya from Nicaragua and these efforts continued for several years to come. But with no landing by Butler, Mahoney's group was soon back aboard ship.[8]

In the latter part of 1910, the American minister to Panama, Thomas C. Dawson, was directed to proceed to Nicaragua to present the views of the United States to General Estrada. In October 1910, the Dawson agreements were signed. Elections were held in November; Estrada was elected and assumed office on 1 January 1911.[9]

The Zelaya party began again to be a constant source of annoyance, and riots and vandalism were frequent throughout the Republic of Nicaragua. The Chamorro faction within the Conservative Party sought to control the administration. This faction prevented Estrada from carrying through desirable reconstruction legislation, failed to cooperate in carrying out the Dawson agreements, and, on 5 April 1911, President Estrada dissolved the assembly. The president then appealed to the United States for assistance, as in addition to his difficulties with the Conservative (Diego M.) Chamorro faction, the Liberal leaders in the neighboring republics were actively fomenting a revolution against his government. General Luis Mena, Estrada's minister of war, was arrested on 9 May 1911, by the president's orders. And on the same day, Estrada resigned, turning over his office to the vice president, Adolfo Diaz, who in turn released Mena. On 31 May 1911, as a result of a Liberal plot, Loma Fort in Managua was blown up, killing over 60 people, and two days later a magazine was exploded with additional casualties. A well defined revolution broke out on 29 July 1912, and because of this unsettled

8. Nicaragua

state of affairs, the United States despatched several naval vessels to Nicaraguan waters.[10]

At the request of the president, a detachment of seamen from the *Annapolis* landed at Corinto, Nicaragua, on 4 August and proceeded to Managua to protect American lives and interests during a period of unrest.[11]

Then, on the 10th of August a battalion of Marines, consisting of 13 officers and 341 men, under Major Smedley D. Butler, was hurried from Panama via the *Justin*. They arrived at Corinto on the 14th, immediately landed and proceeded by rail to Managua.

Seven days later a detachment of 19 Marines and 38 seamen, under naval Lieutenant Bradford Barnette, landed from the *Tacoma* at Bluefields, Nicaragua, at the request of the local governor and U.S. consul, to protect American and foreign lives during a revolutionary period. They remained until the 13th of October.

Second Lieutenant Earl C. Long, with 15 of his Marines, was landed from the *Denver* at San Juan del Sur on 27 August to reconnoiter the railroad at Corinto and vicinity. He established a guard at Chinandega to protect the railroad, which was retained there until the 22nd of October, when the unit was withdrawn.

First Lieutenant Hermann T. Vulte and a detachment of 63 enlisted Marines from the *California* landed at Corinto on 28 August to protect Americans during the revolution. At this point, Rear Admiral William H. H. Southerland assumed command of the entire American force in Nicaragua.

On the 4th of September more Marines, now a provisional regiment of 29 officers and 752 enlisted Marines, and 11 naval enlisted men, commanded by Colonel Joseph H. Pendleton, landed at Corinto from the *California*, for the same reasons as above.[12]

The following day 12 officers, 250 seamen and 61 Marines, commanded by First Lieutenant Lauren S. Willis, landed at Corinto from the *Colorado* for the same reasons as stated above. That group remained ashore until 11 November.

Ten days later the Marine detachment from the *Cleveland*, commanded by Second Lieutenant Daniel M. Gardner, Jr., with a company of seamen, one section of artillery and two Colt automatic guns, landed at Corinto. The entire force, commanded by Lieutenant Commander Edward Woods, remained ashore until 23 October.

A Marine battalion aboard a train, commanded by Major Butler, was ambushed at the pass at Masaya on 19 September. Several Marines were wounded. Butler stopped the train and the Marines went after the rebels. They killed 56 and wounded 70 more in a few minutes. Their train, following that interim, was then allowed to pass. Butler soon had a reputation among the Nicaraguans.

About 800 rebels held the double fortress hills of Coyotepe and Barranca. Butler's battalion and two batteries of Marine artillery moved into position west of Coyotepe on 3 October. Colonel Pendleton offered the rebel commander Zeledon, a chance to surrender, but his effort was ignored. The First Battalion of Marines, commanded by Major William N. McKelvy (see Appendix A) and the Third Battalion, by Butler, which was composed of two companies of Marines and one of sailors, and a battalion of sailors from the *California*, were to take part. McKelvy's men were in the center, the seamen were on the east of the hill, and Butler's mixed unit was on the left. The rebels had a strong, well-defended position but the Americans went up the hill and took the top. McKelvy's losses were the heaviest. The Nicaraguan army, seeing how well things were going, joined in the attack at the last moment. (For a list of Marine officers involved, see Appendix C.)

A Marine detachment under the command of Lieutenant Colonel Charles G. Long engaged with revolutionaries at the Battle of Leon on 5 October, defeating them once again.[13]

On 30 October the *Denver* then proceeded to San Juan del Sur, arriving there on the morning of the 30th, and at once landed a force of bluejackets to protect the American Consulate.

It was much later the following month, on the 21st of November, when the greater part of the Panama battalion, under Major Butler, and the 1st Provisional Regiment, under Colonel Pendleton, was withdrawn aboard the *Buffalo*. That left only a legation guard at Managua, under the command of Lieutenant Colonel Charles G. Long, which consisted of one battalion of 400 officers and men. This battalion was relieved on 9 January 1913 by a regular legation guard of about 105 officers and men, under the command of Captain Edward A. Greene.[14]

During the latter part of 1921 and the first part of 1922, conditions in Nicaragua became somewhat unsettled, and it was deemed advisable to increase the legation guard to enable it to handle the situation should circumstances so require. The *Galveston*, under Captain Clarence S. Kempff, and the *Denver*, under Captain Austin Kautz, were at Corinto in late January, when the commandant, 15th Naval District, ordered that the legation guard be reinforced.

On 25 January 30 Marines commanded by First Lieutenant Edward E. Mann from the *Galveston* landed at Corinto, Nicaragua, to reinforce the legation guard at Managua during a period of anti–American activities.[15] They were followed four days later by First Lieutenant Arnold C. Larsen and 52 men.[16] Following on 8 February were First Lieutenant William S. Fellers and 46 Marines, who had been transported to Corinto on the *Nitro*.[17] Lieutenant Larsen and 13 of his men returned to the *Denver* on 11 February, and the *Galveston*'s Marines did likewise.

During an attempted revolt on 21 May, rebels had seized the La Loma fortress. A warning was sent to them by the American minister, John E. Ramer, that the Marines would open fire upon them if the seizure continued. The rebels immediately left the fort. The Marine legation guard, without firing a shot, had prevented the contemplated destruction of Managua, and through American officials, an amicable settlement was reached by the rival parties without bloodshed.

Meanwhile, according to several authors, a number of individual Marines of that 100 or so man garrison were in constant trouble with the Nicaraguan authorities. They sometimes fought with or shot at natives; a few deserted, including one sergeant who was killed in a standoff with Nicaraguan police. The presence of just a few Marines as legation guards did not sit well with the local populace.

Before 1925, the United States government had informed the government of Nicaragua of its intention to withdraw the Marines then stationed at Managua as a guard for the American Legation. President Bartolemé Martinez endeavored to have that policy changed, but was informed that owing to the notification of some 14 months previously, in which time the Nicaraguan government had ample opportunity to perfect plans, the policy would be carried out.

Carlos Solorzano, who had been elected on a coalition ticket to succeed President Martinez, was inaugurated on 1 January 1925. The United States formally recognized the Solorzano government six days after Solorzano took office. The constabulary, which had been provided for, had not as yet been organized, and President Solorzano requested that the Marines remain until its organization, under American instructors, could be effected. This request was granted and the date of withdrawal was changed to 1 September.

The constabulary was finally organized and trained by three Americans, and by the latter part of July, it was thought that the constabulary had progressed to such an extent as to permit them to assume the duties of maintaining order, and allow the contemplated withdrawal of the Marines.

Instructions were accordingly issued to Major Ralph S. Keyser,[18] who was then commanding the guard, to make preparations for abandoning the post on the 1st of August. These instructions were carried out as planned, and the Legation Guard left Managua on that date, and sailed from Corinto three days later.

Some apprehension surrounded the Marine withdrawal, due to a lack of confidence in the ability of the Nicaraguan government officials to maintain order and furnish proper protection to foreigners and foreign interests. How well grounded were these fears will be clearly shown in subsequent incidents which occurred in the affairs of the republic.

Within a short time after the withdrawal of the Marines, various Liberal leaders, including the minister of finance, were arrested—it being alleged that these persons were implicated in a revolt against the government. Disturbances increased, martial law was declared, and the railway was temporarily suspended through revolutionary activity.

On the 25th of October, supporters of General Emiliano Chamorro seized the Loma Fort in Managua and announced their purpose of driving from the cabinet the Liberal members, and the restoring of the Conservatives. The pact entered into by the political parties whereby the Solorzano-Sacasa had come into being was immediately broken, and Solorzano signed instead a pact with Chamorro, by which the latter was appointed, general in chief of the army and his supporters placed in the cabinet. In the following month, November, Vice President Juan B. Sacasa fled from the republic—stating that he was compelled to do so because of threats against his life. In December, the Nicaraguan Congress ordered Sacasa to appear to answer charges of conspiracy, but he did not return to Nicaragua.

General Chamorro, continuing his climb to power, saw to it that his supporters in the cabinet elected him to the first congress in 1926, and, having gained a seat in that body, had himself elected first designate for the presidency. On 12 January, the congress impeached Vice President Sacasa and banished him for a period of two years. Four days later President Solorzano was granted an indefinite leave of absence by the Nicaraguan congress, and General Chamorro assumed the executive power of the government, even though he had been advised on several occasions by the United States Government that he would not be recognized if he assumed that office.

Notwithstanding this refusal, and the refusal of the Central American governments, General Chamorro proceeded in his administration, apparently in the expectation that he could force recognition. Revolutionary activities broke out in May which resulted in the necessity of again landing American Marines to protect the interests of the United States.

Captain John W. Wainwright, commanding the *Cleveland*, arrived at Bluefields on the east coast of Nicaragua on 6 May. The following day, the Marine detachment, under First Lieutenant Charles S. Finch, together with a detachment of seamen, went on shore to look after their country's interests.[19] This landing party was overall commanded by Lieutenant Commander

Spencer S. Lewis, and remained ashore until the 5th of June, when they were withdrawn.

About two months later, on 27 August, Captain Julius C. Townsend, in the *Galveston*, arrived at Bluefields, and, in accordance with orders of the commander, Special Service Squadron, despatched a landing force ashore consisting of the Marine detachment, under Captain Joseph W. Knighton, and of 6 naval officers and 132 bluejackets.[20] This force landed on the afternoon of 27 August and remained until the 1st of November.

In the meantime, the *Rochester*, on 2 September, under command of Captain Burrell O. Allen, with a Marine company of two officers and 103 men commanded by Captain John W. Thomason, Jr. (see Appendix A), anchored off Bluefields.

Nine days later, Lieutenant Commander Clarence Gulbranson, Captain Thomason, and two squads of Marines boarded the steamer *Dictator*, which was lying in the harbor. They remained aboard, then returned a few hours afterward. On the 13th they again boarded this steamer, remained a few hours then returned; a little later in the day this same party boarded the steamer *Camaguey*, remained aboard a short time, and returned. Then the *Denver*, under command of Captain Henry L. Wyman, arrived at Corinto on 25 September.

On 10 October Captain Wyman sent his landing force ashore. This force consisted of the Marine detachment under First Lieutenant Henry T. Nicholas,[21] five naval officers and 63 bluejackets, the whole under Commander Selah L. La Bounty. They all remained ashore until the 27th, when all were withdrawn except a Marine patrol of 12 men under Lieutenant Nicholas.

Beginning with the 28th, this patrol was quartered aboard the *Denver*, but went ashore about 1:00 each afternoon, remaining until 6:00 p.m., which practice was maintained until 13 November. Shortly after this the *Denver* sailed for Panama, but returned to Bluefields on the 27th, and on the 30th sent its landing force ashore there. This force was the same as that landed previously at Corinto, and the last day of this year found them still ashore.

Two detachments of the *Rochester*'s Marines were landed—one, commanded by Second Lieutenant Kenneth B. Chappell,[22] in Bluefields proper, and the other, commanded by Captain Thomason, at El Bluff, both on 31 October. They were withdrawn on 30 November. The *Rochester* sailed for Rio Grande on 23 December, arrived the same day, and immediately despatched a landing force of one battalion, including the Marines, for duty ashore, and they were still on this duty on the last day of the year. On the same day, 23 December, the *Cleveland* again landed its force of Marines and sailors, at Bragman's Bluff, where they remained until 4 January 1927.

It may be well to give a very brief outline of the political set-up in the Nicaraguan Republic as it existed in the closing days of 1926. A conference had been negotiated between the two political factions—Liberal and Conservative—which, after reaching an impasse in the latter part of October, abruptly ended, and hostilities were again resumed. On the 11th of November, the Congress designated Adolfo Diaz for the presidency, and the United States accorded recognition on the 17th of the same month. Two days prior to this recognition Diaz through the American chargè d'affaires sought the assistance of the United States to protect American and foreign lives and property. Doctor Sacasa (the former vice president) landed at Puerto Cabesaa on 1 December and, surrounded by a small group of followers, was on the same day inaugurated by them as the "constitutional president." He, in turn, named a cabinet and became commander-in-chief of the revolutionary forces. General Chamorro, who had previously deposited the executive power with Senator Uriza, resigned his office as general-in-chief of the Army on 8 December, and on the 15th, he turned over the Army to the Diaz government.

The revolutionary activities begun in the latter part of 1926 increased to such an extent that additional American forces were deemed necessary to furnish the proper protection to all foreigners and to maintain the neutral zones. Marine detachments from *Cleveland*, *Denver*, and *Rochester* went ashore on 1 January 1927. Many were stationed at Pearl Cay Lagoon and at El Bluff. They remained at those places until the 27th of May. The *Cleveland*'s Marines at El Bluff were withdrawn on 4 January. Marines and seamen from the *Galveston* went ashore at Corinto, Nicaragua, two days later and proceeded to Managua to protect the U.S. legation, remaining there until 1 February.

The following day 30 Marines from the *Cleveland*, under the command of First Lieutenant Charles S. Finch, were landed at Rio Grande, remaining there until 6 June.[23] Two days later 22 Marines under the command of naval Lieutenant E. G. Hanson landed at Prinzapolca, also remaining until 6 June. A few days later, on the 10th, the Second Battalion of the Fifth Regiment, commanded by Lieutenant Colonel James J. Meade, landed at Bluefields.[24]

On the 19th of February, Marines and seamen from the *Galveston* went ashore, again taking up a position at Outpost 1 at Leon, where they remained until 15 June.

Marine detachments from the *Arkansas*, *Florida*, and *Texas* went ashore two days later in February, and detachments from the *Florida* and *Texas* later

Opposite, top: **The 11th Marine Regiment boarding a battleship bound for Nicaragua, c. 1927.** *Bottom:* **Marines marching to board a troop transport for Nicaragua, c. 1927.**

joined the Fifth Regiment. A total of 200 Marines arrived and landed at Corinto for guard duty at Chinandega and Leon.

Observation Squadron No. 1 and a Marine rifle company, all under command of Major Ross E. Rowell (see Appendix A), sailed for Nicaragua on the 27th.[25] The Marine detachment from the *Tulsa*, was sent ashore on the 4th of March. On 7 March, the Second Brigade and the Fifth Regiment, less two fifths that had already arrived, landed at Corinto. Brigadier General Logan Feland was in command. On 19 May the Eleventh Marine Regiment arrived in Nicaragua. Then, two days later, Observation Squadron No. 4 arrived in Nicaragua. The 11th Regiment and Observation Squadron No. 4 were under the overall command of Colonel Randolph C. Berkeley and were dispatched to Corinto.[26]

In June a political solution to the revolution occurring in Nicaragua was settled sufficiently and Observation Squadron No. 1, consisting of three officers and 66 enlisted men, was returned to the United States. About 38 officers and 1,100 enlisted men of the Fifth and Eleventh Regiments were also returned to the United States in July 1927. The balance of the expeditionary force remaining at the time consisted of the Second Brigade and the officers and enlisted men serving with the *Guardia Nacional of Nicaragua*. The dispersion of Marines to the U.S. in 1927 was very pre-mature. They would soon return.

Captain Franklin A. Hart and the *Rochester* Marine landing force was withdrawn from shore duty on 13 June. On the 15th of July, First Lieutenant Henry T. Nicholas and 20 of his Marines from the *Denver* landed at El Gallo, remaining there until 8 August. This same date, First Lieutenant Charles Connette,[27] with 19 Marines from the 51st Company, left for Puerto Oabezas via the *Robert Smith*.

The following day, outlaw leader Augusto C. Sandino began his active operations by attacking the Marine garrison at Ocotal with about 500 of his men. On 17 July, Sandino and his mob of about 500 natives continued their attack upon the small Marine detachment and *Guardia* at Ocotal. He was badly defeated and retired after a large number of his band had been killed.

That was not the last of him. His name, Augusto Sandino, was a nom de guerre. He and his followers had decided to oust Diaz from office before the 1928 elections. Diaz was, as Sandino so loudly proclaimed, a handmaiden of the U.S. State Department. He said, "It is preferable ... to die as rebels and not live as slaves." Like him or not, Sandino was the most zealous patriot in all of Nicaragua. He would fight a guerrilla war unlike any seen by Marines before that time. He did not often win any great battles, but he continued fighting long after everyone else had given up. Patriot or not, he and his followers did some really despicable things to Marines and fellow Nicaraguans. His name alone was an "army in being." That was his real claim to fame.

In May 1927, Sandino married his lovely paramour, Blanca Arauz. Despite the uplift in his personal life, the general rebel situation looked bleak to him at the time, and he made some efforts to communicate his willingness to negotiate terms. In effect, he was looking for an honorable way out of what appeared to be an impossible dilemma. The 21st was a busy day. Sandino sent a telegram to General Feland asking that the Americans remove Diaz and take over the reins of government until the elections. Feland responded by ordering the 5th Marines into northern Nicaragua to disarm Sandino and his forces or force them over the border into Honduras. Then General Moncada joined in, sending Sandino a telegram instructing the rebel leader to come in with his men and weapons. Sandino refused—unless the United States agreed to take over the reins of government and, when the time came, guarantee a fair, honest election. This was something the U.S. representatives refused to do. Even when Sandino's father visited his encampment in the department of Nueva Segovia, he refused to relinquish his arms for fear that the Americans would renege on their promises. He swore to continue fighting until his country was free from the men who had ruled and ruined it. That would be never, but he must have held some hope that it would happen someday. There is a story, which is difficult to verify, that Sandino went so far as to offer all the Marine officers in Nicaragua a large monetary settlement if they would cease serving in the country. It never happened, but stranger things did during the next five years.[28]

Although Sandino was willing to make an accommodation with the government and the U.S. forces, some of the rebels were not. One, a man named Cabulla, the leader of the band that attacked Buchanan's Marines at La Paz on 16 May, tried to shoot a Marine officer on 26 May but picked on the wrong man. His intended target, Capt. William P. Richards, was considered to be the best pistol shot in the corps, and he proved it that day at El Viejo.[29] Cabulla paid with his life. According to a 27 May newspaper article: "Captain Richards had gone to a house in which Cabulla was staying to remonstrate against the maltreatment of several inhabitants by the bandit leader. As he entered the door the officer was attacked by a woman in the house with a machete, while Cabulla leaped from his bed and drew a pistol. Capt. Richards thereupon drew his own weapon and fired, killing Cabulla instantly and then was forced to kill the woman in self-defense.... [Cabulla] was reputed to have 60 killings to his credit."[30]

Fifty Marines led by Maj. Harold Clifton Pierce left Managua on 31 May to establish control over Nueva Segovia.[31] They were to "peaceably disarm everybody" and deliver the new governor, Arnoldo Ramirez Abaunza, to

Ocotal. With Pierce were Capt. Gilbert Hatfield, of whom we will learn more later, and 2d Lt. Lawrence Norman.[32] Feland instructed Pierce to "secure information that will facilitate the coming supervision of elections, but do not fire a shot unless imperatively necessary; and conciliate with firmness, tranquilize without force of arms, avoid combat, if possible; do everything compatible with dignity and self preservation to help the big mission of the brigade."

Anyone with a modicum of common sense could see that most if not all the instructions were impossible for anyone to satisfactorily fulfill, even a Marine. Abaunza was a Liberal for a Liberal territory, per the Tipatapa agreement, and Ocotal was his capital. The Marines went first to Matagalpa in trucks, a journey that took them an entire day. There, Pierce met Maj. Maurice E. Shearer, who commanded the 3d Battalion, 5th Marines—the same outfit he had led at Belleau Wood so many years before. During the next four days, Pierce got his men ready for an overland march. He bought 50 riding mules and 56 pack mules and hired 11 mule-skinners. On 5 June they came to San Rafael del Norte, a town that Sandino had held up and robbed just two weeks before their arrival. Second Lieutenant Wilburt S. "Big Foot" Brown and his platoon of Marines from the 20th Company, 3d Battalion, 5th Marines, occupied the town.[33] While they were there, Governor Ramirez visited Blanca de Sandino. She informed him that her husband would never intentionally fire on the Marines, but he knew the rebel leader could not control all his men. The next day the party continued its march. It quickly became evident to Pierce that he was being trailed. When they came to Santa Rosa, he learned that an armed rebel band had passed through the day before. At Totogalpa on 8 June, the Marines found and disarmed about 20 Liberals without incident. That same day, 1st Lt. Frank H. Lamson-Scribner and Cpl. Lawrence Pabst took off with their observers, Capt. Francis E. Pierce and Sergeant Nash, and made a reconnaissance flight for Major Pierce's mounted detachment. They found nothing to report.[34]

Pierce's patrol reached Ocotal on the 9th. The town was located at the 2,000-foot level in a broad valley a bit north of the western end of the Coco River. The weather was good, as was the water supply, and it was on the path to Honduras. The town soon became well known to all Marines.

Upon arrival, Pierce learned that only a few families remained out of a population of 1,400. A small detachment of Liberals defended the town, but Pierce immediately relieved them of their weapons and responsibilities. A band of Conservatives had the town under siege. Pierce sent a message to their leader calling for him to surrender his arms. After several discussions, the Conservative commander, being of sound mind, decided to comply. In they came with flags flying and trumpets blaring: some cavalry, some infantry, 168 men with 98 rifles.

Air activity was on the increase. Two Marine de Havillands, flown by Lieutenant Lamson-Scribner with Gunnery Sergeant Geer as his observer, and Captain Robert J. Archibald with Second Lieutenant Harmon as his observer, made a reconnaissance flight to Ocotal on 11 June.[35] They again observed nothing. On the thirteenth, First Lieutenant Swarthout with Second Lieutenant Frank D. et Weir as observer and 1st Lt. Hayne D. "Cuckoo" Boyden with Sergeant Morgan as observer scouted San Isidro, Esteli, Telpaneca, and Ocotal but observed nothing.[36]

Pierce next tried to communicate with Managua. Because the distance for telegraph service was extremely limited, he chose a different course of action. He ordered his men to spread out signal panels for the air patrols keeping tabs on his expedition, then erected two long poles 75 feet apart in an open field with a message in a bag strung between them. The pilots of the two de Havillands dropped down, read the panel message, and then one of them dropped a weighted line to the message string and pulled it off the poles. Pierce's first message was a request for an American flag and money to pay for the repossessed rifles.

After the pick-up, Pierce had some of his men construct a landing field. The job was completed in three days. Word then came that Sandino was holding a couple of shopkeepers for ransom in Telpaneca and Pierce was ordered to investigate. The new governor did not feel safe remaining by himself in Ocotal, so Pierce left Capt. Gilbert D. Hatfield and ten Marines to protect the governor and hold the town. In early July, Capt. Grover C. Darnall of the Guardia Nacional and two officers and 48 men from the Guardia's 1st Company arrived to strengthen the garrison.[37]

They were soon followed by two Marine officers and 28 enlisted Marines, who joined Pierce's command. Meanwhile, Sandino and Hatfield engaged in an exchange of letters. Sandino began writing to Hatfield in a vitriolic fashion, and Hatfield responded in kind. Sandino's letters were always threatening, and he would terminate them with phrases such as: "Your obedient servant who wishes to put you in a handsome tomb with flowers." Hatfield's replies were mostly tongue-in-cheek, with just enough official sounding language to keep Sandino guessing. It is obvious now that Hatfield was having fun with Sandino, who truly seemed to take the exchange seriously.

The Marines and Guardia troops resided in a substantial adobe building in the center of the town of Ocotal. After a few days, Hatfield noticed that the few remaining native families had begun abandoning the town. Because the natives were pro–Sandino, Hatfield believed that something was about to happen. On 15 July he doubled the guard and prepared for the worst. It was not long in coming. Shortly after dark, Sandino's men started to drift quietly into town in twos and threes. A little after midnight a Marine sentry saw something moving in the shadows and fired a shot in that direction.

Three companies of Sandinistas had infiltrated the town: one to attack the Marines in the city hall, another to attack the Guardia barracks, and the third to drive out any Conservatives who were still in town and take their money or valuables. The Sandinistas had at least two machine guns. One, emplaced on the second floor of a building, worked over the street in front of the city hall. The other, located in Governor Ramirez's office, was positioned to fire diagonally across the plaza from the other gun. In addition to effectively deploying their machine guns, the rebels also used dynamite to advantage.

The Guardia lost no time going into action. Led by 1st Lt. Thomas G. Bruce, the men immediately set about firing from their quarters.[38] The attackers were not the only people with machine guns, however. Bruce hauled their Browning out into the street and, although unprotected, scored hits on the enemy's gun in the governor's office. While this was going on, Marine and Guardia officers residing across the plaza dashed through the crossfire to join their units.

At about 3:00 a.m. Sandino reorganized his forces while several Marines poured desultory Browning automatic rifle and sniper fire upon them. The defenders quickly figured out that an all-out attack was soon coming and prepared to receive it. Within an hour, one of Sandino's lieutenants launched an attack from the church on the tree-studded plaza in front of the city hall. That was the moment when the Marines' marksmanship training showed its value. Machine guns and rifle fire took a heavy toll on the rebels. Three headlong rushes did nothing except provide targets for the Marines and Guardia troops. The leader of the rebel assault, Rufo Mann, tried to rally his men but was shot down and mortally wounded when he appeared on the corner of the plaza. That effectively ended the attack.

At dawn several rebels came out under a flag of truce and delivered a note from Sandino. It requested that the garrison surrender and promised that the defenders would not be harmed if they threw their weapons out into the street. A second note was delivered at 10:00 a.m. Each time Hatfield was urged to consider that his water supply was low. What Sandino did not know was that Hatfield had a large water supply in tanks. It was enough for at least two weeks, perhaps more. Sandino also specified that failure to surrender would result in the town being put to the torch. The defenders would then die in the flames or be killed as they fled the burning buildings. Hatfield's response to both messages was succinct: "Received your message, and say, with or without water, a Marine never surrenders. We remain here until we die or are captured."[39]

As soon as the messengers rounded the corner the firing resumed. A rebel machine gun in the church belfry opened up on the city hall. Seconds later, a sniper killed a Marine trying to scale the wall of an adjoining courtyard.[40] A Marine sergeant killed the sniper with his pistol.

Shortly after dawn, two Marine patrol planes flew over the town and quickly recognized that there was fighting in the town. One of the pilots, 1st Lt. "Cuckoo" Boyden, landed on the airfield the Marines had constructed outside Ocotal. There he learned from a local peasant what was going on in town. He returned to his plane and took off in a hail of bullets. After making a few passes strafing the rebels, Boyden headed off to Managua for help. Meanwhile, the pilot of the other plane, CWO Michael Wodanczyk, exhausted his ammunition as he poured fire into the rebel positions.[41] He had to leave, but more planes were coming. Flying in those mountains was difficult at best, and the Marine pilots had to learn quickly or risk crashing in that rugged terrain.

At 1435 a flight of five de Havillands led by Maj. Ross Rowell appeared over Ocotal. Each plane was loaded with four 17 pound fragmentation bombs and 1,200 rounds of .30-caliber ammunition for their two Lewis guns. Bombing was something the rebels had not yet experienced. As the planes came over, the rebels looked up and saw eternity floating down upon them. It may well have been the first dive-bombing attack in history. The pilots peeled off in sequence, dived toward the rebel positions, released their bombs, and pulled out of their dives. During the dives the pilots fired their fixed machine guns, and the observers cut loose when the pilots pulled up, wreaking further havoc. "Rusty" Rowell said he "led off the attack and dived out of column from 1,500 feet, pulling out at about 600. Later we ended up by diving in from 1,000 and pulling out at 300. Since the enemy had not been subjected to any form of bombing attack, other than the dynamite charges thrown from the Laird-Swallows by the Nicaraguan Air Force, they had no fear of us. They exposed themselves in such a manner that we were able to inflict damage which was out of proportion to what they would have suffered had they taken cover."[42]

There is no question that the tactic proved effective against the rebels. Although they expected strafing attacks, they had no idea what bombs were. The shock of the explosions was more than they could take, so they ran. A few stalwarts hid behind stone walls and made a show of it, but as the planes continued their low-flying attacks and Hatfield's men outflanked them, they, too, fled the scene. At least 56 of the rebels perished and as many as hundreds more were wounded. The Marine defenders suffered two casualties, one dead and one wounded; three Guardia troops were also wounded. The casualties were surprisingly light compared to the fury and magnitude of the attack. Hatfield later acknowledged that Rowell's dive-bombing attack "was the deciding factor in our favor ... the firing slackened and [rebel] troops began to withdraw."

A few hardy souls stayed behind and peppered the Marines with sniper fire that slowed down but failed to stop the Americans from going out to look at the results. When the Marines killed one of the snipers, six others came out of their positions and surrendered to Lieutenant Bruce of the Guardia. Hatfield, according to his patrol reports, counted more than 50 dead rebels on the main street alone. Four days later, after viewing numerous funerals in the town, Hatfield upgraded his estimate of Nicaraguan dead to nearly 300. Many of those were probably townspeople who did not take part in the battle. They were usually the people who suffered from any military action in built-up areas.

In his orders to Maj. Oliver Floyd, Col. Louis Gulick, commander of the 5th Marines, said: "Captain Hatfield and the men under his command did wonderful work and made a brilliant defense in fighting off overwhelming numbers of the enemy, against great odds and conducted themselves with great courage and judgement."[43] Captain Hatfield states that the work of the Guardia was highly commendable; that they fought like Marines. The attack by plane was entirely unexpected by Sandion [*sic*] and the heavy losses he suffered from bombs and machine gun fire caused the complete rout of his forces, forcing their immediate retreat."[44]

Gulick further informed Floyd that 10,000 rations would be coming through Leon and El Sauce to Ocotal "guarded by one officer and one section of men from the 11th Regiment who are to remain in Nicaragua for sometime to come." He further instructed Floyd that if the trip to Ocotal proved too difficult, "part of these rations would be available at Esteli by diverting them at El Sauce. In addition Captain Edgar S. Tuttle with his 23d [Company] consisting of three officers, 67 Marines and one hospital corpsman are pushing forward to Sebaco tonight with as many rations as the transportation will take and 12,000 rounds extra ammunition.[45] I do not expect that these men will necessarily be taken north of Esteli." Gulick continued, "It is important that you get contact with McQuade's column taking rations forward to Ocotal and secure them right away."

Another reporter, a well-known activist, 40 years later described what the Marines had accomplished: "The Marines at Ocotal held their ground masterfully. They fought with all the tenacity, courage, and skill for which the Corps was famous. Sandino's scrawny brown peasants fought less skillfully, but no less bravely. If nothing else, they showed that they knew how to die."[46]

Before the shooting began, Sandino's attack plan made him look like a real general to his peasant followers. That image lasted about as long as it took for modern weapons to destroy his band of rebels. The ever-present planes curtailed his propensity to expose his men to death from above, and the survivors of the dive-bombing attack would follow him for many years to come—regardless of how many planes the Americans threw at them.

Although that battle was the biggest in the entire intervention, the action in Nicaragua was not over First Lieutenant John A. Tebbs and his command, the Marines aboard the *Tulsa*, landed on 17 September at Bragman's Bluff. Nearly a week later, on the 23rd, 1st Lt. Charles S. Finch and his 27 Marines from the *Cleveland* relieved Tebbs and his detachment at Bragman's Bluff.[47] First Lieutenant Charles Connette with 25 Marines from the 51st Company, 5th Marine Regiment, relieved Lieutenant Finch and his command at Bragman's Bluff on 26 September.

While all of these landings were taking place, especially those during the month of January, the commander of the Special Service Squadron deemed that the ships' detachments were not of sufficient strength to care for the situation, and requested additional Marines from the United States. This request was answered by despatching the 2d Battalion of the 5th Regiment, under command of Lieutenant Colonel James J. Meade, which was at Guantanamo Bay, on the 7th of January via the *Argonne*. This battalion landed at Bluefields three days later.

The opposing factions in the Republic reached an agreement on the 7th of May whereby the armed forces were to disarm. In view of this, it was desired to have additional Marines to act as intermediaries in carrying out the pact. In pursuance of this plan, the 11th Regiment and Observation Squadron No. 4, the whole under Colonel Randolph C. Berkeley, was despatched to Corinto, the different units arriving between May 17th and 22d. Every indication made it appear that Sandino and his rebels were finished. Consequently changes were made, the Marine forces on shore in Nicaragua were gradually reduced, beginning about the middle of June, and the 11th Regiment was returned to Haiti and there disbanded. By the last of September, the Marines in Nicaragua consisted only of the 5th Regiment, less one battalion, together with one aviation squadron.

"Bandit" activity continued in the northern part of the country. Captured rebel documents continually referred to a supposed hideout of Sandino's known to them as "El Chipote." Finally, after a lengthy search, Rowell discovered it. "It was a well-fortified mountain, with a great many trenches, and they had machine guns there. They had fields of fire cleared, and they had constructed shacks at each defensive position for the shelter of their men, and on top of the mountain were quite a number of these shacks they had built, some for storehouses, apparently, and some for dwelling places."[48]

The withdrawal of the forces was apparently inopportune, because in the first part of 1928, it was necessary to reinforce the Marines who were retained in the republic, due to a renewal of bandit activities by Sandino and his followers. The attack by Sandino on Ocotal was apparently the signal for increased activity on the part of the banditti throughout the mountainous part of the country, and it was necessary to distribute the units of the Marine Brigade at all strategic points. These points were then held until the *Guardia Nacional de Nicaragua* had been well organized, trained, and properly fitted to take them over and maintain them against opposition. This would go on until 1933.

The 11th Regiment, of two battalions, under the command of Col. Robert H. Dunlap, together with one squadron of aviation, were again despatched to Nicaragua early in January. General Logan Feland was also ordered to return to command the brigade. The different units of this last force arrived and disembarked between 9 and 19 January 1928. Meanwhile, Sandino and his followers weren't doing all that well. The year 1929 was not a very good year for them. The *guardia* had been built well and was coming on strong when led by Marines.

However, there were several air attacks against the rebel forces. Major Ross E. Rowell led his planes in successful dive bombing and strafing attacks on entrenched forces at El Chipote on 14 January. Sandino was wounded in an air raid and looked for ways to exit the combat area. He begged the president of Mexico, Emilio Portes Gill, for permission to enter Mexico. Gill had been trying to mend fences with the United States and was not very happy at being put in this very difficult position. However, finally he relented and in June, Sandino was in that nation.

Several important happenings occurred during the next few years. A Marine captain in command of the detachment aboard the *Denver* was given permission to take 56 of his command ashore and to hunt for bandits. Captain Merritt Edson was sure that he would be able to bring Sandino to justice. What he accomplished was to become known as the Coco River Reconnaissance. The Marines went ashore on 8 March 1928 and spent about a month on the river in boats meeting with resistance at several points and being successful. Meanwhile Sandino was still in Nicaragua and especially harassing American and other foreign property owners. The two groups never met up. Edson decided to do a reconn on the Wanks River, which caused him more problems than he had expected. On 7 April they set out. Meanwhile Sandino spread the word that the Americans were going to destroy Nicaraguan property and harm the women.

8. Nicaragua

A group of what became known as "Horse Marines" in Nicaragua, c. 1928.

Neither reconn improved the situation for the Americans as much as it has been touted to have. Edson received a substantial increase in men when the *Tulsa* headed back to the United States to go into dry dock. Captain John A. Tebbs and that detachment joined Edson. There were several encounters which the Marines won, but one just barely.

A number of the Marine officers attached to the brigade and many non-commissioned officers were temporarily detached from their units and detailed to duty with the *Guardia Nacional* (GN) as instructors and unit commanders—many remaining on this duty until a short time before the entire Marine force was withdrawn from Nicaraguan soil on 3 January 1933. Unfortunately, due to continual misunderstandings and personal conflicts, several Marines in command of GN detachments were murdered in mutinous affairs. However, eventually, the disagreements quieted down and the two groups became more compatible.

The actual contacts between the GN and Sandinista forces are listed as beginning on 16 July 1927, at Ocotal. This one lasted much longer than most, at 14 hours. One Marine enlisted man, Private Michael A. Obleski, was killed, and one wounded, Private Charles E. Garrison.

Two Marines that led many patrols were First Lieutenant Lewis B. Puller (see Appendix A) and Gunnery Sergeant William A. Lee.[49] Their organization, Company M, became known throughout the nation, and frightened nearly every Nicaraguan rebel, if not all. Both men were awarded multiple Navy Crosses for their actions, two to Puller and three to Lee.

The actions of Marines and *Guardia* lasted until 26 December 1932 when a force led by Captain (GN) Lewis B. Puller, Lieutenant (GN) William A. Lee and six other Marines met and killed at least 30 Sandinistas and an untold number of wounded in patrols until 31 December 1932.

Top: **Senior officers inspecting Horse Marines in Nicaragua, c. 1928.** *Bottom:* **Marines in Nicaragua taking prisoners to their jobs, c. 1928.**

USMC Units That Served in Nicaragua

Expeditionary service was continuous since the landing on 6 May 1926 until the Marines were recalled on 3 January 1933.

Second Brigade: Brigade headquarters (organized 15 January 1928). Constabulary detachment designation changed to Nicaraguan National Guard detachment, 13 December 1928.

Fifth Regiment: Headquarters Company; Service Company; Fifty-first Company (10 August 1929 to Second Battalion, Fifth Regiment); First Battalion, Headquarters Company, Seventeenth Company; Twenty-third Company; Forty-ninth Company; Sixty-sixth Company (disbanded 10 August 1929); Second Battalion, Headquarters Company (organized 1 April 1928, disbanded 4 January 1929, reorganized 14 February 1929); Eighteenth Company (organized 25 March 1928, disbanded 5 January 1929); Forty-third Company (organized 25 March 1928, disbanded 4 January 1929, reorganized 10 August 1929): Forty-eighth Company (organized 25 March 1928, disbanded 4 January 1929); Seventy-seventh Company (organized 25 March 1928, disbanded 5 January 1929, reorganized 10 August 1929); Third Battalion, Headquarters Company; Eighth Company; Sixteenth Company; Twentieth Company; and Forty-fifth Company (disbanded 10 August 1929).

The following organizations were attached to expeditionary forces in Nicaragua. except those marked transferred:

Second Brigade: Brigade headquarters; Nicaraguan National Guard detachment.

Fifth Regiment: Headquarters Company; Service Company; First Battalion. Headquarters Company; Seventeenth Company; Twenty-third Company; Forty-ninth Company; Second Battalion; Headquarters Company; Forty-third Company; Fifty-first Company; Seventy-seventh Company; Third Battalion; Headquarters Company; Eighth Company; Sixteenth Company; Twentieth Company.

Eleventh Regiment: Headquarters Company (joined 19 January 1928, transferred to Quantico, 20 August 1929); Service Company (joined 19 January 1928, transferred to Quantico, 20 August 1929); First Battalion (The First Battalion, less the Forty-seventh Company, was transferred to Port-au-Prince, Haiti, 24 August 1927, and rejoined the Second Brigade 15 January 1928, transferred to Quantico, 29 August 1929), Headquarters Company; Second Machine Gun Company; Forty-sixth Company; Forty-seventh Company; Second Battalion (joined 16 January 1928, transferred to Quantico, 20 August 1929), Headquarters Company; Fiftieth Company; Fifty-second Company; Fifty-fifth Company; Fifty-seventh Company; Third Battalion (joined 31 March 1928, disbanded 15 June 1929); Headquarters Company; Fifty-eighth Company; Fifty-ninth Company; Sixtieth Company; Sixty-first Machine Gun and Howitzer Company; Aircraft squadrons—Headquarters detachment, Service Company 3-M (organized 1 March 1929); Observation Squadron (VO) 6-M (joined 16 February 1928); Observation Squadron (VO) 7-M.

Marine detachments from the following named ships served on shore on expeditionary duty in Nicaragua during the periods stated below: *Arizona*, 15 July 1928 to 24 January 1929; *California*, 15 July 1928 to 24 January 1929; *Cleveland*, 23 to 26 September 1927, and 1 April 1928 to 17 March 1929; *Colorado*, 1 to 4 July 1928, remained on shore until 24 January 1929; *Denver*, 19 February 1928 to 11 April 1929; *Galveston*, 9 to 23 January 1928, and 30 April 1928 to 11 April 1929; *Idaho*, 6 July 1928 to 24 January 1929; *Maryland*, 14 July 1928 to 24 November 1928; *Mississippi*, 14 July 1928 to 24 January 1929; *New Mexico*, 6 July 1928 to 24 January 1929; *New York*, 14 July 1928 to 24 January 1929; *Pennsylvania*, 6 July 1928 to 24 January 1929; *Procyon*, 14 July 1928 to 24 January 24 1929; *Rochester*, 7 January 1928 to 10 February 1929; *Tennessee*, 14 July 1928 to 24 January 1929; *Texas*, 14 June 1928 to 24 January 1929; *Tulsa*, 7 January 1928 to 8 February 1928, and 10 March 1928 to 12 April 1929; and *West Virginia*, 14 July 1928 to 24 January 1929.

9

Paraguay

A strong naval demonstration was made necessary by certain hostile acts of Paraguay. In February 1855, when the U.S. steamer *Water Witch* was making a survey of the Parana River at the boundary between Paraguay and Argentina, it was fired upon by a Paraguayan fort.

One of the crew was killed, and the vessel was forced to retire from its mission. There had also been considerable mistreatment of American citizens in Paraguay, and the property of some had been seized. The U.S. Congress took cognizance of these hostilities and authorized President James Buchanan to "adopt such measurees [*sic*] and use such force as in his judgment may be necessary and advisable." Acting upon that authority, Buchanan sent a commissioner to adjust the difficulties and augmented the Brazil Squadron to the then powerful fleet of two frigates, two sloops of war, three brigs, 12 armed steamers, and two armed storeships, carrying in all 2,500 men, including about 300 Marines. The squadron was especially well equipped for landing force operations. The show of force on the coast of Paraguay and sending part of the steamers up the Parana River as far as the capital were sufficient to induce the government of that country to adjust difficulties and thereafter respect the American flag.

10

PERU

From the date of the Peruvian Congress of 1822 to the administration of President Agustin Gamarra, internal disturbances had continued in this republic. Toward the close of his term of office an incident occurred which finally brought about the revolution of February 1835. The partisans of Orbegoso and Bermudez illegally nominated them as successors to Gamarra, which nearly brought the contending factions to a test of arms. A reconciliation of their differences took place on the eve of battle; Orbegoso was elected to govern the affairs of state.

Prominent in this affair had been General Salaverry, a man anxious to gain control of the nation for himself and his constituents. Therefore, he induced disturbances to distract attention from his activities, secretly organized a considerable army, ousted Orbegoso, proclaimed himself chief of Peru, and galloped into Lima as its master on 25 February 1835. However, Orbegoso was not to be so easily deposed, as indicated by immediate resort to the use of the forces remaining loyal to him. The subsequent actions of these forces brought about deplorable conditions throughout the country, especially at Lima, the capital, and Callao, the chief port of entry.

On 6 December several American citizens petitioned the American chargé d'affaires, Samuel Lamed, "to cause 40 to 50 Marines to be landed" for their protection and the guarding of their property. The United States flagship *Brandywine* under Captain David Deacon, with the commander, Pacific Squadron, Captain Alexander S. Wadsworth, aboard, was in the harbor at Callao at the time. Just prior to the 10th of December, the chargé, believing the American consulate to be in danger, requested Commodore Wadsworth to send a Marine guard for his protection. This request was executed on the 10th, and Corporal Henry Bell and Privates John Batham, Deodatur Nicklin and George Preston were sent to Lima.[1] Both factions having temporarily transferred their activities to other points, Lima was left without either military or civil government for several days, and conditions in the city became more chaotic.²

The American chargé again having requested Marines, Wadsworth on the 17th sent the remainder of the Marine Guard ashore under Captain Charles C. Tupper. These Marines were quartered in different American houses, but the majority were at the consulate. Captain Wadsworth said in his report: "There is no doubt but the presence of the Marines prevented a general plunder. As it was no foreign houses were plundered. The English and French Marines were sent up a few days after our own."

Early 1836 found the United States Marines of the ship *Brandywine* still on duty in the capital city, Lima. All communication between this city and Callao had been severed, and a blockade of the port had been decreed. President Orbegoso then made Chorillos the port of entry, but Colonel Solar—one of Salaverry's men, who was commandant of Callao—notified Commodore Wadsworth that this port, too, had been declared in a state of blockade. The commodore denied the commandant's right to declare a blockade, informed him that American vessels would be protected against molestation for any infraction of it, and immediately sent the *Boxer* to that port to enforce his decision.

The Marines under Captain Charles C. Tupper remained on duty at Lima until 24 January, when they were withdrawn, and returned to their ship.³ The *Brandywine* sailed from Callao on 1 March but returned several times during the remainder of the year. One of these occasions was on 31 August, at which time Private Alexander Cady was sent to Lima for duty at the American consulate. He remained until 2 December, when he rejoined the ship at Callao; one Marine was sufficient.

From 19 to 23 January 1836, several people were given shelter on board the *Brandywine* because of the serious conditions in Callao. After that, no further difficulties existed between the United States and Peru.⁴

11

Puerto Rico

The first contact the U.S. appears to have had in this island was on 14 November 1824 when Commodore David Porter (see Appendix A) landed his Marine detachment at Fajardo to avenge an insult to the American flag.[1]

In the latter part of 1824 an American mercantile house in St. Thomas, Virgin Islands, had been robbed, and there was satisfactory evidence that the goods stolen had been carried by pirates into Foxardo, a small port on the east end of Puerto Rico, then a colonial possession of Spain. In late October Lieutenant Charles T. Platt of the USS *Beagle* was in this vicinity and was informed of the robbery. He agreed to aid in recovering the stolen goods and proceeded to the Port of Foxardo. Arriving there on the 26th, he waited upon the proper civil officers, who treated him roughly, demanded his commission, which, when sent for, they pronounced a forgery. They charged him with being a pirate and finally arrested him and Lieutenant Robert Ritchie, who had accompanied him, and detained them both under guard during the day. After enduring various insults on the part of the officials and the inhabitants, they were permitted to return to their vessel.

Lieutenant Platt immediately set sail and, as he was running off the coast, met the *John Adams* standing in, with Commodore David Porter aboard. He went aboard and reported the treatment he had received to the commodore. The decision of the latter was soon formed; he deemed this an insult to the American flag, which must be atoned for. The commodore's ship could not enter the harbor at Foxardo because of shallow water, so instead it was anchored outside. Taking its boats and the *Beagle* and *Grampus*, he proceeded into the harbor to carry out his plans. On the way into the harbor, and when the ships were about to anchor, it was perceived that a shore battery was preparing to fire upon the landing party. A boat was immediately sent with a detachment of 14 Marines under Lieutenant Thomas B. Barton[2] (a passenger on board the *Grampus*) to spike the guns; meeting no resistance from the Spaniards, they quickly accomplished their mission and returned.

Later that same year, Commodore Porter landed with 200 Marines and sailors (officers and men), and addressed a letter to the Alcalde, dated 12 November, reciting the facts of the injury, demanding explanation and atonement, threatening to make the town responsible in case of refusal, and despatched it by Lieutenant Cornelius K. Stribling under a flag of truce.[3] One hour was given for a reply. Second Lieutenant Horatio N. Crabb, with 27 of his Marines, was ordered to place himself in advance of the column and escort the flag of truce to the town.[4] When within a short distance of the town, the Marines halted to await the return of Lieutenant Stribling. A short time afterward he returned, in company with the governor and captain of the port, who humbly apologized for the wrong they had done and promised thereafter to respect the rights of American officers. This apology was accepted and after marching through the town the party returned to their vessels.

After the fall of Santiago de Cuba on 17 July the U.S. government became anxious to seize Puerto Rico before an armistice or cessation of hostilities, so as to be able to lay claim to the island during peace negotiations.

After a naval officer, Lieutenant Greenlief A. Merriam went ashore on 25 July with a letter of capitulation for the Spanish governor to sign and returned to the *Dixie*. Marines led by First Lieutenant Henry C. Haines landed from the *Dixie* at Playa del Ponce, Puerto Rico, and for the first time, raised the American flag over that island.[5] The following morning U.S. Army troops, anxious to precede any naval action, went ashore to occupy the island at Guánica. The army actually was the occupying force.

First Lieutenant John A. Lejeune went ashore on 10 August from the *Cincinnati* leading 37 Marines to protect a lighthouse that U.S. forces had previously captured.[6]

12

SANTO DOMINGO/ DOMINICAN REPUBLIC

Much like Haiti, its partner on the island of Hispaniola, from its creation, Santo Domingo was in constant turmoil. United States Marines landed there as early as 6:00 p.m., just two years after the Marine Corps' founding. The first serious affair, however, began in 1903 when the American consul at Puerto Plata requested that Commander William H. Turner of the USS *Atlanta* land a party of Marines to protect American citizens. First Lieutenant Richard G. McConnell proceeded ashore with 25 of his men on 1 April 1903 and remained ashore until 19 April.[1]

The following year another insurrection broke out and the president and his staff were forced to flee for their lives. Revolutionaries perpetrated numerous indignities upon Americans and their property—killing their livestock, burning property, and destroying sugar cane, among other happenings. A Marine detachment from the *Detroit* commanded by Commander Albert C. Dillingham landed on 3 January and another smaller force on the 7th.[2]

These depredations continued and more Marines were landed. The Dominicans even fired upon a U.S. ship, the *New York*, and U.S. warships fired back upon insurgent positions.

At this time, at least four other nations with heavy investments were looking at this island republic with a jaundiced eye. After several years of murder, mayhem, and civil war, Santo Domingo was bankrupt. Several times Germany and Great Britain had landed troops in various nations in the Caribbean, and the U.S. worried that the next time they would stay. That would be testing the Monroe Doctrine. The nation's governing bodies, especially the president, didn't want any excuses available for that to happen.

The British government had noted the apparent seriousness of the revolutionary movement in Santo Domingo and had despatched the HMS *Pallas* under Commander C. Hope Robertson as their representative at this place. Commanders Dillingham and Robertson collaborated in establishing protective zones against the operations of the opposing Dominican factions. On the 15th the Marine detachment which had been landed at Sosua on the 7th was withdrawn, and the *Detroit* proceeded to Puerto Plata. On the morning of the 17th the opposing forces engaged in a pitched battle causing the Jiminez soldiers to retreat to the fort, firing as they ran. In the meantime the *Hartford* had arrived to reinforce the *Detroit*, and upon this serious outbreak of firing, Commander Dillingham deemed it advisable to despatch a considerable force on shore for the protection of the lives of all foreign residents. Accordingly, the Marine guard and a detachment of sailors were despatched early in the morning, while the *Hartford* "sent half of landing party ashore." About midafternoon this party returned to their respective ships, with the exception of the Marine guard of the *Detroit*, which remained ashore to guard the American consulate until the 23rd.

On the 1st of February an incident took place which prompted the United States government to send an armed force to the Dominican Republic in order that adequate protection might be afforded its citizens. J. C. Johnston, a crew member of the launch from the auxiliary cruiser *Yankee*, then at Santo Domingo City, was fired upon and killed by the revolutionary forces under Jiminez.

Captain Richard Wainwright, who was temporarily in command of the South Atlantic Squadron, was ordered to proceed to the troubled area on 8 February, and he arrived at Santo Domingo City aboard the *Newark* on the 11th, finding that the *Colombia* had preceded him, having arrived on the 8th. Captain James M. Miller, of the *Colombia*, who was senior to Captain Wainwright, had sent an officer and a Marine sergeant ashore to confer with the insurgents relative to the entry of the Clyde Line steamer *New York* into the harbor to discharge its cargo. This was on the 9th, and on the 11th, after the arrival of Captain Wainwright, the steamer *New York* stood in under convoy of the steam launch of the *Colombia*, and when near the dock the insurgents fired upon and struck the steamer several times, some of the bullets grazing the launch, which was flying the American flag.

This was a flagrant violation of an armistice which was supposed to be in force between the contending parties, and Captain Miller was apparently determined not to let such an incident pass without exacting redress for the insult to the American flag. A conference was held aboard the *Colombia*, and it was decided to shell the insurgents' position and then land Marines and bluejackets from both ships. Having informed the government authorities and the American chargé d'affaires of this intention, the *Newark* opened fire at

Senior officers inspecting Marines in Santo Domingo, c. 1917.

1525, and ten minutes later the landing forces left for the shore. Each ship despatched one battalion of approximately 160 officers and men, including the Marines under the command of Captain Albert S. McLemore[3] (*Newark*) and First Lieutenant Henry D.F. Long (*Colombia*), the whole force being under the direct command of the executive officer of the *Colombia*, Lieutenant Commander James P. Parker.

The boats carrying this landing force had nearly reached the beach when they were fired upon by the insurgent forces from shore, but no casualties were suffered. They pushed on, however, and landed at 4:30 p.m. When the insurgents' fire was observed from the deck of the *Colombia*, orders were issued to open a bombardment on their position from the 4-inch guns. The first shot was fired at 4:32 and this continued until 4:47. The fire from the *Newark* was continued until 5:00 p.m., when the bombardment ceased. The units returned to their respective ships between 9:00 and 10:00 p.m.

The de facto governments which had ruled the affairs of the republic since the last declaration of its independence in February 1844, and more particularly that under the leadership of Ulises Heureaux (1882–89), had borrowed from foreign governments until the finances were in such a state as to make the repayment of loans an impossibility, unless the revenues received were controlled by some responsible party or foreign state. Under this state of affairs, and at the request of the Dominican government, the United States took over control of the Dominican finances in 1905.

President Theodore Roosevelt issued the so-called Roosevelt Corollary to the Monroe Doctrine, which stated: "Chronic wrongdoing ... may in America, as elsewhere, ultimately require intervention by some civilized nation, and in the Western Hemisphere the adherence of the United States to the Monroe Doctrine may force the United States, however reluctantly, in flagrant cases of such wrongdoing or impotence, to the exercise of an international police power."[4]

The next step for Roosevelt was to take over the revenue producing custom houses of the Dominican Republic. With a bit of arm twisting, the weaker nation was forced to "invite" the Yankee big brother in. However, the U.S. Senate would not approve the pact and Roosevelt went ahead and prepared an executive agreement, bypassing Congress. The Democrats in Congress denounced the agreement and it took a couple of years for a new treaty to be approved in 1907.[5]

Between 1911 and 1916, six presidents held office for various periods of time. In the early part of 1916, the Dominican government was in a state of collapse. General Arias, who was then secretary of war, launched an insurrection against the government headed by Juan Isidro Jiminez, and a state of anarchy followed.

The contending forces were contending for the possession of the capital, Santo Domingo City, and the American Legation being in the direct line of fire, was struck several times by shells. Advices as to this state of affairs were furnished to the State Department by the American minister, William W. Russell. The Navy Department, in turn, was requested to despatch a naval force to the troubled area to furnish protection for United States citizens.

Rear Admiral William B. Caperton, commanding the cruiser force, ordered the 6th and 9th Companies of Marines from Haiti to the naval transport *Prairie*, despatched it to Santo Domingo City, and upon its arrival May 5, these companies were landed. A little later this force was reinforced by the 1st, 4th, 5th, 13th, 14th, 19th, and 24th Marine companies, and Santo Domingo City was occupied. This caused the withdrawal of the forces under General Arias, who reestablished his headquarters at Santiago in the interior.

Admiral Caperton requested the Navy Department to send an additional regiment of Marines, for service in conjunction with those already landed, in order to quickly put down the revolution and effect the pacification of the interior. The 4th Regiment of Marines, under Colonel Joseph H. Pendleton, ordered from San Diego, arrived at Monte Cristi and disembarked on June 21. Marines from the *New Jersey* and *Rhode Island* had been landed previously at Puerto Plata, as well as some of the companies originally landed at Santo Domingo City, including the artillery battalion which landed at Monte Cristi.

Marines fighting rebels in Santo Domingo, c. 1917.

When Colonel Pendleton arrived with the 4th Regiment, he was designated to command all forces ashore, and combining his force with the other Marine companies and detachments then on shore, he was directed to start an expedition to the interior, capture Santiago (Arias' headquarters), and in this manner bring about tranquil conditions. The expedition started on its mission on the 26th headed by Colonel Pendleton himself. Several engagements occurred, the first at Las Trencheras, where the Marines found two trench lines which interfered with their further passage. The Marines' single battery of artillery and the machine gun company quickly brought an end to that position, though they lost one Marine killed and another wounded.

A second unit under the command of Major Hiram I. Bearss had been moving from Puerto Plata to join Pendleton at Navarette, which they did on 2 July. They had been engaged several times but also were successful.

Before the Marines reached their objective, Santiago, a peace commission had negotiated an agreement whereby the revolutionists would lay down their arms and a provisional government would be organized. The expedition then

The 4th Marine Regiment's senior officers, Colonel Joseph H. Pendleton, Major Robert H. Dunlap and Major John T. Myers, aboard the USS *New Jersey*.

advanced into Santiago without further opposition, entering the city on July 6th.[6]

Every effort was made on the part of the American government to negotiate a treaty which would safeguard the tranquility of the republic. These efforts met with failure. Consequently, the United States proclaimed a military occupation and military government in Santo Domingo from November 29. This government was organized upon the usual plan—foreign relations, finance, public works and communications, justice and public instruction, agriculture, and immigration and interior (under which was the Departments of War and Navy). The Department of Sanitation was subsequently established. The military government brought order out of chaos and placed the government on a sound basis in all respects.

From the end of 1916 forward, the Second Brigade was deployed as the Army of Occupation in Santo Domingo to enforce the military government's decrees and to maintain order. In the beginning, the military government divided the country into two parts; the Northern District with headquarters in Santiago was garrisoned by the 4th Regiment; the Southern District headquarters was located at Santo Domingo City and was the responsibility of the 3d Regiment.

Fort Ozama on the Caribbean waterfront in Santo Domingo City, c. 1917. The city was occupied by the United States until 1924.

There was trouble at San Pedro de Marcoris on 10 January 1917 when a force of Marines was landing. Rebels on shore killed Second Lieutenant James K. Bolton and slightly wounded Captain John R. Henley.[7] It later came out that the shots were fired by a 16 year old boy standing with two adult males who were in a crowd on the wharf. Life was still dangerous for American Marines in the Dominican Republic, also know as Santo Domingo.

On 22 January, First Lieutenant Harry W. Weitzel with another officer and 50 enlisted men of the 48th Company joined Hiram Bearss at Consuelo after a long, tiring trip via train and gunboat, and for five days struggling over mountain trails.[8] They served with Bearss until the 31st, when Bearss decided he didn't need them any longer and ordered Weitzel and the 48th to return to La Vega.

A provisional government was installed on 21 October 1922, and all of the functions of civil government were delivered into its hands. The military governor was charged with the approval of expenditures not provided for in the budget and the task of quelling disturbances when, in his opinion and in the opinion of the provisional government, the local constabulary was unable to cope with it.

Regular elections having been previously held, a constitutional government was inaugurated at 10:30 a.m. on 12 July 1924; Fort Ozama was turned over to the new government in the afternoon, and the American forces commenced their withdrawal. This withdrawal was completed on 17 September 1924.

The military governorship was held by Rear Admiral Harry S. Knapp,

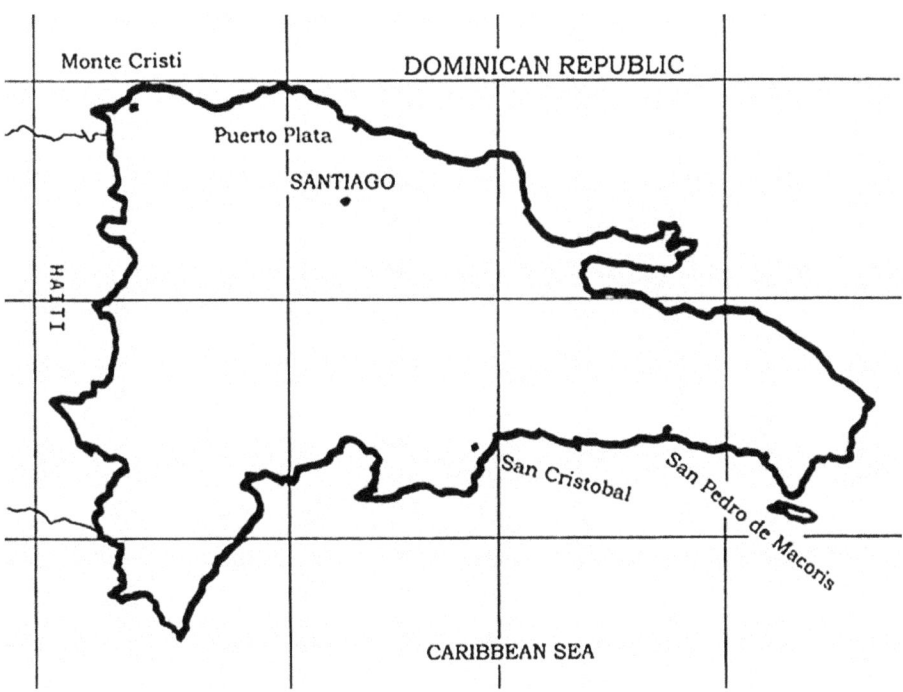

Map of Santo Domingo/Domincan Republic.

Rear Admiral Thomas Snowden, Rear Admiral Samuel S. Robison, and then Brigadier General Harry Lee of the United States Marines, whose tenure of office was from 5 December 1922 to the withdrawal of all troops.[9]

During the occupation the Marines were divided into detachments and placed strategically to put an end to banditry, which had grown to serious proportions due to the absence of a civil government. This situation was soon under control. The American forces varied in strength from the 280 who first landed to three regiments (3rd, 4th, and 15th) of approximately 3,000 officers and men. The Marines suffered casualties of four officers and 10 men killed; one officer and one man died of wounds, three officers and 51 men died of disease; two officers and 37 men died through accident; two officers and 29 men died due to other causes, and five officers and 50 men were wounded in action.

In October 1917, a *guardia* (or constabulary) was organized, commanded and trained by the Marines, and used extensively in subduing bandit activities throughout the island. Upon the withdrawal of the United States forces, this organization took over all police duties of the Republic under their own officers.

A Brief History of the Guardia Nacional Dominicana

To somewhat relieve the few Marines of some of their onerous duties it was decided to duplicate what the Marines had done in Haiti and would later accomplish in Nicaragua, in other words to design and create a police force to aid the Marines. On 7 April 1917, Adm. Knapp, the military governor, formally dissolved the remaining shreds of a Dominican armed force. He then ordered the Marines to form a police force like that formed in Haiti which would be commanded by Marines, officers and noncommissioned officers (NCOs). It was originally termed the *Guardia Nacional Dominicana*, and appointed as its first commandant was Lieutenant Colonel George C. Thorpe.[10] The total allowed was 1,234 natives with 40 Marines seconded by the U.S. government. The *guardia* utilized the U.S. Marine Corps as a model for its formation and later, in combat and faithfulness it lived up to its parent corps.

Major problems in the beginning were that the better educated Dominicans refused to serve in leadership positions. Consequently some of the earliest recruits were not what the founders were aiming for. Some had been in the previous Republican Guard, or had questionable backgrounds.[11] When the war in Europe interfered with the leadership by drawing off many of the Marine officers, NCOs that were often corporals or sergeants were placed in command. Most of them were "followers" rather than bona fide leaders, so the command structure was weakened. In addition, the enlisted Marines usually had a weak command of the local language. However, training commenced and proceeded and eventually, through trials and tribulations, as long as the Marines were in charge, the *guardia* came through.

This is probably the best place to tell their story with the understanding that how it eventually turned out will vary considerably with the intent of its origins. First, it was the intention of the U.S. government to stabilize the nation. It was certainly not considering semi-permanent occupation of Santo Domingo. It was, however, a mistake to apply U.S. standards and attitudes toward the various nations of Latin America, as they had in Haiti, Nicaragua, and Cuba, among numerous others. It was considered appropriate to create a police force with U.S. values, rather than those of the nation involved. It worked rather well while the U.S. occupied Santo Domingo, but fell apart afterwards.

This attitude ignored Latin attitudes and traditions and the strength of the local culture. The imposition of this "cure all" formula in several different nations was based on the assumption of Anglo-Saxon superiority and a disdain for other peoples. It reflected a total lack of appreciation of local cultures that the United States considered inferior and entailed ignoring what the U.S. authorities regarded as unstable political systems which rendered countries ungovernable. This attitude was substantially true in many instances, but the solution created new problems.

The creation of such a constabulary became the centerpiece of U.S. policy in the island nation. Executive Order No. 47, dated 7 April 1917, established the *Guardia Nacional Dominicana*, and appropriated funds for its training and equipping. The *guardia* was conceived primarily as an internal police force, not a replacement for the army, and was designed to bring chronic rebellions under control and to maintain law and order. It was initially authorized for a strength of 1,200 men, although its organization and recruiting proceeded slowly. The United States had sufficient control to assure the disbanding of the previously ill-trained military and police forces and to enforce the disarming of the local populace. These measures alone reduced the incidence of violence in the nation.

The Dominican elite had rejected the military government and refused to cooperate with the conquerors in any way, including serving in the new police force. This deprived the *guardia* of leadership by the most educated members of the society. Recruiting problems compelled U.S. leaders to induct individuals with questionable backgrounds and to enlist individuals who had previously been members of the local Republic guard to bring the *guardia* to its targeted strength. Officers were drawn from the middle class, who often viewed the military as a means to achieve power and status. Even securing sufficient numbers of enlisted men proved problematical, despite the attractions of a regularly paid position in the face of widespread unemployment. Besides the approximately $15 a month, there was clothing, food, and housing. These were generally unattainable for the lower classes. Unfortunately, the individuals who did agree to serve were often illiterate and ill-prepared and that made training them most difficult.

Although the force was initially commanded by Marine officers, the war in Europe caused a shortage of them, requiring that Marine NCOs be put on temporary duty with the *guardia* as officers. Hence, a newly commissioned Dominican was limited to the rank of second lieutenant and often found himself reporting to a Marine sergeant or corporal, temporarily commissioned as a captain or major in the Dominican *guardia*. This was an unattractive position and resulted in poor training for the Dominicans. The Marine officers and enlisted men assigned to this duty were ill-prepared for their tasks and responsibilities, lacking a knowledge of the local culture, training in combating guerrillas, and in many cases even a knowledge of the Spanish language. Many of them came from a society which looked down upon other peoples, especially Latinos, and they were frequently harsh in their methods.

The situation was further complicated when the revolt in the East compelled the occupation authorities to rush newly recruited *guardia* units into the field after only brief training. The result was an unruly force leading to charges of abuses and a high number of court-martials.

Recognizing the problems resulting from poor training and reflecting political negotiations that resulted in orders to "Dominicanize" the *guardia*, the force was reorganized in 1921 under the auspices of Brigadier General Harry Lee, who commanded the 2d Marine Brigade, and Colonel William C. Harllee, who now commanded the 15th Regiment. The changes included the establishment of a military school in Haina for training officers and renewed recruiting efforts, along with an authorization to expand the force, renamed the *Policia Nacional Dominicana*, to 3,000 men. A second training center was established in Santiago.

Early in 1922 the commandant decided to reorganize the 4th Regiment, at 58 officers and 1,510 enlisted men still on duty in Santo Domingo. These were to be divided as follows: a headquarters and headquarters company, service company, howitzer company, and three infantry battalions. Each battalion included a machine gun company and three rifle companies. This was more than twice the size of the regiment in February 1922. However, lack of personnel made it impossible to implement the new organization. Actually, all that happened was the addition of the howitzer company which, in fact, ran the regimental training center near Santiago, and a Headquarters Company, 1st Battalion. For the remainder of the occupation the 4th Regiment looked like the following: Hdqs. Co., Howitzer Co, Service Co., 25th Co., 33d Co., 69th Co., and the 1st Bn. The 1st Bn. had the following units attached: Hdqs Co., 10th Co., 28th Co., and the 32d Co.[12]

Lee authorized a series of home guard units in the eastern district. Fifteen Dominicans, generally those who had been hurt by the "Bandits," were allowed weapons, and four Marines; a leader, plus three with automatic weapons. During 15 to 30 April those law enforcement groups literally wiped out organized banditry in that eastern section.

By August 1922 the recruiting effort had brought the PND to a total of 800 men. Lieutenant Colonel Presley M. Rixey, Jr., who assumed command of that unit on 1 June 1921, did more than any other individual to make the PND a success. He established bases at Santiago and another at Santo Domingo City, each with 500 officers and men. They had a supply of trucks in order to move rapidly anywhere that rebel activity occurred.[13]

The reorganization and training were shortened because of the negotiations to arrange the end of the occupation. The withdrawal agreements established deadlines for control of the force by the government and the Dominicanization of the officer corps that were more rapid than Marine officers desired. Control of the force was turned over to the Dominican government at the time of the U.S. withdrawal in 1924. After the withdrawal the Dominican government instituted numerous changes, including installing officers who were members of the ruling party. After that it became just what it shouldn't have: an instrument of control rather than a moderate police force.

Additional problems came from American entrepreneurs who demanded preference in dealing with the locals. One group, said to have been aligned with United Fruit, complained that the military government showed them less support than the Dominican government. Of course, those hucksters eventually got their way and caused more problems for the United States and especially the Marines.

Meanwhile, Hiram Bearss was doing his thing. Soon after assuming command, he sent Major Jay McC. Salladay with a Marine detachment to the San Pedro de Macoris area.[14] To back him up, he also sent Captain John Quincey Adams by land with a troop of mounted Marines. It wasn't long before the latter sent Bearss a telegram attesting to the fact the he was held up by rebels and couldn't cross the Macoris River. He added that Salladay couldn't land at that

Prisoner line-up in Santo Domingo, c. 1919.

A rest for the 4th Marine Regiment on a hike somewhere in Santo Domingo.

town because armed insurgents at the wharf were holding him up. Bearss blew up. No damned peasants were going to hold up his Marines. Taking another cutter, he headed for San Pedro de Macoris, and as soon as he arrived pushed his men, armed with machine guns, into the town. He left standing orders that when he signaled them, the cutter crew were to begin shelling the town.

His next move was to send a message to the town officials that he wanted all arms turned in to him, otherwise he would have the town flattened, and he added the same would be true if there was any sniping. The arms began coming in and by nightfall the place was fairly quiet. Salladay and his men were able to disembark and Adams' Marines came riding into town. Hiram and his command were able to occupy all the strategic points and within a few days the situation was in fine shape. Or so it seemed.

Nonetheless, there was still a bandit in the hen house. His name, was Chachá and he waltzed around the Marines, at least in the beginning. The 16 year old that killed 2d Lt. Bolton was said to have been a member of his band. They were heavy with weapons, mostly oldies but still able to kill. They were armed and dangerous. Chachá was a magnet not only for patriots, but also the criminal element.

12. Santo Domingo/Dominican Republic

Marines fighting rebels in Santo Domingo, c. 1918.

Bearss was aware of his style and decided to move at him. He and his men went to a sugar plantation with mills at Consuelo. The Marines included artillery, Adams' cavalry and Bearss' infantry. Reaching the plantation, the Marines came under heavy fire from the enemy. Bearss ordered Adams to charge, which he did in a fearless and gallant manner. Chachá's heroes beat it in great disorder. They weren't used to such tactics.

Bearss began cleaning up the neighborhood, spreading his men about the area even to utilizing a narrow gauge railroad which connected each plantation. He received orders to report back to San Pedro but ignored them. The Marine chief of staff, Lieutenant Colonel Robert H. Dunlap, another superior Marine, sent him a well-intentioned message that he should withdraw, otherwise he might find himself in severe difficulties.[15] Hiram believed that if he left his command and the local Americans, he deserved to be court-martialed.

Instead he went to work on Chachá and his crowd with an intensity that soon had the latter reeling. No matter where he went, Bearss and his Marines followed him. Finally Chachá had his belly full and worked out an agreement to surrender.

Another source of trouble was the advent of union organizers from the

U.S. They were engaged in trying to protect the laborers' rights and interfering with Marine operations. Also, unfortunately, a large number of Black Jamaicans had been brought in and they began joining the rebel armies and killing Marines. Marines were also killing them and the local British consul protested. "They are British subjects and you shouldn't be killing them," or words to that effect. The matter went back and forth between the U.S. and British governments and somehow got straightened out.

A compatriot of Chachás named Vicentico Evangelista remained at large. He called himself Jesus Christ and was commonly known to his followers as the Messiah. He claimed to be invincible and bullet-proof. His followers also decided that they too must be safe from all the Marines could hurl at them. They weren't, as many soon found out.

Eventually, Bearss and his 67 Marines caught up with Evangelista and his force. He had First Lieutenant Ellis B. Miller with his machine guns posted to the left, and First Lieutenant Samuel L. Harrington, now commanding the Horse Marines, to his right.[16] The firing of the "sprinkler guns" and the deadly aim of the Marine riflemen, plus the shock of the cavalry rushing in upon them, scared hell out of the rebels. Many of them went down, but few Marines were casualties. Bearss himself was mounted on a white horse and yelling directions at his command. Either the superstitious natives feared this devil on a white horse or perhaps were afraid to even consider firing. At any rate, Bearss came through without a scratch.

Later that month of March, the remnants of Evangelista troops were caught up by Captain Ross S. Kingsbury and his Marines, who killed another 15 of the 40 or so and wounded many of the others; Evangelista was one of those.[17] So, he wasn't bullet-proof after all.

Bearss' tour as commander of the 3d Provisional Regiment technically terminated on 20 March 1917 but he remained at headquarters, Santo Domingo City, until 10 May when he received orders to "report at the Philadelphia Navy Yard ASAP." He was soon on his way to France and a real war.[18]

In April the Marines came across another group in a strong position at Las Canitas in western Santo Domingo. After a fight lasting seven hours the Marines succeeded in driving off the enemy, killing nine and wounding at least 20. Two Marines were wounded.

In May, Thorpe was appointed to replace Bearss in command of the 3d Regiment and went out to command in person. Fortunately, Thorpe had First Sergeant William West in his command who was a successful "diplomat." West, in command of a Marine outpost at Hato Mayor, went out to the rebel Vicentico's camp and made arrangements for him to surrender, for a price. West got Thorpe and Vicentico together in a meeting in which Thorpe convinced the rebel to surrender himself and his band. On 4 July 1917 the rebels came in and all were disarmed and allowed to go to their homes, except for Vicentico and two of his relatives. They were sent under guard to San Pedro de Macoris, where, surprisingly, Vicentico was killed while trying to escape.[19]

Meanwhile, Major William H. Pritchett and a detachment of the 32d Company was functioning on the south shore of Samana Bay during May, June, and July.[20] They were also looking for Vicentico, but due to poor communications were unable to connect with Thorpe, who was north of the mountains. So, for the time being, they continued searching for the man who wasn't there.

After these Marine victories, the rebels avoided further conflict during 1917 and the Marine commandant was able to broadcast that "all the bandit leaders have been captured or killed and their followers dispersed"—a somewhat premature conclusion.

One of the earliest "bandit" contacts was in January 1918 when a combined Marine and *guardia* patrol moved at least 250 miles through the mountainous region in western Santo Domingo against the camp of the group led by Dios Olivorio. It failed to surprise Olivorio and many of his followers fled at their approach. A few were captured and their camp was destroyed, but overall it was a grave disappointment. Few other contacts were made during the first six months of this year.

One sergeant, William R. Knox, was ambushed and killed on 21 March, and the local Marine garrison took the field looking for the killers. Because Marine numbers had been reduced to provide men to serve in France, they didn't have enough manpower to cover the period successfully. With that reduction, the rebels increased their activity. With that, Lt. Col. Thorpe decided to wage an aggressive campaign against them.

Later in the year, depredations started up again. In July Captain Charles F. Merkel made camp in a horseshoe valley whereupon they were attacked from three sides. Merkel's men finally fought their way out by going up the hill toward the rebels and driving them off. The fight lasted about 20 minutes and one Marine and two of the *guardia* were wounded. However, the rebels paid for it with eight dead and two wounded.[21]

That same month, much activity in the 4th Marine Regiment's area took place. It was to conform with the increased activities of the 3d Regiment. Captain Harry L. Jones and his 33d Mounted Company including two other officers and 54 enlisted men; a 30 man detachment from the 25th Company led by Captain James M. Bain; and a 30 man detachment from the 48th Company led by Captain James T. Moore were active during this period.[22]

Bain and his 25th Company departed from Sabana de la Mar on 31 July, and on 2 August were climbing a mountain ridge just south of the village of La Loma. About a quarter mile up they encountered fierce rifle fire from above. Corporal Clyde R. Darrah, in command of the point, ordered his men to return fire. They did and their accuracy soon broke the spirit of the Dominicans, who fled. Bain failed to follow the raiders; it was a failure in anti-guerrilla activities and in fact this was their last contact with the enemy.

Jones' mounted company had a zone of 180 miles to cover southwest of Hato Mayor, Bain a 150 mile zone southeast of Hato Mayor, and Moore a 190 square mile territory to the east. There were many frustrations in attempting to put down these excursions of the rebels. They, in their peasant clothing, would melt into the terrain if cornered by a Marine detachment, having disposed of their weapons in the brush. The various Marine detachments were hiking vigorously over the countryside but accomplishing little. The only time the rebels would stand was if they greatly outnumbered the Marine groups. Overall, while serving with the 3d Regiment, neither Moore's nor Bain's detachments made contact with the quarry.

However, Capt. Harry Jones' mounted company was either more active or perhaps more daring. On one occasion, Second Lieutenant Jack H. Tandy, Assistant Surgeon Herbert L. Shinn, and ten enlisted men on a patrol north of La Paja stopped at a farmhouse for supper. The occupants seemed friendly, inviting the Marines in to sit by the fire. However, the husband soon disappeared, saying "I'm gonna check on my animals." The men obtained their food and went outside to eat. Not long after, a bullet pierced the building and passed through Private John M. Poe's hat. Then bullets were hitting and missing all over that side of the house. About 80 men, armed with various weapons, closed in on the sitting Marines. Soon locked in hand-to-hand combat, the rebels found the fight was not going well and they started evacuating the field. They left 17 dead.

The only Marine missing was 2d Lt. Jack Tandy, who couldn't be found and was presumed dead. Shinn had assumed command and directed the defense. The next morning they rounded up their horses and headed for their home base. Two days later Tandy showed up at La Paja, having made his way through the woods alone for fear of being discovered.[23]

Two days later a patrol of two officers and nine enlisted Marines escaped disaster. They were eating supper in a native house and were fired upon from three sides. They reacted vigorously by running outside and firing in every direction which within minutes drove off their adversaries.

On the 28th of August the insurrectionists raided the town of Dos Rios and absconded with all the food in the local stores, meanwhile picking up some recruits. Colonel Thorpe and his ten man detachment, in the same area,

12. Santo Domingo/Dominican Republic

Marines on parade in Santo Domingo, c. 1918.

was ambushed on 7 September while crossing a stream just west of the town. A sharp fight forced the rebels to disperse after losing at least nine dead. No Marine casualties occurred, but most of their ammunition was exhausted.

The 33d Company continued to be very active during the month and until the end of the year. During September and October, a number of Marine patrols in other parts of Santo Domingo participated in similar encounters with groups of rebels. One of them, led by Captain William C. Byrd, occurred on 24 October.[24] He and his band were planning on attacking a rebel camp in the mountains near El Seibo. Completely surprising the natives, after just a few shots they fled. But, just a few hours later the Marines were ambushed as they were crossing a river. Prompt fire from their machine gun drove the native attackers away and all Marines survived.

Overall, it wasn't the best year for replacement Marines. It was a time of draftees, and they were poorly trained and most had little interest in being in the service, let alone after the armistice. Several officers complained about the quality of not only the enlisted men but also the junior officers. The war in France was getting the best the Marines could turn out, leaving lesser quality men for this duty.

The balance of this year saw a slowing down of rebellious activity, though partly because the sugar plantation owners were bribing the bandit leaders not to bother them. That simply encouraged more bandit activity, but most of each incident was so small and spread out, the Marines couldn't cover all the ground necessary. It also saw, on 21 October, the great Col. Pendleton leave

Marines in a chow line in Santo Domingo, c. 1919.

for command of the barracks at Paris (then) Island. His successor was a future commandant, Brigadier General Ben H. Fuller.[25] Admiral Knapp actually put Pendleton's name in for a Navy Cross, which was awarded.

At the beginning of 1919, Rear Admiral Thomas Snowden relieved Adm. Knapp as military governor. However, that was not the best situation, because while Knapp was close to what was happening and close to the necessary people, Snowden held himself aloof and matters deteriorated. A rigid disciplinarian, Snowden was poorly prepared to govern. He was abrasive and almost immediately strained relations between the occupiers and occupied. He inaugurated press censorship and issued regulations barring all criticism of the military government and of the U.S. "Helped" by U.S. citizens, he issued new land laws, which, you can guess, favored who?

On 26 February elements of the 15th Marine Regiment, commanded by Colonel James C. Breckinridge and numbering 50 officers and 1,041 enlisted Marines, landed at San Domingo City to assist the 2d Brigade in ending banditry.[26] Now about 3,000 Marines were soon joined by the 1st Marine Air Squadron. This was a new formation composed out of the recently disbanded unit at Miami, labeled at Quantico as Squadron D. Equipped with six JN-6 (Jenny) biplanes, the squadron began operations from an airstrip hacked out of the jungle near Consuelo. It was commanded by Captain Walter E. McCaughtry, a Marine who had risen from warrant rank.[27] This would be the first time Marine ground forces would be supported by Marine air.

There were dozens of bandit contacts during this period. One was that of Second Lieutenant Harold N. Miller's mounted patrol of 19 men with the 44th Company, who ran into about 125 rebels near Hato Mayor mid-morning on 22 March 1919.[28] The Dominicans lay on both sides alongside the road where the road made a sharp turn to avoid an animal pen. There was heavy brush at this point. Both groups opened a heavy but badly directed fire upon the Marines. Miller had his men dismount, formed a skirmish line and returned fire. Their machine gun concentrated on the animal pen, which quickly silenced the fire from that post. Then Miller had his men charge those on the opposite side of the road and the rebels fled. They stopped and returned fire but the machine gun got them moving again. Less than a hour passed and the fighting was over. The Marines suffered no losses but the natives lost at least 15 men.

One of the newly appointed officers of the 15th, and only a Marine since August 1917 himself, complained about his men. "Very poorly trained, they were practically mutinous when I arrived there."[29] Another commentator stated: "Most of the marines serving in Santo Domingo had been enlisted during the World War; many, who expected to serve only in France, had been retained in Santo Domingo long after the close of the War. This condition together with the many hardships led to some dissatisfaction, which had a noticeable effect on the morale of the command."[30]

Increased activity in the Eastern District caused elements of the 15th Regiment to provide an expedition during the latter part of this year. This caused a third district to be formed. During this year there were 50 major contacts between Marines-*guardia* and insurrectionists and at least 100 minor contacts. Casualties were rather light, despite the increased tempo of patrolling; three Marines were killed (two of whom were officers) and four were wounded.[31]

The 33d Mounted Company was reassigned to the 15th Regiment on 25 February 1919, while the other two led by Captains Moore and Bain rejoined their 4th Regiment, and for all purposes, that was the end of the 4th in antiguerrilla campaigns in the country.

The 15th, supported by the 3d Regiment, was kept busy in 1919 with about 200 contacts with guerrillas. Captain William Byrd, whom we met the previous year, was busy in February in eastern Santo Domingo. He and his command struck a camp of about 60 rebels in a very difficult location and managed to kill a dozen while also collecting a large stock of weapons. In April another 20 man Marine team, led by First Lieutenant Donald G. Oglesby, struck three different rebel camps all the same day. In a May patrol Second Lieutenant Frederick H. Biebush and his command also hit a camp and succeeded in killing 15 enemy.[32]

Meanwhile, the aviation squadron was functioning as well. It began service after arrival on 27 February 1919 after the Marines on the ground had been frustrated in their efforts to engage the various guerrilla bands operating through the entire region. Given the nature of the small unit action, there were few suitable targets for bombing or strafing attacks. They managed to bring down bombs and machine guns upon the helpless enemy and brought back a lot of useful data to the ground troops. This caused the guerrillas to become more cautious in their moves and they began to tell the locals the planes were there to bomb them as well.

One example of the aircraft becoming closely involved with the guerrillas on the ground was when 2d Lt. Manson C. Carpenter and observer 2d Lt. Nathan S. Noble, flying in response to a telephoned report to the air base about a ground skirmish near Guaybo Dulce, caught about 30 horsemen fleeing across an open meadow.[33] Diving to about a hundred feet, Carpenter launched a strafing attack, maneuvering so that both his front and Noble's cockpit guns were brought to bear. As he climbed to regain altitude the enemy fled to nearby trees. On their second pass, the open ground was now empty of horsemen, but they counted six bodies on the ground. However, this sort of successful opening was less and less available as the time went on.

In reality, the more successful intervention using airplanes was to improve communications among the small Marine garrisons scattered throughout the country, and to bring about military mail, supplies and occasionally personnel. While most of the casualties were among the guerrillas, of the air personnel, four Marines were killed and perhaps a dozen were wounded in the year.

Because the guerrilla bands usually greatly outnumbered the Marine combat patrols, they could and did sometimes rush the Marines with machetes and knives, initiating short but savage hand-to-hand clashes. On 13 August a patrol of three privates from the 44th Company led by Cpl. Bascome Breedon had such an encounter with tragic results. At a stream crossing a large group surrounded and attacked the four Marines with rifles and knives. Though the Marines managed to kill a half dozen natives, three Marines were killed. The lone survivor, Pvt. Thomas J. Rushforth, though wounded in both hands and in his hip, managed to mount a horse and fight his way through the enemy.

Brigadier General Logan Feland, a veteran of the 4th Brigade in France, relieved Gen. Fuller in command of the Second Brigade on 27 November 1919.

The year 1920 in Santo Domingo wasn't all bad. The military government managed to incorporate some number of social reforms, including improving economic conditions and, importantly, the health situation. Enrollment of school children increased from 18,000 to 100,000; a system of roads was being constructed, and the country grew wealthy from the sale of sugar.

On 12 October men of the 4th Marine Regiment helped fight a severe fire in the center of the business district in Santiago. And on 24 October, Brigadier General Charles G. Long replaced Feland in command of the 2d Brigade.

In December the air squadron received a new commander, Major Alfred Cunningham, the first Marine to qualify as an aviator and the first man in Marine aviation. He had led Marine aviation in France during World War I.

The incoming Warren Harding administration replaced Admiral Snowden in June 1921. His replacement was Rear Admiral Samuel S. Robison.

Brigadier General Harry Lee, formerly commanding the 6th Marines in France, relieved Gen. Long in command of the Second Brigade on 8 August 1921. He retained command until the Marines left the Dominican Republic in 1924. As previously mentioned, then Lt. Col. William C. Harllee assumed command of the 15th Marine Regiment on 28 September 1921. He soon launched a systematic drive to finish off the "bandits" in the eastern district. Thomas Steele, a British subject who had been in charge of the Angelina sugar plantation, was abducted by a rebel named Ramon Nateras and his band. Harllee ordered his regiment, 36 officers and 814 enlisted men, into action. On 29 September, Marine Gunner Robert W. Reid led his detachment of eight Marines up close to the high ground held by a native group of about 80 men. Reid and his men successfully drove that group off the precipice and their stronghold.

Harllee continued using his 15th Regiment reinforced with elements of the *Policia Nacional* between October 1921 and 11 March 1922. This was a series of nine large-scale cordon operations in the provinces of Seibo and Macoris. His style was to surround batches of area known to house bandits, then squeeze them. After collecting the suspicious ones, he put them up to be identified by hidden native informers. Those selected, over 600, weren't put in prisons. Instead they were set to work building a network of roads, ten feet wide, to enable automobiles to easily traverse them. And, in collecting those 600, not one of Harllee's Marines was killed.

However, Gen. Lee called a halt to Harllee's tactics because of developing Dominican opposition and because Lee claimed that it had failed to capture the leaders and hard core. And besides, there were more depredations than previously. So, back to patrolling went the 15th Regiment.

Early in the year 1922 the commandant decided to reorganize the 4th

Senior Marine staff officers with their commanding officer in Santo Domingo, c. 1922.

Regiment at 58 officers and 1,510 enlisted men still on duty in Santo Domingo. These were to be divided as follows: a headquarters and headquarters company, service company, howitzer company, and three infantry battalions. Each battalion included a machine gun company and three rifle companies. This was more than twice the size of the regiment in February 1922. However, lack of personnel made it impossible to implement the new organization. Actually, all that happened was the addition of the howitzer company which in fact, ran the regimental training center near Santiago, and a Headquarters Company, 1st Battalion. For the remainder of the occupation the 4th Regiment looked like the following: Hdqs. Co., Howitzer Co., Service Co., 25th Co., 33d Co., 69th Co., and the 1st Bn. The 1st Bn had the following units attached: Hdqs. Co., 10th Co., 28th Co., and the 32d Co.[34]

Lee authorized a series of home guard units in the eastern district. Fifteen Dominicans, generally those who had been hurt by the "bandits," were allowed weapons, and four Marines; a leader, plus three with automatic weapons. During 15 to 30 April those law enforcement groups literally wiped out organized banditry in that eastern section.

On 1 August the 3d and 15th Marine Regiments in Santo Domingo were disbanded and their personnel transferred to the newly reestablished 1st

12. Santo Domingo/Dominican Republic 165

A Marine patrol in camp, Santo Domingo, c. 1924.

Marine Regiment with Col. Charles C. Carpenter in command, and then they joined the 4th Marine Regiment and 1st Air Squadron as the 2d Brigade.[35] The 2d Brigade had a total of 467 contacts with rebels, or bandits as the Marines reported them. In those contacts, the Marines killed or wounded 1,137 Dominicans, while Marine casualties totaled 20 killed and 67 wounded.[36]

The Marine air was still supporting the ground Marines. Now it was especially helping ground commanders to control the operations of their widespread patrols by dropping messages to them and keeping regimental headquarters informed of their whereabouts. In fact, in later evaluations, air was most important in this nation, indeed indispensable to Marines operating on the ground and to their commanders. Major Edwin A. Brainard, a future director of Marine Aviation, relieved Cunningham in command of the aviation force and would retain that post until the Marines left Santo Domingo.

All during the period that Marine air served in this mainly jungle environment it had continuous trouble with service, spare parts, fuel, and the long time for the delivery of any parts.

The Marines received orders in 1922 to withdraw to specific areas and by the beginning of 1923 had mostly complied with those orders. Major efforts were being made by the Dominicans with background help and advice from various American officials to develop democratic ideals and a form of government.

On 15 March 1924 over 100,000 Dominican citizens went to the polls and elected a popular hero, Gen. Horacio Vasquez, president, and his *Alianza* party, large majorities in both houses of congress.

The first Marine unit to leave, on 18 July, was the 1st Air Squadron. On 6 August the 4th Marine Regiment, after nine years, left Santo Domingo bound for San Diego, California. The 1st Marine Regiment left intermittently until finally, on 18 September those last Marines left. They had been left behind to settle administrative details.

The Marines learned some valuable lessons in jungle warfare while in that republic which they were to utilize in their future relations in other nations, including Nicaragua and the fight against Japan many years later.

13

Uruguay

It appears that the first intervention by Marines in Uruguay took place on 28 August 1855 when the Marine detachment aboard the sloop *Germantown* went ashore at Montevideo to protect American lives and property. It appeared to the ship's commanding officer, Commander William F. Lynch, the revolution would affect those Americans, but the trouble ashore ended almost at once and the Marines returned to the ship the following day.

At the end of November, First Lieutenant Augustus S. Nicholson, together with landing forces from ships of three other nations, guarded the consulates of the nations.[1] Conditions on 27 November became worse and more naval forces were sent ashore to support the Marines. Nicholson prevented the massacre of a group of insurgents who had already surrendered to government troops by interposing himself and some of his Marines between the two factions.

Less than three years had passed when another revolution broke out in the small republic of Uruguay in 1858. No one faction seemed able to hold the reins of government for more than two or three consecutive years before it would be deposed and another of revolutionary origin take its place. The lives of foreigners were jeopardized, and their property imperiled by this almost constant strife between the different factions who strove to control the administration of government.

Naval Flag Officer French Forrest, flying his broad pennant from the *St. Lawrence*, with the *Falmouth* in company, was at Montevideo when conditions became so chaotic that he deemed a landing of Marines necessary for the protection of his countrymen and the American consulate. Britain was also represented by a war vessel in the harbor. The American and English commanders conferred as to action to be taken, and agreed, as they had some two years previously, to combine their efforts in the form of a joint landing. Flag Officer Forrest was to command the combined force.

In accordance with the prearranged plan, Forrest selected the entire Marine Guard of the *St. Lawrence*, under the command of Captain and Brevet Major John G. Reynolds, with Captain William B. Stark as an assistant, and despatched them ashore on 2 January.[2] After the British had joined them on shore, the forces were combined and distributed between the American and British consulates and the Custom House. The American Marines remained on this duty until the 27th of the same month, at which time they were relieved by an increased force from the British ship, when they returned aboard the *St. Lawrence*.[3]

Little more than ten years of comparative tranquility was accorded the people of this revolution-ridden country before another outbreak occurred in 1868. On this occasion an armed force from the warships of six different foreign nations then present in the harbor of Montevideo were landed. These foreign vessels represented Brazil, France, Great Britain, Italy, Spain and the United States.

General Flores was governor, while his son Colonel Fortunio Flores was in command of the Battalion de Libertad, which was the regular guard of the city. This battalion had been turned against constituted authority and was in armed revolt against the governor. The governor feared for his personal safety and those who were loyal to him. Consequently, he applied to the American consul, James D. Long, for protection for himself, his loyalists, and the custom house in the port.

This request was communicated to Rear Admiral Charles H. Davis, U.S. Navy, commanding the South Atlantic Squadron of the United States, who was then in the harbor with his flagship *Guerriere* which was accompanied by the *Quinnebaug, Shamokin, Kansas* and *Wasp*. Admiral Davis received the consul's letter on the 6th of February, and a little later in the day, also received a letter from the British admiral relative to participation in a combined landing in the city. After considering the matter, he decided to cooperate with the foreign forces present, who, it seems, had received a like request from the governor for the landing of armed forces.

The combined landing took place "at 5:50 a.m." on 7 February. The United States forces consisted of Second Lieutenant of Marines R.R. Neill, with 15 of his Marines and 30 sailors, the whole under the command of Lieutenant Commander Henry B. Rumsey of the *Guerriere*.[4] When the various forces arrived on shore, they were placed under the direct command of Rear Admiral Amilcare Anguissola, who was in command of the Italian squadron then present in the harbor of Montevideo. This was done in consequence of his seniority of rank to all others.

These several forces remained ashore until shortly after noon of the following day, when upon receipt of a letter from the governor stating that the difficulties had ceased to exist, the foreign forces were returned to their respective ships.

This uprising had little or no political significance; it was devoid of any fixed purpose, Colonel Flores (the son) appointed no officials and made no attempt to exercise political authority nor enforce police regulations. His conduct appeared to be that of a mutineer at the head of some three or 400 armed soldiers who lawlessly threw into consternation and a state of siege a city of 70,000 inhabitants, two-thirds of whom were actually foreigners, and left the sole reliance for security of lives and property to the support of foreign men-of-war.

Admiral Davis in his report of this affair stated: "The predominance of foreign interests here [Montevideo], and in the large cities of the Argentine Republic will probably render it expedient at no distant period, to confer upon them a permanent defense against these frequent insurrections or revolts, very few of which possess any color of a motive, such as would justify resistance of legal authority."

The *Quinnebaug* and *Shamokin* sailed a few days later and Admiral Davis followed them in the *Guerriere* on the 19th of February, leaving the *Kansas* with detailed instructions to look after the interests of the United States during his absence. It appears that he had hardly cleared the harbor before a new outbreak occurred with disastrous results. Late in the afternoon of this date Governor Flores "was butchered in the street" by agents of the opposite party, and his friends rose in return and killed 30 or 40 of those belonging to the party of the assassins. This incident, of course, threw the city into a state of chaos, and the assistance of the foreign warships was again requested to protect the custom house and resident foreigners.

Following Admiral Davis' instructions and in compliance with this later request on 19 February, the commanding officers of the *Kansas* and *Wasp* landed 56 Marines and seamen, officers and men, who guarded the custom house, and the American consulate from the evening of the 19th to the 27th. On the latter date they were withdrawn at the request of the president of the Republic.[5]

Appendix A: Biographies

George Barnett was born in Wisconsin in 1859, graduated from the naval academy in 1881 and was appointed a second lieutenant of Marines two years later. He mainly served aboard ships until 1901. In 1902 he assumed command of a battalion of marines sent to Panama to protect the railroad. Then he was assigned to Cavite, then back aboard ships in the Pacific. In 1906 he accompanied the battalion to Havana, Cuba. Later, in 1911, 1912, and 1913, he commanded Marines in Cuba, which was followed by his appointment as major general commandant on 25 February 1914. He continued in that position until relieved on 30 June 1920. He continued serving until retirement on 9 December 1924.

Hiram I. Bearss was born in Indiana on 13 April 1875. He, like so many other Marine officers of that time, joined the Marines for the war with Spain. He re-upped and served in the Philippines from December 1899 till he went in Waller's brigade to serve during the Boxer war in China. He made a reputation there, much like his friend Butler. His service during these early years was in Panama, Cuba, Mexico and Santo Domingo. Then he went to France with the 5th Regiment, later the 6th, and then served as the regimental commander of the 102nd Infantry Regiment, the 26th Division. His service with every unit was distinguished but especially with the 102nd, which he led at St. Mihiel, straight through large German formations. Later he was promoted, in the Army a brigadier general, and commanded the 51st Infantry Brigade through the Meuse-Argonne battle. He was placed on the retired list as a Marine colonel on 22 November 1919 and advanced in retirement to brigadier general. He was awarded a Medal of Honor on 13 March 1934 for his 1902 actions in the Philippine Islands.

Smedley D. Butler was born in West Chester, Pennsylvania, on 30 July 1881. Though from a family of peace-loving Quakers, Butler desired war and joined as a second lieutenant on 20 May 1898. Released after that war, he re-upped in April 1899 and was soon on his way to Manila, then Peking in 1900. He was wounded several times but served notably. Afterwards, he served in Panama, Puerto Rico, and Nicaragua, where he led the assault on Coyotepe. He went back to Panama in 1912, then to Vera Cruz, Mexico, where he was awarded his first Medal of Honor. The following year he served in Haiti, where he was awarded his second Medal of Honor. He commanded the 13th

Regiment of Marines in France, where he was awarded both the Army and the Navy Distinguished Service Medals. In 1927 he commanded the 3d Brigade of Marines in China, after which, as major general, he requested retirement, on 1 October 1931.

Merritt Edson was appointed a second lieutenant on 15 September 1917 and first lieutenant 1 July 1918. He had already served on the Mexican border with the Vermont National Guard in 1916. He served in France with B Company, 11th Marine Regiment, the 5th Brigade, in France in 1918. After the war he tried to take up aviation but it wouldn't take him. He went to sea and served aboard the *Denver* in Nicaragua, earning a Navy Cross. Promoted to major in 1936 over many senior officers, he then served with the 4th Marines in Shanghai, then was made Lieutenant Colonel on 1 April 1940. He formed the 1st Raider Bn., led it on Guadalcanal and was awarded a second Navy Cross and a Medal of Honor. He was made colonel on 21 May 1942, brigadier general on 1 December 1943, and the aide-de-camp of the 2d Division. His arrival in Washington following the war was at the time the Army was trying to wipe out the Marine Corps. He, now a major general, purposely gave up any further chances in his career to speak his mind. He retired from the corps and not long after was found dead in his Vermont home.

George Elliott was born in Alabama but was appointed a second lieutenant of Marines from New York on 12 October 1870. Sea duty and shore duty was his fate until being assigned to Huntington's Battalion and making a creditable reputation during the Guantanamo Bay excursion in 1898. He was transferred to the Philippines on 21 September 1899. His performance at the battle of Novaleta earned him distinction and his lieutenant colonelcy. On 3 October 1903 he was appointed commandant, being chosen over many senior officers of the corps. As brigadier general commandant he was soon in action at the landing at Panama in 1904. He, like several of his predecessors, pushed education in the corps; he fought back an attempt to remove Marines from navy ships. He was promoted to major general commandant on 13 May 1908 and retired on 30 November 1910.

Logan Feland was first a training officer in the U.S. Army during the Spanish American War. He liked what he saw of Marines and was awarded a commission as a first lieutenant on 1 July 1899. He served in the Philippines, Cuba, at Vera Cruz, and was an officer accompanying Gen. Pershing to France in June 1917. Then he fought the war with the 4th Marine Brigade, as a major, lieutenant colonel, then colonel. After the war he was sent to Santo Domingo to command the 2d Provisional Brigade. During the mail guard service, he commanded that detail. Brigadier General Feland was in command in Nicaragua in 1927, in 1929 he was promoted to major general, and on 1 March 1933 he retired at that rank. He was awarded a large number of medals including a Distinguished Service Cross and several Silver Stars.

Herman H. Hanneken was born at St. Louis, Missouri, on 23 June 1893. He enlisted in the Marine Corps as a private in July 1914, serving the following five years gaining rank to sergeant. While at this rank he personally, with the aid of Corporal William Button, killed the rebel leader Charlemagne in Haiti on the night of 31 October 1919. For other actions he was awarded a Navy Cross in April 1920. He was promoted to second lieutenant in 11 April 1921 and received the Medal of Honor. After a number of years in various assignments, Hanneken was sent to Corinto, Nicaragua, in December

1928 for service with the 2d Brigade of Marines. Less than a month after arrival he captured another notorious bandit leader, General Jiron, Sandino's chief of staff. For that he was awarded a second Navy Cross. Schooling and various assignments then brought him to major, lieutenant colonel, and finally, colonel. He served with the 1st Marine Division during World War II, earning a Silver Star at Guadalcanal, Legion of Merit at Peleliu, and a Bronze Star at Cape Gloucester. Brigadier General Hanneken retired on 1 July 1848.

Charles Heywood was from Maine and entered the Marine Corps as a second lieutenant on 5 April 1858, serving in the U.S. Civil War, in which he broke all Marine Corps records rising from second lieutenant to brevet lieutenant colonel in 1864. As commandant he managed to increase the corps from 2,200 officers and men to 7,600; also increasing Marine stations from 12 to 21. His greater distinction was to be the first commandant to be promoted to major general. He made many improvements and additions to the Marine Corps during his tenancy, stepping down 2 October 1903.

John A. Lejeune was born in Louisiana and graduated from the United States Naval Academy in 1888. Commissioned a second lieutenant of Marines on 1 July 1890, he served aboard ship during the War with Spain and in 1903 led a battalion of Marines in Panama. Later he commanded a brigade of Marines at Cavite, served in Cuba in 1912, at Vera Cruz in 1914 and became assistant to the commandant until he went to France and eventually commanded the 2d Division. Returning to the U.S., he was soon appointed the 13th major general commandant of the corps. He retired from that post in 1929.

Charles G. "Squeegee" Long was a long-serving field Marine. Appointed a second lieutenant on 1 July 1891, he served mainly as a leader of Marines in various interventions. Made a captain on 3 March 1899, he served at Guantanamo, Philippines, China, Panama, Nicaragua, Vera Cruz, and Haiti. He was promoted to colonel on 29 August 1916, serving at the commandant's office, then to brigadier general in November 1918. He was in command of the 2d Brigade in Santo Domingo in 1920 and retired a major general on 31 December 1921.

James E. Mahoney was born in Massachusetts, graduated from the United States Naval Academy and on 1 July 1883 became a second lieutenant of Marines. He was a first lieutenant in 1890, and was named captain on 8 March 1899. He served with Company E, Huntington's battalion, at Guantanamo. As a result of Mahoney's distinguished conduct in Cuba, he was promoted to captain, and many years later, in 1921, he would receive a brevet medal for that action. In 1902 he was ordered to Cavite to command a battalion of Marines. On 14 October 1903 he was promoted to major and awarded "special duty" in Panama. Then, as a lieutenant colonel, Mahoney was ordered to expeditionary duty in Panama, once again, then to the Philippines again. Colonel Mahoney and his command left for Nicaragua, arriving there on 22 February 1910, but it was a brief action. He was in Cuba in 1912, Vera Cruz in 1914, and then, as a temporary brigadier general on 1 July 1918, on watch at Galveston, Texas, with his brigade. The war in Europe over, he like so many other Marine officers was reduced in rank to colonel. At his request he was placed on the retirement list with his many medals.

John Marston was born in Pennsylvania in 1884 and attended university there. He waited until 1908 to accept a commission as a second lieutenant of Marines. He served in Hawaii and soon after at the naval prison in Portsmouth, New Hampshire, for a number of years, Then in Haiti, and was promoted to major. In February 1922 he was made the commanding officer of the Marine Guard at the Managua, Nicaragua Legation, remaining there two years. Four years later he commanded the *Guardia Nacional* in that same city. From 1931 he served mainly stateside, except for a few years at Peking in command of all Marines in China. His first post during World War II, as now a major general, was command of the 2d Marine Division until 1 April 1943. He returned to the U.S. at that date and commanded the Department of the Pacific then Camp Lejeune until he retired in August 1946.

Bowman McCalla was a sailor from 30 November 1861. He had spent three years at the U.S. Naval Academy. After many years at sea he spent some time teaching at the academy. He served with Marines in Panama, and again in China. He served as assistant chief of the Bureau of Navigation from 1881 to 1887. He was advanced in numbers for his service against Spain and three numbers for his services in China in 1900. He served extremely well with and was liked by Marines. He retired a rear admiral on 19 June 1906 and died four years later on 6 May 1910.

Charles G. McCawley was born in Pennsylvania but appointed from Louisiana, entering the Marine Corps on 3 March 1847. He served with great distinction during the Mexican-American War, being brevetted twice, and again during the American Civil War. He was promoted to colonel-commandant on 1 November 1876, as the eighth in that line. McCawley was one of the outstanding "reformers" of the period. Among his many notable attainments was the commissioning of Naval Academy graduates as Marine second lieutenants beginning with the class of 1881. He died 13 October 1891, less than a year after stepping down as commandant.

William N. McKelvy, a graduate of the U.S. Naval Academy in 1893, was appointed a second lieutenant on 1 July of that year. He had a distinguished career which lasted for many years. He served aboard ships with Huntington's battalion in Cuba and earned a brevet rank of captain, served in China during the Boxer Rebellion, then in the Philippines, served under Butler in Panama, was back in 1906 Cuba, and held various state-side appointments. McKelvy served in Nicaragua in 1912, Vera Cruz in 1914, in Nicaragua in 1916, and in Santo Domingo commanding the 3rd Regiment of Marines. He was made a colonel in October 1917 and retired at that rank in 1925.

Wendell C. Neville, the 14th major general commandant of the corps, entered the U.S. Naval Academy in 1886, graduated and was appointed a second lieutenant of Marines in 1892. He served in the war with Spain in the Huntington Brigade in Cuba, where he earned the brevet medal and brevet captain. He served in China in 1900, then the Philippines and at Vera Cruz, where he was one of the many Marine officers to be awarded a Medal of Honor. This was followed by service in Cuba, Nicaragua, Panama, then in Hawaii. He would command the 5th Marine Regiment in France, then assume command of the 4th Marine Brigade. He served as assistant to the commandant, Lejeune. Then in 1929 he was appointed to that post, but died the following year on 8 July 1930.

Joseph H. Pendleton was a native Pennsylvanian born on 2 June 1860. He graduated from the U.S. Naval Academy and was commissioned a second lieutenant of Marines on 1 July 1884. He boarded the *Pensacola* in 1885, served at the Marine Barracks in New York, cruised the Bering Sea, and was advanced to first lieutenant on 28 June 1891. He had more sea duty, then was made captain in 1899 and major in 1903. He joined the 1st Brigade of Marines at Cavite in May 1904, then went on to command the Marine battalion at Guam. He was promoted to lieutenant colonel on 1 January 1908, and was back with the Marines in the Philippines in 1909. Promoted to colonel on 23 May 1911, he was detached and returned to Portsmouth, NH, in August 1912 to command the Marine battalion. He and most of his command were transferred to Nicaragua in 1912 with him in total command of the Marines. Next was Guantanamo, then back to Portsmouth. Next was his command of the 4th Regiment, which lasted until 22 November 1916, when he was sent to Santo Domingo. Brig. Gen. Pendleton was military governor of that republic until September 1918, when he was reassigned to command Parris Island. His duties were mainly stateside after that. He was promoted to major general and retired on 2 June 1924.

David Porter was one of five of his family, all named David, in military service, in the Navy and one a Marine. This David Porter was commissioned a lieutenant on 8 October 1799. He was made captain 2 July 1812, and for various reasons, mainly an unwarranted court-martial, resigned 18 August 1826. He would never accept any further advancement in the U.S. Navy, even though President Jackson tried very hard to get him back.

Lewis Puller, from Virginia, joined the Marines as an enlisted man on 27 June 1918 and was appointed a reserve second lieutenant on 16 June 1919, but on 27 June was forced to resign. He enlisted as a private the following day and served enlisted for five years. Commissioned a second lieutenant in March 1924, he also tried aviation but washed out in that field. His major occupation became Nicaragua in which he served in the *Guardia Nacional* and led many patrols along with his companion, William "Iron Man" Lee. Both men were awarded Navy Crosses, two for Puller and three for Lee. Lee was captured by the Japanese on Wake Island; Puller survived and fought all through that war, earning two more Navy Crosses and becoming a lieutenant general. He has mostly admirers among the corps, though a few have complained about his handling of the 1st Marines at Peleliu.

Ross E. Rowell, born in Iowa, was appointed a second lieutenant on 3 August 1906. His first assignment was in Cuba, then Cavite, followed by sea service. He was promoted to first lieutenant in November 1908, captain in September 1914, and in October 1917 he was promoted to major. He was in Panama in 1909, Nicaragua 1914, and Haiti in 1921. He went back to Cuba, then had flying lessons in 1923. Aviation was where he made his name and fame. Assigned to Nicaragua in 1927, he was named director of Marine Corps aviation. He was promoted to colonel in 1935, brigadier in 1939, and when World War II came he was in command of aviation in the Pacific. After the war he retired a lieutenant general. He had earned the Distinguished Flying Cross and the Distinguished Service Medal for his acts in Nicaragua.

John W. Thomason was one of the giants of the corps. He was an artist, writer, and fighter famous for about 10 books, mainly about Marines. He joined and served in

France, coming out a captain with a Navy Cross. In 1925, he was appointed to the command of the Marine detachment aboard the *Rochester*, which was the flagship of the Special Service Squadron, formed to keep a watchful eye on the Central American and Caribbean republics. Landing in Nicaragua in 1926 provided him with many stories for his later works. Thomason served in many climes and places, especially China. He made a major contribution to the corps in his many books and especially his illustrations. He died a colonel on active service in 1944.

Alexander A. Vandegrift, born in Charlottesville, Virginia, on 13 May 1887, became the 18th commandant of the Marine Corps on 1 January 1944, after serving with great distinction in World War II. He was appointed a second lieutenant of Marines on 22 January 1909, and after a few stops went to serve under Major Butler in Panama. He was at the Battle of Coyotepe in Nicaragua and at Vera Cruz in 1914. Soon afterward he was in Haiti and in 1916 became a member of the *Garde de Haiti*, until December 1918, when he was returned to the States. That lasted a brief time; he was returned to Haiti the following July to again serve in the *garde*. Most of the balance of his career was stateside or in China. In March 1940 he was appointed assistant to the major general commandant, then command of the 1st Marine Division following the relief of Major General P.H. Torrey. Next was Guadalcanal, then in 1943 command of the 1st Marine Amphibious Corps, several more landings then home to assume the commandant role. He was in office during the toughest war the Marines ever engaged in and its great reduction following its termination. He retired a general on 31 December 1947.

Littleton W. T. Waller was an old hand. He'd been appointed a second lieutenant on 16 June 1880 and served aboard several ships, including the *Indiana*, during the war with Spain. He served extremely well in various places including the Philippines. In China, he was a major, then brevetted a lieutenant colonel on 28 March 1901, and was always in the forefront during his career. His major misfortune was in the march across the island of Samar in the Philippines. It cost him a court-martial, in which he was exonerated, but also cost him his chance to be the commandant. He led a regiment of Marines in Panama in 1904, and then a provisional brigade in Cuba in 1911. This was followed by his command of the First Brigade at Vera Cruz in April 1914. Waller was in Haiti and commanded the Marines in 1915, and then a brigadier general on 29 August 1916, and major general on 1 July 1918. His final command was of the Advanced Base Force in Philadelphia from January 1917 until his retirement. He was a Brevet Medal recipient along with many other awards. He retired 27 March 1920.

Frederick May Wise, son of a naval officer, was born in New York City on 6 October 1877. He had the usual schooling and was appointed a second lieutenant of Marines on 1 July 1899. After service in the Philippines, China in the Boxer Rebellion, he returned to Cavite. When his father died he was returned to stateside and service at the Marine Barracks, Brooklyn Navy Yard. He again went to Cavite, followed by a sojourn in a hospital in Japan until he was well. His next assignment was Cuba in 1906, then two years aboard ship once again. He was with the Marines landing at Vera Cruz, Mexico, in April 1914. Trouble in 1915 Haiti found him there followed by the intervention in Santo Domingo. Major Wise was with the 5th Marines in France, then was promoted to lieutenant colonel. After trouble with Brig. Gen. Harbord he was sent to join the 59th Infantry of the 4th Division as regimental commander. He led that regiment, and later the 8th Brigade it was part of, and was made a colonel. He was awarded two Distinguished Service Medals, Army and Navy, plus two Silver Stars and a Croix de Guerre at Belleau Wood leading 2/5. At the end of that war he was back in Haiti as a major general of the *gendarmerie*. In April 1921 he was back at Quantico. After nearly 27 years of service he decided to retire a colonel on 19 January 1926. He was promoted to brigadier general in 1937.

Appendix B: Officers of the First Provisional Regiment, Nicaragua, 1909–1910

The officer rolls of the First Provisional Regiment of Marines on 31 December 1909, serving in Nicaragua during that year's rebellion. All sergeants listed were the company first sergeants.

Regimental Field and Staff
Colonel James E. Mahoney, Commanding
Major Philip M. Bannon, unattached
Captain Louis McC. Little, Adjutant
Captain Hugh L. Matthews, Quartermaster
Sergeant Major Thomas F. Hayes, Sergeant Major

First Battalion
Major Wendell C. Neville, Commanding
First Lieutenant Arthur E. Stokes, Adjutant

Company A
Captain Louis M. Gulick, Commanding
First Lieutenant Harry G. Bartlett
Second Lieutenant Richard H. Tebbs, Jr.
Second Lieutenant Leon W. Hoyt
First Sergeant Joseph J. Franklin

Company B
Captain Richard H. Clifford, Commanding
First Lieutenant Holland M. Smith
Second Lieutenant Thomas S. Clarke
Second Lieutenant Joseph D. Murray
Gunnery Sergeant George Heinsohn

Company C

Captain Harry R. Lay, Commanding
Second Lieutenant Francis T. Evans
Second Lieutenant Donald F. Duncan
Second Lieutenant Sydney N. Raynor
Gunnery Sergeant Robert Carrigan

Third Battalion

Company G

Captain James C. Breckinridge, Commanding
First Lieutenant William H. Buckley
First Lieutenant William D. Smith
First Sergeant Charles D. Meginness

Company H

Captain William H. Parker, Commanding
First Lieutenant Edward H. Conger
First Lieutenant Charles F. B. Price
First Sergeant Charles A. Pennington

Company I

Captain Robert M. Gilson, Commanding
First Lieutenant Edward S. Willing
Second Lieutenant Robert E. Adams
First Sergeant Daniel J. McNamara

Company K

Captain John A. Hughes, Commanding
First Lieutenant Charles A. Lutz
First Lieutenant Ralph L. Shepard
First Sergeant Robert E. Slingluff

Five months later, on 27 May 1910, Major Smedley D. Butler landed again with two companies, A and C, including six officers, 200 enlisted Marines and two corpsmen.

Company A

Captain James C. Breckinridge, Commanding
First Lieutenant Ralph L. Shepard
Second Lieutenant Donald F. Duncan
First Sergeant Charles D. Meginness

Company C

Captain Robert M. Gilson, Commanding
First Lieutenant Edward S. Willing
Second Lieutenant Thomas S. Clarke

Appendix C: Officers at Coyotepe and Barranca, Nicaragua, 1912

Officers who participated in the assault on Coyotepe and the Barranca on 4 October 1912.

Regimental Headquarters
Colonel Joseph H. Pendleton, Commanding
Captain Harry Lee, Regimental Adjutant
Surgeon Robert E. Hoyt, Regimental Surgeon
Pay Inspector Thomas H. Hicks, Aide-de-Camp
Captain Russell B. Putnam, Regimental Paymaster

First Battalion
Major William McKelvy, Commanding
First Lieutenant Emile P. Moses, Adjutant
Passed A.S. Fletcher H. Brooks, Surgeon

Company A
Captain Edward A. Greene, Commanding
First Lieutenant Henry M. Butler
Second Lieutenant Alfred M. Robbins

Company B
Captain Robert Y. Rhea, Commanding
First Lieutenant William A. McNeil
Second Lieutenant Robert W. Voeth

Company C
Captain Eugene P. Fortson, Commanding
Second Lieutenant George W. Martin

Company D
Captain Howard H. Kipp, Commanding
First Lieutenant Thomas E. Thrasher, Jr.
Second Lieutenant Charles A.E. King

Second Battalion

Artillery Company E
Captain Robert O. Underwood, Commanding
Second Lieutenant Robert E. Messersmith
Second Lieutenant Roy S. Geiger

Third Battalion

Major Smedley D. Butler, Commanding
First Lieutenant Edward A. Ostermann, Adjutant
Passed A.S. Benjamin H. Dorsey, Surgeon

Company A
Captain John C. Beaumont, Commanding
First Lieutenant Harold F. Wirgman
Second Lieutenant George C. DeNeale

Company B
Captain Nelson P. Vulte, Commanding
Second Lieutenant Alexander A. Vandegrift
Second Lieutenant Richard A. Tebbs, Jr.

Company C
First Lieutenant Edward H. Conger, Commanding
Second Lieutenant Arthur J. White

Fourth Battalion (USS California)

Lieutenant Commander George W. Steele, Jr., Commanding
Ensign Francis G. Marsh, Adjutant

First Company
Lieutenant (jg) John M. Schelling, Commanding
Ensign Daniel J. Callaghan
Ensign Beriah M. Thompson

Third Company
Ensign Kinchen L. Hill, Commanding
Ensign Robert H. Skelton
Ensign Stanley G. Womble

Appendix D: The Roll of Honor

Dates represent time of action.

Marines Killed While Serving with the Guardia Nacional de Nicaragua

First Lieutenant Albert R. Bourne, USMC. 19 September 1931.
First Sergeant Thomas G. Bruce, USMC. 1 January 1928.
Second Lieutenant Laurence C. Brunton, USMC. 21 April 1932.
Corporal Laurin T. Covington, USMC. 21 April 1932.
First Lieutenant Veryl H. Dartt, USMC. 18 April 1930.
Sergeant Norman G. Freeman, USMC. 2 August 1930.
First Lieutenant Leo Healey, USMC. 17 February 1931.
First Sergeant Johnny F. Hemphill, USMC. 30 December 1927.
Sergeant Robert W. Leake, USMC. 30 August 1929.
Sergeant Charles J. Levonski, USMC. 4 April 1932.
Sergeant William E. McGhee, USMC. 15 June 1931.
Captain Harlan Pefley, USMC. 11 April 1931.
First Lieutenant Lester E. Power, USMC. 15 June 1931.
Sergeant Luis A. Ramirez, USMC. 1 July 1931.
Gunnery Sergeant Edward H. Schmierer, USMC. 30 June 1932.
First Lieutenant Edward Selby, USMC. 9 March 1930.
Corporal Lewis H. Trogler, USMC. 6 October 1929.
Sergeant Russell White, USMC. 10 November 1930.
Phm. First Class Finis H. Whitehead (MC), USN. 21 April 1932.
Sergeant James O. Young, USMC. 18 April 1930.

Marines of the Guardia Nacional Killed During the Earthquake at Managua on 31 March 1931

Major Hugo F. A. Baske (Lt. Cmdr. MC, USN)
First Lieutenant James F. Dickey (Chief Q.M. Clerk, USMC)
Second Lieutenant William H. Pigg (Sgt. USMC)

Injured at Earthquake in Managua on 31 March 1931

Second Lieutenant Robert G. Crawford (1st Sgt., USMC, internal injuries, broken pelvic bone, severe body bruises)

First Lieutenant Charles Davis (SgtMaj. USMC, bruises)
Captain James L. Denham (1st Lt. USMC, scalp injuries)
Colonel Robert L. Denig (Lt. Col. USMC, fracture of right leg)
Second Lieutenant McKinley D. Hoskin (Sgt., USMC, bruises)
Second Lieutenant Hugo Makus (Sgt., USMC, bruises)
First Lieutenant George Occhionero (GySgt, USMC, internal injuries, fracture right hip, etc. Completely disabled)
First Lieutenant Louis Rossich (GySgt., USMC, internal injuries, fractured bones right knee and hand, etc.)

Marines Decorated for Service During Earthquake

Major Horace R. Boone (Lt. Cmdr., MC, USN)
Captain Evans F. Carlson (1st Lt., USMC)
First Lieutenant Charles Davis (Sgt. Maj., USMC)
Captain H.M.H. Fleming (Captain, USMC)
Major Maurice C. Gregory (Captain, USMC)
First Lieutenant Nicholas M. Greico (1st Sgt., USMC)
Colonel Gordon D. Hale (Commander, MC, USN)
Captain Herbert S. Keimling (1st Lt., USMC)
Major General Calvin B. Matthews (Lt. Col., USMC)
Major Otto Salzman (Captain, USMC)
Colonel Walter G. Sheard (Major, USMC)
Captain Edward J. Trumble (1st Lt., USMC)

Recipients of the Medal of Honor

Schilt, Christian F. (Quilali) 21 February 1928.
Truesdale, Donald L. (Constancia) 1 August 1932.

Recipients of the Navy Cross

(* denotes Gold Star in lieu of second award)

Lt. Col. Archer, Percy F. 19 April 1929–3 September 1930.
Capt. Archibald, Robert J. March 1927–July 1928.
PFC Aron, Irving W. 31 December 1930.
1st Lt. Atkinson, Benjamin W. 3–4 April 1928.
PFC Ballinger, Earnest F. 3 April 1928.
Lt. Col. Beadle, Elias R. 11 July 1927–14 March 1929.
Col. Berkeley, Randolph C. Spring of 1927.
*Capt. Blake, Robert. 10 February 1929–30 June 1929.
Capt. Bleasdale, Victor F. 25 July 1927.
Capt. Brown, Julian P. 12–15 May 1927.
1st Sgt. Bruce, Thomas C. 16 July 1927.
Capt. Buchanan, Richard B. 16 May 1927.
Cpl. Bunn, Bennie M. 26 December 1932.
Pvt. Bush, Lambert. 31 December 1930.
Col. Buttrick, James T. 25 September 1929–18 April 1930.
1st Lt. Carlson, Evans F. 18 May 1930–1 May 1931.
Capt. Challacombe, Arthur D. 12–15 May 1927.
1st Lt. Chappell, Clarence J. 6 November 1927–8 November 1928.

Cpl. Clark, Cecil H. 24 February 1932.
Cpl. Cobb, John N. 7 June 1930.
1st Sgt. Darrah, Clyde R. 11–12 April 1931.
Sgt. Davis, Chester H. 28 March 1928–30 June 1929.
Sgt. Eadens, Alva. 19 September 1927.
Capt. Edson, Merritt A. 7 August 1928.
Pvt. Elliott, Edward E. 31 December 1930.
Pvt. Erpelding, George H. 23 August 1930.
Maj. Floyd, Oliver. July 1927.
Pvt. Gale, Eugene B. 6 June 1930.
Sgt. Gayer, Harry. 7 December 1928.
Capt. Geyer, Peter C. 1 April 1928–30 June 1929.
1st Lt. Gould, Moses J. 30 December 1927.
Cpl. Gray, Earl T. 22–26 May 1932.
Col. Gulick, Louis M. Spring of 1937.
1st Lt. Guymon, Vernon M. 31 December 1927–26 May 1929.
1st Lt. Hakala, Edwin U. 11 December 1928–30 June 1929.
Gy Sgt. Hamas, John. 23–26 April 1932.
*1st Lt. Hanneken, Herman H. 11 December 1928–30 June 1929.
Pvt. Harbaugh, Joseph A. 31 December 1930.
Capt. Hatfield, Gilbert D. 16 July 1927.
Capt. Holmes, Maurice G. 6 December 1928.
Capt. Hunter, Robert S. 14 May 1928.
Pvt. Hutcherson, Mack. 31 December 1930.
2d Lt. Jack, Samuel S. 12 April 1931.
Pvt. Jackson, Frank A. 31 December 1930.
Pvt. Jackson, Marvin A. 16 May 1927. Killed in action.
1st Lt. Keimling, Herbert S. 19 September 1927.
Sgt. Kerns, Paul. [unknown date]
1st Lt. Kilcourse, Thomas J. 30 December 1927.
Pvt. Kosieradzki, Frank. 31 December 1930. Killed in action.
* Maj. Larsen, Henry L. 1 April 1928–26 March 1929.
Gy Sgt. Lee, William A. 20 March–19 August 1930.
* Gy Sgt. Lee, William A. 11–20 December 1930.
* Gy Sgt. Lee, William A. 20 September–1 October 1932.
PFC Lester, Herbert D. 30 December 1927.
2d Lt. Letcher, John S. 10 December 1928.
Pvt. Litz, Richard J. 31 December 1930.
Capt. Livingston, Richard. 30 December 1927.
Pvt. McCarty, Joseph A. 31 December 1930.
1st Sgt. McGhee [McGee], William E. 15 June 1931.
1st Lt. McHenry, George W. 1 February 1928–6 May 1929.
Capt. MacNulty, William K. 27 February 1928.
Lt. Col. Meade, James J. Spring of 1927.
Capt. Moore, Edward B. 16 January 1928–21 March 1930.
Sgt. Mosier, Melvin. 7 August 1928.
1st Lt. O'Day, Edward F. 30 April 1928.
1st Lt. O'Shea, George J. 9 October 1927.
Sgt. Palrang, Arthur M. 31 December 1930.

MTSgt. Paschal, Archie. [unknown date]
Capt. Pierce, Francis E. 19 March 1928.
Maj. Pierce, Harold C. 31 January 1928–5 April 1929.
2d Lt. Piper, Earl S. 13 May 1928.
1st Lt. Power, Lester E. 15 June 1931.
1st Lt. Puller, Lewis B. 16 February 1930–19 August 1930.
* 1st Lt. Puller, Lewis B. 20 September–1 October 1932.
1st Lt. Richal, Meron A. 1 January 1928.
1st Lt. Ridderhof, Stanley E. 1 April 1928–30 June 1929.
* Capt. Roberts, Harold C. 4 September–10 November 1928.
* Maj. Rockey, Keller E. 19 January 1928–11 November 1928.
Sgt. Roos, Otto N. 30 December 1927.
Lt. Col. Rossell, Joseph A. August 1928.
2d Lt. Salzman, Elmer H. 28 September 1928.
Maj. Schmidt, Harry. 5 February 1928–6 June 1929.
Sgt. Schoneberger, Russell. 7 August 1928.
Gy Sgt. Shephard, Millard T. 4 December 1927–25 March 1929.
Sgt. Simmons, Orville B. 22 July 1931.
Maj. Simon, Allen E. 10 June 1929–11 April 1930.
Cpl. Smith, George C., Jr. 13 May 1930–6 August 1930.
Maj. Smith, Julian C. October 1930–2 January 1933.
Pvt. Stengel, Meyer. 7 August 1928.
Capt. Stockes, George F. 28 September 1928.
Maj. Thacher, Miles R. 11 July 1929–18 April 1930.
Pvt. Toro, Rafel. 25 July 1927.
Pvt. Turner, Charles E. 30 December 1927.
1st Lt. Walraven, John G. 1 December 1928.
Sgt. White, Russell. 7–9 November 1930.
Gy Sgt. Williams, Charles. 6 December 1928.
1st Lt. Williams, Gregon A. 3 October 1931.
Capt. Wood, John C. 11–13 April 1931.
PFC Yelanich, Anthony G. 7 August 1928.
1st Lt. Young, John S. 12–13 April 1931.

Recipients of the Distinguished Service Medal

Berkeley, Randolph C. CoS 2d Brigade, 1928–1929.
Dunlap, Robert H. CO 11th Marines and CG 2d Brigade, 1928–1929.
Feland, Logan. Cdr. Naval Forces ashore, Western Nicaragua 1927.
Feland, Logan. CG 2d Brigade 1928–1929.
Matthews, Calvin B. MajGen. Jefe Director *Guardia Nacional* 1931–1933.
McDougal, Douglas C. MajGen. Jefe Director *Guardia Nacional* 1929–1931.
Price, Charles F.B. Vice Chairman and Inspector U.S. Electoral Mission, 1932.
Rhea, Robert Y. CO 5th Marines, Organizer *Guardia Nacional* CoS 2d Brigade, 1927 and 1929–1930.
Rowell, Ross E. Nicaragua 1927–1928.
Sanderson, Charles R. Supply and Quartermaster 2d Brigade 1928–1929.
Utley, Harold H. Cdr. Eastern Area 1928–1929.
Wallace, Rush R. Cdr. 5th Marines 1928–1929.
Williams, Dion. CG 2d Brigade and U.S. Naval Forces ashore 1929–1930.

Appendix D

Distinguished Flying Cross
1st Lt. Becker, Herbert P. 16–22 July 1931.
Maj. Bourne, Louis M. 14 January 1928.
1st Lt. Boyden, Hayne D. 16 July 1927.
2d Lt. Fike, Charles L. 2 May and 19 June 1930.
Hart, John N. 2 May and 19 June 1930 (enlisted pilot).
Heritage, Gordon W. 16–22 July 1931 (enlisted pilot).
Capt. Johnson, Byron F. 19 June 1930.
1st Lt. Lamson-Scribner, Frank H. 18 November 1927 to 17 January 1929.
Maj. Mitchell, Ralph J. 19 June 1930.
Munsch, Albert S. 5 November 1927 to 4 November 1928 (enlisted pilot),
Maj. Rowell, Ross E. 16 July 1927.
Rutledge, Raymond P. Nicaragua 1932 (enlisted pilot).
Weir, Frank D. 22 May 1927 to 12 December 1928 (enlisted Pilot).
Williams, Neal G. 6 July 1932 (enlisted pilot).
Chief Marine Gunner Wodarczyk, Michael. 28 February and 19 March 1928.
2d Lt. Young, John S.E. 19 June 1930.

Officers and Enlisted Members of the Guardia Nacional
(* Killed or ** Wounded; GN = *Guardia* rank)

Ackerman, 1st Lt. James A.
Adams, Cpl. (2d Lt. GN) George H.
Alban, 1st Lt. Harvey B.
Alexander, Lt. GN M. O.
Anderson, Capt. GN R.A.
Anderson, Gy Sgt. (1st Lt GN) Walter E.
Anderton, Lt. GN F.
Arnett, Capt. Roscoe.
Ashbrook, Lt. GN C.
Atha, Lt. GN S.D.
Atwell, Lt. GN J. F.
Bain, Capt. James M.
Bales, 1st Lt. William L.
Barnes, Lt. GN.
*Baske, Lt. Cmdr. (Maj. GN) Hugo F. A.
Bateman, Lt. GN.
Beadle, Lt. Col. Elias R.
Beans, Lt. GN F. O.
Bell, 2d Lt. GN James R.
Bell, 2d Lt. GN L. H.
Bernheim, Lt. GN J.
Berueffy, Lt. GN M.
Biebush, 1st Lt. Frederick C.
Blackburn, Cadet Ollie.
Blanchard, Lt. GN J. L.
Bleasdale, Capt. Victor F.
Bourne, 1st Lt. (Capt GN) Albert R.
Boyle, Lt. GN H.
Bradman, Brig. Gen. Frederick L.
**Brannon, (Lt. GN) C. T.
Brauer, 2d Lt. (1st Lt. GN) James O.
Broderick, (Lt. GN) J. M.
Brown, (Lt. GN) C. A.
Brown, 1st Lt. Wilburt S.
*Bruce, 1st Sgt. (2d Lt. GN) Thomas.
*Brunton, 2d Lt. (1st Lt. GN) Laurence C.
Bryson, 2d Lt. (2d Lt. GN) William F.
Buckner, 1st Sgt. (1st Lt. GN) Arthur E.
Bunn, (Lt. GN) B. M.
Burns, (Lt. GN) J. A.
Burt, (Lt. GN) O. K.
Burwell, 1st Lt. (Capt. GN) Edward L., Jr.
Calvert, (Lt. GN) W. M.
Carlson, 1st Lt. Evans F.
Chappell, (Lt. GN) Clarence J.
Cheatham, Maj. Thomas P.
Chenoweth, (Lt. GN) M. K.
Christy, (Lt. GN) W. J.
**Clark, (2d Lt. GN) Cecil H.
Clauson, 1st Lt. (Capt. GN) Nicholas E.
Cobb, (Lt. GN) J. M.
Coffman, 2d Lt. (1st Lt. GN) John H.
Colsky, Gy Sgt. (1st Lt. GN) Robert.
Conklin, Lt. Cmdr. Frederic L.
Corbett, Capt. Murl.
*Covington, Cpl. (2d Lt. GN) Laurin T.

The Roll of Honor

Cox, Capt. Max.
Craig, Capt. Edward A.
Cramer, 2d Lt. (2d Lt. GN) Mercade A.
**Crawford, 1st Sgt. (1st Lt. GN) Robert O.
Croka, Capt. William B.
Cronmiller, 1st Lt. (Capt. GN) LePage, Jr.
Cunningham, 2d Lt. (1st Lt. GN) Francis J.
Curcey, Lt. GN L.
Darnall, 1st Lt. Grover C.
Darrah, Lt. GN C. R.
*Dartt, 1st Lt. (Capt. GN) Veryl H.
Daudy, Lt. GN O. B.
Davies, 1st Lt. (Capt. GN) William W.
**Davis, Sgt. Maj. (1st Lt. GN) Charles A.
**Denham, 1st Lt. (Capt. GN) James L.
**Denig, Maj. (Col. GN) Robert L.
*Dickey, Chief QM Clerk (1st Lt. GN) James F.
Downey, Lt. GN D. R.
Dumas, Lt. GN H. E.
Dye, Capt. Leon L. (Paymaster).
Elliott, Lt. GN H. J.
Elmore, Capt. Willett.
Erskine, Capt. Graves B.
Erwin, Pay Clerk (1st Lt. GN).
Fagan, (Capt. GN) R.
Farrar, Lt. GN T.
Fellers, 1st Lt. William S.
Ferguson, Lt. GN F. W.
Fleming, Capt. (Capt. GN) Hamilton M. H.
Forsyth, 1st Lt. Ralph E.
Forsyth, 1st Lt. (1st Lt. GN) MC Ralph E.
*Freeman, Sgt. (2d Lt. GN) Norman O.
Fricke, 1st Lt. (Capt. GN) Augustus H.
Frisbie, 1st Lt. Julian N.
Frisch, Lt. GN W.
**Gaitan, Lt. F.
Gale, Lt. GN P.
Gardner, Lt. GN G. E.
Garrett, Lt. Col Franklin B.
Gaspar, Capt. Walter S.
Gladden, Capt. Alton A.
Good, 1st Lt. (Capt. GN) George F., Jr.
Gould, 1st Lt. Moses J.
Graves, 1st Sgt. (1st Lt. GN) Avery.
Gray, (2d Lt. GN) Earl T.

Gregory, Capt. (Maj. GN) Maurice C. (QM).
Grieco, Gy Sgt. (2d Lt. GN) Nicholas M.
Griffin, 1st Lt. (Capt. GN) Robert L.
Griffith, 1st Lt. Samuel B. II.
Gumaelious, Lt. GN O. E.
Hakala, 1st Lt. (Capt. GN) Edwin U.
Hale, Cmdr. (Col. GN) Gordon D.
Hall, Lt. GN F.C.
Hamas, Lt. GN John.
Hancock, Lt. GN J. B.
Haralson, Lt. GN R. C.
Hardin, Lt. GN M.
Harrington, Maj. Samuel M.
Harris, Lt. GN R. F.
Hatfield, Capt. Gilbert D.
Haubensack, Lt. GN O. F.
Hayes, Capt. Glenn E.
**Hays, Lt. GN V.
*Healey, 1st Lt. (Capt. GN) Leo.
Helm, Cmdr. Jesse B.
*Hemphill, 1st Sgt. (2d Lt. GN) Johnnie F.
Henderson, Lt. GN L.
Hennrich, Lt. GN C.
Hogaboom, 2d Lt. Robert E.
Holmes, Capt. Maurice G.
Hopper, 1st Lt. James O.
**Hoskin, Sgt. (2d Lt. GN) McKinley D.
Howard, Capt. Frederick M.
Hoyt, Maj. Leon W.
Huefe, Capt. Edward O.
Hughes, Lt. GN C. G.
Hunt, Capt. LeRoy P.
Hunter, Lt. GN H. N.
*Hunter, Capt. Robert S.
Hurst, 1st Sgt. (1st Lt. GN) Harry E.
Hussa, Lt. GN N.
Hutchcroft, Lt. GN H. D.
Inman, Capt. (Capt. GN) Orrel A.
James, Capt. William C.
Johnson, 2d Lt. (2d Lt. GN) Chandler W.
Kalman, Lt. GN L. A.
Keimling, 1st Lt. Herbert S.
Keller, Lt. GN J. G.
Kelly, 1st Lt. (Capt. GN) William P.
Kemp, Lt. GN O.
Kerns, Lt. GN Paul.
Kessler, Lt. GN A. W.
Kipp, Lt. GN H. E.

Klein, Lt. GN B.
Krawie, Sgt. (2d Lt. GN) John W.
Krebs, Lt. GN W. F.
Krieger, Lt. GN Emil M.
Kurchov, Lt. GN F. L.
Larson, 1st Lt. Emory E.
*Leake, Sgt. (2d Lt. GN).
Ledbetter, 2d Lt. (1st Lt. GN) Otho C.
**Lee, Lt. GN William A.
Leech, Maj. Lloyd L.
*Levonski, Sgt. (1st Lt. GN) Charles J.
Linscott, Capt. Henry B.
Livermore, Lt. GN E. L.
Livingston, Capt. (Maj. GN) William J. (Paymaster).
Long, Lt. (MC GN) H.F.A.
Lynch, Lt. GN T. M.
McAfee, 1st Lt. (Capt. GN) Ralph D.
McClung, Lt. GN J. L.
McDonald, Gy Sgt. (Lt. GN) Donald.
McDougal, Col. Douglas C.
*McGhee, Sgt. (2d Lt. GN) William E.
McHenry, 1st Lt. George W.
McOorkle, (McCorkle?) (2d Lt. GN) F. M.
McQueen, 1st Lt. (Capt. GN) John C.
Mahoney, Lt. GN M. M.
**Makus, Sgt. (2d Lt. GN) Hugo A.
Manning, Lt. GN G. M.
Marcos, Lt. GN E.
Marston, Maj. John.
Martin, Lt. GN W. D.
Matthews, Lt. Col (MO GN) Calvin B.
Maynard, 1st Lt (Capt GN) George L.
Mays, Lt. GN V.
Meeks, Lt. GN L. C.
Merritt, Cadet GN Norman L.
Miller, Capt. (Maj. GN) Glenn D.
Mitchell, Maj. Ralph J.
Mitchell, Sgt. (2d Lt. GN) Robert J.
Mixson, Capt. James A.
Neel, Lt. GN J. L.
Nicholas, 1st Lt. Henry T.
Occhionero, Gy Sgt. (1st Lt. GN) George.
O'Leary, 1st Lt. (Capt. GN) John D.
O'Neill, Capt. Stewart B.
O'Shea, 1st Lt. George J.
Parker, Capt. John H.
Patchen, Capt. Fred O.

Pattison, Lt. GN J. R.
Paul, 1st Lt. Albert W.
Payne, Lt. GN P.
Peard, Capt. Roger W.
*Pelfey, Capt (Capt GN) Harlen.
Pennington, Lt. GN O. E.
Peterson, 2d Lt. (2d Lt. GN) Robert L.
Pierce, Maj. Harold J.
*Pigg, Sgt. (2d Lt. GN) William H.
Pilcher, Lt. GN.
*Power, 1st Lt. (Capt. GN) Lester E.
Price, Lt. Col. Charles F. B.
Pugh, 1st Lt. Lloyd R.
Puller, 1st Lt. (Capt. GN) Lewis B.
Radford, Col. Cyrus S.
Ragsdale, Lt. GN S. M.
Ramirez, Sgt. (2d Lt. GN) Luis A.
Rea, Capt. Leonard E.
Reid, Lt. GN R. C.
Rewie, Lt. GN F.
Rhea, Lt. Col. Robert Y.
Richal, Lt. GN M.
Ridderhof, Lt. GN S. E.
Rimes, Sgt. (2d Lt. GN) James C.
Rittman, Lt. GN E. J.
Roberts, 1st Sgt. (2d Lt. GN) Joseph K.
Rogers, Capt. William W.
Ross, Lt. GN E. C.
**Rossich, Gy Sgt. (1st Lt. GN) Louis.
Russell, Capt. GN E. L. (?)
Ryan, Lt. GN D.
Sabater, 2d Lt. (2d Lt. GN) Jamie.
Sage, Capt. Albert B.
Salzman, Capt. Otto.
Satterfield, Gy Sgt. (1st Lt. GN) James H.
Savage, 1st Lt. Eli.
Schmidt, Capt. Carl S.
*Schmierer, Gy Sgt. (2d Lt. GN) Edward H.
Schneeman, Sgt. Robert E.
Schwerin, Capt. (Capt. GN) James P.
Scott, 1st Lt. William W., Jr.
*Selby, 1st Lt. (Capt. GN) Edward.
Shannon, Capt. Harold D.
Sheard, Maj. (Col. GN) Walter O.
Sinkule, Lt. GN B. O.
Skinner, Capt. Rees.
Small, Capt. GN A. C. (?)
Smith, Sgt. F. C.

Smith, 1st Lt. (Capt. GN) James M.
Smith, Maj. Julian C.
Smith, Capt. GN Max D. (?)
Smith, Lt. GN M. E.
Smith, Lt. GN O. C.
Smith, Lt. GN W.C.
Snyder, Lt. GN O. D.
Snyder, Capt. William K.
Spotts, Capt. George W.
Stafford, 1st Lt. David A.
Stanko, Lt. GN J. M.
Stanley, Lt. GN P. C.
Stearns, Lt. GN C. B.
Stent, Capt. Howard N.
Stephenson, Lt. GN T. M.
Stevens, Lt. GN W.W.
Stevenson, Lt. GN T. M.
Stone, Lt. GN W. J.
Stuart, Lt. GN T. R.
Suprenaut, Lt. GN E. J.
Synn, Maj. Charles A.
Thompson, 2d Lt. GN R. A.
Thrasher, Maj. Thomas E., Jr.
*Trogler, Sgt. (1st Lt. GN) Lewis E.
Trosper, Lt. GN R. A.
Truesdale, (Lt. GN) Donald L.
Trumble, 2d Lt. (1st Lt. GN) Edward O.
Turville, Lt. Cmdr. William H. H.
Urig, Lt. GN.
Villegas, Lt. GN E. D.
Voeth, Maj. Robert W.
Vogel, Lt. Col Clayton B.
Vogel, (Voge?) Lt. GN R. E.
Wallace, Lt. GN D. H.
Walraven, Lt. GN.
Watson, Maj. Thomas E.
Webb, Capt. James W.
Weeks, Lt. GN O. R.
Wells, Lt. GN D. E.
Whaley, Maj. Louis W.
*White, Sgt. (1st Lt. GN) Russell.
*Whitehead, PhM 1st (2d Lt. GN) Finis H.
Whitford, Lt. GN.
Williams, QM Sgt. (1st Lt. GN) Frank.
Williams, 1st Lt. (Capt. GN) Oregon A.
**Williamson, Lt. GN W. H.
Wilson, Lt. GN M. K.
Wise, Lt. Col. William C.
Wood, Capt. John C.
Wood, Capt. GN U. C.
Wriston, Lt. GN L. S.
Wynn, Maj. Charles A.
Wysaski, Lt. GN F. M.
Yandle, 1st Lt. Marvin V.
York, 1st Sgt. Joseph.
Young, Maj. Archibald.
*Young, Sgt. (2d Lt. GN) James O.

Later Arrivals

Below are Marines who arrived in Nicaragua at a later date and do not show up in some records. The arrival date is in parentheses.

Battin, 1st Lt. Ralph C. (5 December 1928)
Benson, 2d Lt. William W. (1 May 1930)
Fox, Capt. Donald R. (6 August 1929)
Hamel, 2d Lt. Lester S. (27 October 1931)
Hanneken, 1st Lt. Herman H. (6 May 1929)
Holdahl, 1st Lt. Theodore A. (13 November 1929)
Hunt, 1st Lt. Robert O. (24 March 1930)
Leach, 1st Lt. Ralph D. (29 December 1928)
Linsert, 1st Lt. Ernest E. (29 November 31)
Lowell, Maj. Roy D. (12 August 1928)
Roberts, 2d Lt. Clyde C. (1 July 1931)
Rosecrans, 1st Lt. Harold E. (29 July 1930)
Rowan, Capt. George R. (12 November 1931)
Shaughnessey, 1st Lt. Ernest E. (1 October 1929)
Sims, 1st Lt. Amor L. (20 August 1929)
Withers, 2d Lt. Hartnoll J. (3 August 1930)

Chapter Notes

Chapter 1
1. Miller, *A Chronology of the United States Marine Corps, 1775–1934*, p. 68.
2. Ellsworth, pp. 9–10.
3. Uruguay was heavily involved in this assault upon Rosas and his government.
4. Ellsworth, p. 11.
5. Tattnall was one of the many officers of the United States Army, Navy, and Marines who elected to leave the service and return to their birth states in the South in 1861.
6. Herring, pp. 715–17; Ellsworth, pp. 10–13.
7. Leonard, *The Story of the United States Marines, 1740–1919*, pp. 46–47.

Chapter 2
1. Brown was a lieutenant on 2 June 1856 and advanced through all the ranks to rear admiral on 27 September 1893. He retired on 19 June 1897. McCann was a lieutenant on 18 September 1865, rose through the ranks to commodore on 26 January 1887, then retired on 4 May 1892 and was advanced one grade for "efficient and faithful service during the Civil War."
2. Ellsworth, p. 17. Muse was one of those unfortunate Marine officers who had served as a second lieutenant in the Civil War and because of slow promotions he had not progressed much many years later. However, in less than ten years he would retire a colonel in August 1900.
3. Schley was a lieutenant on 16 July 1862, captain on 31 March 1888, and rear admiral on 3 March 1899. He disappears from my records in 1916.
4. *Secretary of the Navy Annual Report* for 1891.

Chapter 3
1. Howland, *American Relations in the Caribbean*, pp. 198–99.
2. Garland was appointed a second lieutenant on 17 October 1834. He died on 20 June 1864.
3. *Secretary of the Navy Annual Report*, 1873. p. 8.
4. The entire following pages are taken from Clark, *The Landing at Panama*. Brasshat publication.
5. The terms "liberal" or "conservative," or just about anything else, were terms without substance. If your opponents were liberal you by necessity were conservative. This was true in many nations in the Western Hemisphere in the 19th and the 20th centuries.
6. McCalla and the Marines served frequently and well together.
7. The term "brigade" was used officially during this entire affair. The only previous use for the term "Marine Brigade" was that unit formed by the U.S. Army for duty on and along the Mississippi River during the U.S. Civil War. Even though the numbers were similar, the Marine force that landed at Guantanamo in 1898 was labeled "Huntington's Battalion." The next time the term "brigade" would be used would be in 1918 when two regiments and a machine gun battalion were formed into the 4th Marine Brigade, 2d Division, Regular, American Expeditionary Forces.
8. In 1903 President Theodore Roosevelt, while authorizing U.S. forces to once again land in the isthmus, prevented Colombian national troops from landing in their effort to put down another rebellion, and thereby openly supported the rebels. This in turn caused the Colombians to lose out and insured

the satisfactory establishment of an independent state of Panama, which Roosevelt recognized immediately or perhaps sooner. The canal dig was becoming very important in making national policy.

9. McCalla and Marines would serve well together again in 1898 during the Spanish-American War and again in 1900 during the Boxer Rebellion, when he again briefly commanded the Marine-Navy ground forces.

10. Meade, the nephew of the famed Civil War general, would be a competent Marine for many years, attaining the rank of brigadier general in 1900 and retiring in 1903. He briefly commanded all Marines in China during the Boxer Rebellion.

11. Collum entered service from Indiana as a midshipman in 1854 and resigned on 7 May 1857. He was commissioned a second lieutenant in the Marine Corps on 7 September 1861, then served mainly aboard ship off the southern U.S. coast. He resigned on 26 June 1897. He is most famous for compiling the material for the first known history of the corps, written by a man named Aldrich in 1875, then publishing his corrected version in 1890 and the revised edition in 1903.

12. Russell was appointed from Pennsylvania a second lieutenant of Marines on 16 October 1869. He retired a lieutenant colonel on 1 March 1903.

13. Burton was appointed a first lieutenant from Massachusetts on 1 July 1899. He eventually joined the Quartermasters Department as a lieutenant colonel in 1917 and served until he retired at that rank on 8 July 1930. McCreary was appointed from Pennsylvania as a Marine second lieutenant on 27 July 1899. He proceeded to captain and the recruiting office in Buffalo, New York, but for some reason disappears from the records in 1914, which probably means he died. Ramsey was an enlisted Marine appointed a second lieutenant on 5 December 1900. He retired a colonel on 1 July 1931.

14. Lucas was appointed a second lieutenant from Ohio on 1 July 1891. He advanced to captain, then major on 3 March 1903. He served in the Philippines and next mainly stateside until he became ill while a lieutenant colonel and retired in October 1915.

15. On 1 July 1890, Cole was appointed a second lieutenant after graduation from the U.S. Naval Academy. He progressed very well, making captain and then major 3 March 1903 while commanding the Second Regiment in the Philippines. He was the colonel commanding the 2d Brigade of Marines in Haiti in 1916. On 29 August 1916 he was promoted to brigadier general, and on 3 June 1924 to major general, but he perished in 1930.

Chapter 4

1. Huntington was appointed a second lieutenant on 5 June 1861. Rising slowly, like all post–Civil War Marines, he served in the Panama Landing in April-May 1885, was made lieutenant colonel on 2 February 1897 and colonel 10 August 1898. He died on 10 January 1899.

2. Sampson had a long and distinguished naval career. He was appointed a lieutenant on 16 July 1862 and advanced through the ranks to make rear admiral on 3 March 1899. He retired on 9 April 1902 and died 6 May 1902.

3. Heinl, *Soldiers of the Sea*, p. 116.

4. It was learned much later that the ship's crew had witnessed FitzGerald's signal and was preparing to fire when Quick's signal was seen. Quick earned a Medal of Honor, and so did FitzGerald but twelve years later.

5. The entire part played by Huntington's battalion was derived from the *Appendix to the Report of the Chief of the Bureau of Navigation, 1898*, and Nalty, *The United States Marines in the War with Spain.*

6. Howland, *American Relations in the Caribbean*, pp. 18–20.

7. Ibid., pp. 16–18. This was the "special clause" which would have cause to impact on Cuba's freedom of action in the years ahead.

8. Howland, pp. 24–32.

9. Klemann did quite well in his career. Ten years later he was a captain.

10. Catlin served at Havana, Cuba, in 1898 when the *Maine* was wrecked, and several other times. He led the 6th Regiment in France until he was wounded and retired in 1919 a brigadier general.

11. Leonard, pp. 141–42; Ellsworth, p. 62. At this date, the corps had 278 officers and 7,940 enlisted. Thirty-five percent of the total was in Cuba.

12. Harllee was from Florida and commissioned a second lieutenant on 17 February 1900. His first "cruise" was the Cavite in the Philippines as a first lieutenant in August 1900. He was a captain in 1905 and had recruiting duty in Chicago. In 1916 he was director of target shooting. He was heavily engaged in Marine target shooting for many years. He retired

a colonel in June 1935, but apparently was called back for World War II and retired a second time a brigadier general in 1944.

13. Denig was a valuable Marine for intervention service. He was born in New York but appointed a second lieutenant from Ohio on 7 October 1905. He served as a major in France in 1917–19 in the 5th Regiment, later the 6th and even later led the 2d Battalion, 9th Infantry, earning a Distinguished Service Cross and Navy Cross. In 1929 he served in Nicaragua. In 1934 he was a colonel and on 30 June 1941 the Examining Board, at Headquarters Marine Corps, allowed him to retire with the rank of brigadier general. The coming war altered his status, however. He was retained at rank as director of Marine Corps public relations. He is quoted as asking, "What in Hell is public relations?" He served notably.

14. Clyde H. Metcalf, *A History of the United States Marine Corps*, p. 320.

15. Ibid., p. 322.

16. Ibid., pp. 316–24.

17. Upshur earned a Medal of Honor at Haiti in 1915. He was a major general in World War II and died in a plane crash.

18. Benjamin R. Beede, ed., *The War of 1898 and U.S. Interventions 1898–1934, an Encyclopedia*. Anthony R. Pisani, Jr., and Allen Wells, "Cuba, Intervention (1906–1909)," pp. 131–34.

19. Robert J. Kane, *A Brief History of the 2d Marines*. Washington, D.C., Historical Division, U. S. Marine Corps, 1970, p. 3.

20. Ibid.

21. Metcalf, pp. 324–25. Ellsworth, pp. 62–63.

22. Mahoney, p. 112.

23. Ibid., pp. 112–13.

24. Lyman was from Ohio, and accepted a commission as a second lieutenant on 1 July 1890. He served in some island affairs and then, in June 1917, accepted a post in the Adjutant and Inspector's Office. He was promoted to major general in May 1935, and attaining the age of 64, he retired on 1 October 1939.

25. Schmidt became a second lieutenant on 17 August 1909. Had a distinguished career, earning a Navy Cross in Nicaragua, and a Navy Distinguished Service Cross in World War II while commanding the 4th Marine Division at Kwajalein, Eniwetok, Saipan. He became a major general on 28 September 1942.

26. All those numerically named companies became part of the 5th Regiment before sailing for France and service with the 4th Marine Brigade within the 2d Division, Regular.

27. Shaw, from Minnesota, graduated from the Naval Academy and was appointed a second lieutenant 1 July 1896. He moved up the ladder and was a colonel on 26 March 1917, serving mostly in the many small wars before then. He retired at that rank on 5 April 1921.

28. Halford was appointed from Indiana on 23 July 1900. He reached the rank of lieutenant colonel on 23 November 1919 and colonel on 26 December 1929, retiring the following October.

29. Bradman was born in New Jersey but appointed a second lieutenant from Massachusetts on 8 April 1899. He became a colonel on 1 July 1918 and a brigadier general on 20 May 1931. He retired that rank on 1 February 1939.

30. Treadwell was born in the District of Columbia and graduated from the United States Naval Academy. He was appointed a second lieutenant on 1 July 1892 and colonel on 29 August 1916, and retired at that rank in May 1922.

Chapter 5

1. Metcalf, p. 226. Bates was appointed a second lieutenant of Marines on 19 February 1873. He made captain on 2 May 1891 and retired that same day.

2. Howland, pp. 124–25.

3. Ronald J. Brown, *A Few Good Men: The Story of the Fighting Fifth Marines*. New York: Presidio Press, 2001, p. 5.

4. David Healy, *Gunboat Diplomacy in the Wilson Era*. Madison: University of Wisconsin Press, 1976, p. 31.

5. Cacos are variously described as "soldiers of fortune" or as "bandits" who lived on the country in normal times. They also supported various candidates for the presidency or whoever could buy them at any time. Estimates place their numbers at between 25,000 to 50,000 living in the mountains.

6. Healy, pp. 55–57.

7. Healy, p. 61. The Marine and bluejacket numbers were exactly equal. There were 165 sailors and 165 Marines in the landing party. Van Orden was in total command. He, from Michigan, accepted a commission as a second lieutenant on 1 July 1899. His service was noteworthy and he was promoted to colonel on 1 July 1918. He commanded the 11th Regiment from its formation on 3 January 1918 until its deactivation on 11 August 1919. Although the

regiment was never engaged in active combat, the officers and men performed a myriad of duties in Europe. He retired a colonel on 1 August 1923.

8. It seems that an election had been held and the Haitians were celebrating it the way they always did, by firing into the air.

9. Metcalf, p. 376. Subsequent investigations concluded that the two Americans had been killed by the fire from a nervous reaction by their own comrades. That sort of thing happened too often when untrained sailors were sent ashore as landing parties such as at Vera Cruz in 1914.

10. Healy, pp. 63–64.

11. Ellsworth, p. 90.

12. McCrocklin, p. 24.

13. Ibid.

14. Ibid., p. 25.

15. To perhaps confuse the issue more than might be necessary, on 1 July 1916 the 1st Marine Regiment and the 2d Marine Regiment would change designations within a year. The 1st became the 2d and the latter became the 1st in Santo Domingo.

16. Johnstone, p. 10.

17. Schmidt, *Maverick Marine*, pp. 74–75.

18. Venzon, *General Smedley Darlington Butler: The Letters of a Leatherneck, 1898–1931*, p. 155. Also Schmidt, *Maverick Marine*, p. 75.

19. McCrocklin, p. 29.

20. Ibid.

21. Bobo was a man of unusual attainments. He was a graduate of universities in Paris and London. He held degrees in law and medicine and was fluent in many languages.

22. The name was changed in 1927 at the request of the president, Louis Borno. He and many Haitians believed strongly that the term *gendarmerie* hinted at French police oppression. It then became the *Garde d'Haiti*.

23. The treaty was ratified by Haiti on 11 November 1915 and the U.S. on 23 February 1916. It was proclaimed in effect on 3 May 1916. The actual establishment of the *gendarmerie* was begun in September 1915, but recruiting and training took many months before they were ready to pick up their end of the workload.

24. Frederic May Wise, *A Marine Tells It to You*. New York: J. H. Sears, 1929, p. 132.

25. Ibid., p. 133.

26. Those were the instructions from Secretary of the Navy Josephus Daniels.

27. Quoted in Schmidt, p. 77.

28. Quoted in Schmidt, p 77. See also Clark, *With the Old Corps in Nicaragua* for other instances in Nicaragua of Butler's fighting heart.

29. For more details, see George B. Clark, *Devil Dogs: Fighting Marines of World War I*. Presidio Press, 1999, or the reprint by the U.S. Naval Institute Press, 2013.

30. Metcalf, p. 381. Barker was appointed a second lieutenant from Massachusetts on 2 April 1904. He was a major in 1917 when he was appointed provost marshal in France, then assumed command of the First Battalion, 6th Regiment, in August 1918. His service during the ensuing years was mostly stateside until he retired on 1 July 1937 as a brigadier general.

31. Campbell, from West Virginia, was appointed a second lieutenant on 11 September 1900. He proceeded to captain and service in Haiti. In 1919 he was a major in command of the Marine detachment in Camaguey, Cuba. He was promoted to colonel on 29 October 1931 while at the Portsmouth Navy Yard, and retired at that rank on 30 June 1936.

32. Thrasher, appointed a second lieutenant from Texas on 6 January 1909, took the easy way. He got appointed to the paymaster's office as a captain effective on 17 November 1916, then to major on 1 July 1918. He was assigned to Quantico in 1932, then retired a colonel on 30 June 1937.

33. McCrocklin, pp. 33–34.

34. Butler, in *Old Gimlet Eye*, incorrectly writes that this was why he recommended Daly for the second Medal of Honor. See page 194. Musicant picked up this error without change on page 196 without citation.

35. George B. Clark, *Treading Softly: U.S. Marines in China, 1819–1949*. Westport, CT: Praeger, 2001, p. 39.

36. George B. Clark, *Legendary Marines of the Old Corps*. Pike, NH: The Brass Hat, 2002, pp. 66–67.

37. Quoted in Schmidt, *The U.S. Occupation of Haiti*, p. 85.

38. Quoted in Schmidt, *Maverick Marine*, p. 80.

39. In a few years the natives would be convinced that slavery had returned. See below when the Marines would invoke *corvée*, which brought about a worse rebellion.

40. Low joined the corps from Connecticut, though he was born in New Hampshire, on 1 July 1899. He progressed to captain but disappears from my records in 1917 soon after he was promoted to major. Stowell became a

second lieutenant of Marines on 4 April 1913 and served in France with 1/6 as CO. Reduced to his regular rank of captain, he then served on recruiting duty. He was back at major in 1926, then disappears from the records after attaining lieutenant colonel rank. Benet-Mercie .30-caliber machine rifle, Model 1909, weighed 30 pounds and came with a tripod which weighed 50 pounds and was not used very much. It was considered more trouble than it was worth.

41. Iams served seventeen years enlisted, then was appointed a second lieutenant on 17 July 1918. He made captain on 4 June 1920, served with the 2d Brigade in Nicaragua in 1929 and retired at rank of major in January 1932. Gross' real name was Samuel Marguiles and he has been listed as Butler's orderly in *Old Gimlet Eye*, p. 193. Iams is supposed to have yelled to Butler, "Oh, hell, I'm going through." Both enlisted men and Butler were awarded Medals of Honor.

42. Both men were awarded the Medal of Honor, as was their leader, who was third into the breach, although he didn't emphasize that in this report. This was Butler's second Medal of Honor. Ross Iams was later retired as a major. Gross [real name Marguiles] developed epilepsy and wound up in a veterans' hospital in Pennsylvania.

43. Schmidt, *Haiti*, pp. 84–85.
44. McCrocklin, p. 35.
45. Schmidt, *Maverick Marine*, p. 84. Waller, a Southerner, was very critical of the Negro inhabitants of the island and an extreme racist, whereas Butler, a northerner and Quaker, was decidedly less so.
46. Schmidt, *Haiti*, p. 88. Men who joined the Marine Corps tend, then and now, to be desirous of responsibility above and beyond the norm. The number of occasions when they rose to the pinnacle of power and responsibility is many. Examples abound in the corps' long history and are too numerous to recount.
47. Ibid., p. 90.
48. McCrocklin, p. 55.
49. Ibid., pp. 59–63.
50. Ibid., p. 62.
51. One study of 1,200 blood tests found that 95 percent were syphilitic and almost that number had hookworm or other equally enervating diseases.
52. Schmidt, p. 86. McCrocklin, p. 68. The key provisions of the U.S. "approved" new constitution allowed foreigners (Americans) to legally own property in Haiti. Money appears to be the real reason for the U.S. intervention. When running for the vice presidency in 1920, Franklin D. Roosevelt, who had been assistant secretary of the Navy, bragged that he had written the Haitian constitution.

53. McCrocklin, pp. 93–94. Schmidt, p. 92.

54. *Hearings Before a Select Committee, October 31, 1921*, p. 530.

55. Schmidt, *Maverick Marine*, pp. 92–93. At that time the United States was a severely racist society, North and South, and black Americans weren't treated much better than were the Haitians. Consequently, white Marines, not always from the educated classes, reflected the American society they were from.

56. Russell, a later commandant of the corps, was mainly a political officer. He was a naval academy grad appointed a second lieutenant on 1 July 1894. His service consisted mainly of non-combat actions in Latin America. He was a colonel on 26 March 1917 and on 1 October 1919 he was made commanding officer of the 1st Brigade in Haiti. A brigadier general as of 1 January 1922, he would be made the U.S. high commissioner and remain there until the end of the occupation.

57. McCrocklin, pp. 95–98.
58. Miller/Johnstone, p. 117.
59. Inman, *Through Santo Domingo and Haiti*, p. 68.
60. *Hearings*, p. 136.
61. Doxey, from Arkansas, served as a naval cadet for eight years before being appointed a second lieutenant of Marines on 9 June 1911. He was captain on 20 August 1916 and was a major with the 3d Brigade in China in 1927. He was a lieutenant colonel on 1 July 1936 and no longer in China. He disappears from the records in 1942, possibly killed in action.
62. Why Kelly was not awarded a Navy Cross for his exploits amazes me.
63. Hooker, appointed from Nevada on 17 February 1900, was born in California. He served in the Philippines, as a captain in 1908 on special duty at Marine headquarters, then in Haiti in 1916 and was still there in 1920. He was a colonel but disappears from the records in 1933.
64. A few years after that Williams would purposefully disobey an order from Maj. Gen. Smedley Butler, his area commander, to not drink in public. This was during prohibition. He purposely got drunk in front of Butler in a crowded hall before many witnesses, many of them civilians, not allowing Butler any room.

He paid for the stupid mistake with a court-martial.

65. Mims served five years enlisted before being appointed a second lieutenant on 24 July 1917. He was an aviator and captain on 1 July 1918. He disappears from the records in 1922.

66. Sanderson became one of the outstanding Marine aviators. From Washington state, he served a couple of years enlisted and was appointed a second lieutenant naval aviator on 1 June 1919. He went onward until promoted to brigadier general on 5 June 1944 and retired a major general in December 1951.

67. McCrocklin, pp. 117–18. Most of the foregoing was derived from that study.

68. Ibid., p. 118.

69. Santelli, *A Brief History of the 8th Marines*, pp. 3–10.

70. McCrocklin, pp. 120–21.

71. Ibid., p. 124. Kirkpatrick, from Maine, was appointed a second lieutenant on 1 January 1919. He had already served over 10 years as an enlisted Marine. He retired at the rank of major in 1938.

72. Gen. Gerald C. Thomas Oral History Transcript, 23 September 1966, pp. 376–77.

73. Robert B. Asprey, pp. 58–59.

74. *New York Times*, 15 October 1920, p. 17. Franck blamed President Wilson and Navy Secretary Josephus Daniels for failing to take steps to change the prevailing low value placed on Haitian lives.

75. *Hearings Before a Select Committee on Haiti and Santo Domingo*, p. 517.

76. The Samar tragedy occurred on the Philippine island of Samar in 1901 when Marine Colonel L.W.L. Waller led a misguided march across that island and suffered many deaths to his command. Williams was a survivor.

77. This position would actually be the major office Russell would hold as a Marine until he was selected by Franklin Roosevelt to be the 16th commandant in March 1934.

78. Turrill, born in Vermont, entered the corps as a second lieutenant on 2 October 1899. He served with great distinction with the 1st Battalion, 5th Marines, in France, earning a Navy Cross and USA Distinguished Service Cross, two Silver Stars, and two Croix de Guerres. He retired soon afterward.

79. McCrocklin, pp. 192–93.

80. Leonard, pp. 152–161.

Chapter 6

1. See the chapter on Nicaragua for more about Zelaya.

2. Venzon, ed., *General Smedley Darlington Butler: The Letters of a Leatherneck, 1898–1931*, pp. 40–41.

3. Secretary of the Navy Annual Report, p. 633.

Chapter 7

1. Bauer, *Surfboats and Horse Marines, etc.*, p. 136.

2. *Secretary of the Navy Annual Report, 1870*, pp. 142–49.

3. Henley, from Georgia, was appointed a second lieutenant on 10 March 1905. He served mainly aboard ships until he was appointed a captain in August 1916 and served in Santo Domingo with the 2d Provisional Brigade. He was made major in May 1917 and was in command of the Marine brigade at Guam. In the following years he served mainly stateside. He became a lieutenant colonel in August 1930, and retired a colonel on 30 June 1941 but continued on active duty during the war.

4. Herring, p. 340. Ellsworth, p. 115.

5. Metcalf, pp. 298–99.

6. Long was appointed on 1 July 1891 from the U.S. Naval Academy. Made a captain in June 1898 and major in 1903, his service was mainly stateside. He was promoted to lieutenant colonel in 1916 and served at Headquarters USMC. As a brigadier general in October 1918 he was still at headquarters; he retired at that rank on 31 December 1921.

7. President Wilson had a habit of interfering in Mexican politics. He was especially opposed to the current military dictator, General Victoriano Huerta. The U.S. fleet had, and would, spend a great amount of time in the waters off both sides of Mexico during this entire period.

8. That regimental designation is rather complicated. On 19 June 1913 it was changed from the 2d Regiment to the 1st Advanced Base Regiment until 21 April 1914, when it became the 1st Regiment, 1st Brigade. Long remained in command until relieved by Col. James E. Mahoney on 6 May 1914.

9. Metcalf, pp. 299–301.

10. Wise, p. 124.

11. *Secretary of the Navy*, pp. 470–71.

12. Quirk, *An Affair of Honor*, pp. 95–96.

13. John A. Lejeune, *Reminiscences of a Marine*. Philadelphia, Dorrance, 1930, p. 209.

14. A. A. Vandegrift, as told to Robert Asprey, *Once a Marine: The Memoirs of General A. A. Vandegrift*. New York: W.W. Norton, 1964, pp. 43–45.
15. Ibid., p. 44.
16. Schmidt, p. 214.
17. Miller, p. 118.

Chapter 8

1. Ellsworth, p. 77.
2. Clark, *With the Old Corps in Nicaragua*, pp. xiv–xvi.
3. Metcalf, p. 236.
4. Ellsworth, pp. 123–24.
5. Metcalf, p. 408.
6. Howland, pp. 174–75.
7. Hughes was a former enlisted Marine awarded a commission as a first lieutenant on 6 December 1901. He was known as a "Johnny the Hard" because of his rough treatment of enlisted Marines. He was also quite foolhardy and was hurt several times because of it. He served as a major in France and was badly gassed, and soon retired.
8. Schmidt, pp. 38–39.
9. Howland, pp. 175–76. Ellsworth, pp. 124–25. Clark, pp. xviii–xx.
10. Metcalf, pp. 410–11. Schmidt, pp. 42–45.
11. Miller, pp. 112–13 for this and following entries. Ellsworth, pp. 125–27. Schmidt, p. 47.
12. Schmidt, p. 47.
13. Long, born in Massachusetts, graduated from the Naval Academy and on 1 July 1891 was appointed a second lieutenant of Marines. He had a distinguished career, ultimately retiring on 31 December 1921 as a brigadier general. Most of the previous entries were from the same sources, Schmidt, Ellsworth, and Miller, plus Clark, pp. 3–15.
14. Greene, a Georgian, was appointed a second lieutenant from that state on 23 July 1900. He made colonel on 2 January 1929 and retired that rank on 1 September 1931.
15. Mann enlisted in 1917 and was appointed a second lieutenant on 15 August 1918 and first lieutenant on 16 August. He retired a major on 16 October 1928.
16. Larsen enlisted in the Marines in late 1915. He was appointed a second lieutenant on 15 August 1918 and one year later on 19 August 1919 it was re-affirmed. He retired a colonel on 30 June 1941 but remained on active duty through the end of the war.
17. Fellers enlisted in the Marines in 1918 and was appointed a second lieutenant on 1 January 1919 and a first lieutenant on 2 January 1919. He served in Haiti, and by 5 October 1942 he was a colonel, having earned two Navy Legion of Merit awards. One was for 15 November 1942 to 11 October 1943, when he served as executive officer for the Fifth Marines and also later for the 2d Marines, and the second for the New Britain campaign as D4 for the 1st Division between 26 December 1943 and 15 March 1944.
18. Keyser was born in Virginia and was appointed a second lieutenant on 10 March 1905. He had a distinguished career in France with the 3d Battalion, 5th Regiment. He retired in 1937 as a brigadier general, but he was promoted a major general in retirement, on 26 September 1942.
19. Finch had a brief career as a Marine. He was appointed 9 June 1919, made first lieutenant on 4 March 1925 and resigned on 30 June 1936 at that rank.
20. He was appointed from Maryland a second lieutenant on 15 August 1917 and to first lieutenant the following day. He rose to colonel on 20 May 1942. He disappears from the records in 1946, which possibly meant he died in 1945.
21. Nicholas, from Kentucky, graduated from the U.S. Naval Academy and was appointed a second lieutenant on 7 June 1919. He had a modest career: first lieutenant on 3 June 1924, serving in the Nicaraguan *guardia* in 1929, and still a first lieutenant as late as 1935. He disappears from my records after that.
22. From Maryland, Kenneth B. Chappell was appointed a second lieutenant on 22 July 1924. He was a captain on 1 October 1935 and then served aboard the *Chester*. He was a colonel on 5 November 1942. He was the commanding officer of the 1st Marines at Okinawa and later commanding officer of Headquarters, 1st Marine Division. He was still on active duty in 1947 but apparently retired in 1948.
23. Finch was appointed a second lieutenant from the United States Naval Academy on 7 June 1919. He retired a first lieutenant on 30 June 1936.
24. Metcalf, p. 419.
25. Ellsworth, p. 132.
26. Berkeley was appointed a second lieutenant on 13 April 1899, and like so many young officers of that period was a captain by

Notes—Chapter 8

23 July 1900. For the first few years he was based mainly at various naval stations in the U.S., then back aboard ships. He was at Vera Cruz in 1914 and was one of that multitude of Marine officers to receive a Medal of Honor. In 1916 he was a major commanding the Marine barracks on Guam, a lieutenant colonel on 29 August 1916 and colonel on 1 July 1918. On 3 October 1919 he assumed command of the First Provisional Brigade in Haiti. He served in Nicaragua in 1927 and was awarded a Navy Cross. He was promoted to brigadier general on 1 July 1930 and then commanded the Parris Island base. He was made major general on 1 February 1939 and retired that same day.

27. Connette served more than 10 years as an enlisted Marine. In France he was with 1/6 and was awarded several Silver Star citations at the Meuse-Argonne. He was appointed a first lieutenant on 1 January 1919, later changed to 13 April 1922, and participated in several interventions during the period he remained a Marine officer.

28. Clark, pp. 36–37.

29. Richards, born in Washington state, served nearly four years as an enlisted Marine, then to the U.S. Naval Academy, after which he was appointed a second lieutenant on 30 March 1917, a first lieutenant on 23 May that year and captain the same day. He served with the 3d Provisional Brigade in Galveston, Texas, during the war. He retired a lieutenant colonel on 30 June 1940 but apparently served on duty during World War II.

30. *Boston Globe*, 27 May 1927.

31. Pierce, more commonly known in the corps as "Biff," joined in 1912. He was awarded the Navy Cross for his actions in Nicaragua in 1928–29. He was made a colonel on 29 June 1938 and served during the Second World War.

32. Hatfield served as an enlisted Marine, became an officer 15 November 1919 and was named captain on 17 October 1923. He retired a lieutenant colonel on 1 November 1939 but served during World War II. Norman was born in Ohio and served nearly five years enlisted, then was appointed a second lieutenant on 5 March 1926 and a colonel on 15 November 1942.

33. Brown was an enlisted Marine in the 20th Company, 3/5, during World War I. He attended the United States Naval Academy for two years, resigned and re-enlisted in August 1922. Brown was commissioned a second lieutenant in July 1925. In 1927 he went to Nicaragua with the 5th Regiment. Two years later he began his next ten years at sea duty. In 1942 overseas with the 8th Defense Battalion, commanding officer and colonel of the 15th Artillery Regiment, then the 11th Artillery Regiment. In April 1951 he was commander of the 1st Regiment of Marines. He was ultimately major general when he retired and went to school to earn a Ph.D.

34. Lamson-Scribner was appointed a second lieutenant on 8 June 1923. He progressed to colonel on 30 October 1942, serving as the air officer on Admiral Rockwell's Amphibious Force staff during the Gilbert and Marshall combat. He was awarded a Distinguished Flying Cross for service in Nicaragua from 18 November 1927 to 17 January 1929. Pierce was appointed a second lieutenant on 9 April 1921 and a colonel on 1 July 1938. He retired on that date but was recalled for World War II.

35. Archibald was born in West Virginia but appointed a second lieutenant from California on 30 March 1921. He began flying almost as soon as he entered the corps. He disappears from the records in 1930, which probably means that he died in service. I couldn't locate anyone named Harmon in the Marine Corps.

36. I could not locate anyone named Swarthout. Weir from New York attended and graduated from the U.S. Naval Academy and was appointed a second lieutenant on 8 June 1923. He reached the rank of colonel by 25 October 1942 and had earned a Legion of Merit for 26 June to 18 September 1942. He was also the holder of Distinguished Flying Cross in Nicaragua for the period 22 May 1927 through 12 December 1928. Boyden was a distinguished Marine. He was appointed a second lieutenant on 19 August 1919, and was a naval aviator. He progressed to colonel in 1942, and served at Okinawa.

37. Darnall was a first lieutenant in the corps. He made captain just before retiring in December 1932.

38. Bruce was a Marine first sergeant; first lieutenant was his *guardia* rank.

39. *New York Herald Tribune*, 19 July 1927.

40. The Marine killed was Private Michael Obleski. Private Charles E. Garrison was wounded.

41. Mike had been a gunnery sergeant in the 5th Marines in France before becoming a pilot. By the end of World War II he was a lieutenant colonel; he had been awarded a Distinguished Flying Cross for his actions in February and March 1928 in Nicaragua.

42. Edward C. John, *Marine Corps Aviation: The Early Years, 1912–1940*, p. 56.
43. Floyd, was an enlisted man promoted to second lieutenant on 5 August 1909. He became Captain Floyd on 29 August 1916 and earned a Navy Cross in 1927 at Nicaragua; he was serving at Cavite in 1919. Major Floyd disappears from the records in 1935. Gulick was born in Italy, but was appointed from New Hampshire a second lieutenant 26 May 1899. He progressed up to colonel on 1 July 1918, having served at various posts in between. In 1927 he commanded the 2d Brigade of Marines in Nicaragua. In 1932 he was commanding officer of the detachment at Peiping, China, but disappears from the records in 1934.
44. An extract from Gulick's orders to Floyd dated 18 July 1927. In author's possession.
45. Edgar S. Tuttle served as an enlisted Marine for eight years before his appointment as a second lieutenant on 24 July 1917. It was confirmed on 16 September 1919. He retired a major on 1 November 1936.
46. Lejeune Cummins, *Quijote on a Burro: Sandino and the Marines*. Mexico City: private printing, 1958.
47. Tebbs, a Virginian, was appointed a second lieutenant on 15 September 1915, served in France with the 23d Machine Gun Company, 6th Machine Gun Battalion, and became a first lieutenant on 1 July 1918. He didn't progress very far in rank because he retired a major in June 1945.
48. Lejeune, "Testimony of the Marine Corps Commandant," p. 53.
49. Lee was an enlisted man until 1935 when he was promoted to Marine gunner. That rank was changed to commissioned warrant officer on 1 May 1941. Beginning on 19 July 1939 he was serving in North China, when he was captured by the Japanese and spent World War II in a prisoner of war camp. He was slated for promotion to captain but that could not be effected until he was released. My records do not show what happened, although I am positive he survived and was promoted.

Chapter 10

1. Ellsworth, p. 137.
2. Herring, *A History of Latin America*. pp. 595–96. Ellsworth, *One Hundred Eighty Landings of United States Marines 1800–1934*. p. 137.
3. Tupper was commissioned a second lieutenant on 3 March 1819, first lieutenant in 1822, and captain in 1832; he died on 18 January 1838.
4. Ellsworth, p. 137.

Chapter 11

1. Miller/Johnstone, *A Chronology of the United States Marine Corps 1775–1934*, p. 66.
2. Marine Corps Archives. Ellsworth, pp. 139–40.
3. Ibid.
4. Crabb was commissioned a second lieutenant on 7 May 1822 and resigned a first lieutenant on 30 December 1837.
5. Haines was commissioned a second lieutenant from the U.S. Naval Academy on 1 July 1883. In August 1900 he was a major and on Admiral Dewey's staff. The following year he was in the Adjutant and Inspector's Office, remaining there and rising to colonel in 1916. Made brigadier general in January 1920, he retired at that rank on 1 January 1923.
6. Bernard Nalty, *The United States Marines in the War with Spain*, p. 30.

Chapter 12

1. McConnell was appointed a Marine second lieutenant on 2 October 1899 from Pennsylvania. Though promoted to first lieutenant, he disappears from the records in 1906, which, perhaps, means that he died in service.
2. Ellsworth, p. 67.
3. McLemore was appointed a second lieutenant from the United States Naval Academy on 1 July 1893. He served in various posts until, as major, he became part of the Adjutant and Inspector's Office in January 1910. He became colonel in 1916 but disappears from the records in 1922. Long was commissioned a second lieutenant on 26 January 1900, first lieutenant on 28 July 1900, was dishonorably discharged on 30 December 1907, but shows up in the 1920 register as being retired a captain on 21 August 1919.
4. Howland, pp. 80–81.
5. Ibid., pp. 83–84.
6. Metcalf, pp. 349–50. Ellsworth, pp. 69–70.
7. Bolton, from South Carolina, was commissioned a second lieutenant on 29 September 1916. Henley, from Georgia, was commissioned a second lieutenant on 10 March 1905. During 1918 he was a major at Guam. Was made a colonel in 1935 while serving at Pearl Harbor, Hawaii. He retired at that rank on 30 June 1941 but served during the war.

8. Weitzel was from Kentucky and commissioned a second lieutenant on 6 January 1909. He served with the 4th Marines in Santo Domingo even after he was a captain on 29 August 1916, and again in 1919. He was a major in June 1920 and in 1929 serving in Nicaragua. He retired at that rank on 1 June 1935.

9. Harry Lee, born in Washington, D.C., was appointed a second lieutenant on 2 August 1898. He served in the Spanish-American-Cuban War. He served aboard ships and in various locations and capacities until World War I, when he assumed command of the 6th Regiment after Col. Albertus W. Catlin was badly wounded on 6 June 1918. He was brigade commander, 2d Marine Brigade, in Santo Domingo, became a major general and remained in service until his untimely death in 1935.

10. Thorpe was a hero several times over. In 1903 he led the Marine detachment that brought the new ambassador to his office at Addis Abba, the capital of Ethiopia. There the emperor Menelik awarded him the medal Star of Ethiopia. The trip was through much of Africa's worst terrain and tough native tribes. They fought many times during that ascent, always successfully.

11. One of those who rose to a leadership position was Rafael Trujillo, a dictator of the republic.

12. Kenneth W. Condit and Edwin T. Turnbladh. *Hold High the Torch*, Washington, D.C.: Historical Branch, G-3 Division, Headquarters, U.S. Marine Corps, 1960, pp. 81–82.

13. One of the most infamous graduates was a man named Rafael Leonidas Trujillo, who later became the dictator of the Dominican Republic.

14. Salladay was appointed a second lieutenant from his birth place, Illinois, on 8 December 1899, was made a captain in 1903, and was in the Philippines in 1906. He was made a major in 1916 and was in Santo Domingo. After being named lieutenant colonel in July 1918, he retired at that rank on 11 March 1920.

15. Dunlap was truly a superb Marine. He went to France and commanded a regiment (17th) of heavy U.S. Army artillery. Later, passed over for commandant, he earned an assignment at the most prestigious French military school. While there, he was killed while saving a French woman and her child from an avalanche.

16. Miller was appointed a second lieutenant from Iowa on 23 July 1900, served at Cavite aboard the *Oregon*, was back in the Philippines and Santo Domingo with the 4th Regiment in 1919 and then was made major and was assigned to the Philadelphia Navy Yard. In 1927 Lt. Col. Miller was with the 3d Brigade in China, then retired a colonel on 30 June 1936. Harrington, from Delaware, was appointed a second lieutenant 6 January 1909, was aboard the *Idaho* later that year, and was made a first lieutenant in 1911. Assigned to the legation at Peking, China, in 1913, he was appointed a major on 1 July 1918, then served in the Adjutant and Inspector's Office. In August 1922 he was back in service, now with the *Gendarmerie d'Haiti*. Then in 1927 he was assigned to Nicaragua. Promoted to brigadier general on 1 January 1940, he retired at that rank in January 1943, though he continued to serve until 1945.

17. Kingsbury was appointed a second lieutenant on 3 December 1904. He was at Marine Barracks, Honolulu, in November 1910, where he remained for a number of years. Then, he was a first lieutenant commanding the Marine Barracks at Charleston, SC, in 1913. Next he was promoted to major and was with the 2d Brigade in Santo Domingo in 1916. While there, he became a member of the Adjutant and Inspector's organization. In 1919 he was at New London, CT. After this he disappears from the records.

18. Most of the above, about Bearss, is from my book *Hiram Iddings Bearss, U.S. Marine Corps: Biography of a World War I Hero*, McFarland, 2005.

19. 3d Provisional Regiment, Commanding Officer Thorpe's report to the commanding general, 2d Provisional Brigade, Colonel Pendleton, 8 July 1917.

20. Pritchett, a Georgian, was appointed a second lieutenant on 2 March 1900. His service was mainly stateside until assignment to Santo Domingo. He was promoted to lieutenant colonel in 1923, still stateside, then colonel, and retired at that rank on 3 November 1928.

21. I finally located a Marine officer by the name Merkel. In October he was accused of beating and disfiguring one native prisoner and having four others shot during operations against natives near Hato Mayor. He was arrested and while confined killed himself with a hidden small pistol.

22. Jones resigned 29 August 1919. Bain, from Virginia, was appointed a second lieutenant 29 September 1916 and reached captain 23 May 1917. He held that rank with the Nicaraguan National Guard in 1928. He was finally

made a major in 1932 and retired a lieutenant colonel on 30 June 1939. Moore, appointed from South Carolina a second lieutenant on 29 September 1916, was a captain on 23 May 1917. On 4 July 1921 he became an aviator and remained at Quantico. In China in 1927, he flew a plane and lost his wings, parachuting safely. As a major he was sent to Haiti in May 1932. In 1935 Lt. Col. Moore was in the Virgin Islands, named a brigadier general in 1942, was commanding officer of the 4th Marine Base Defense Aircraft Wing, named major general in 1944, and served various locations in the Pacific. He was made a lieutenant general retroactive to 1944 and retired in November 1946.

23. Condit/Turnbladh, pp. 89–91. Not much else is available on Tandy except that he was promoted to captain in 1919 and placed on inactive the same day as his promotion.

24. Byrd, from South Carolina, was appointed a second lieutenant on 29 September 1916. Named captain on 23 May 1917, he became an aviator on 26 July 1926 and was still at Quantico in 1928, but disappears from records in 1929.

25. Fuller, a U.S. Naval Academy grad, was appointed a second lieutenant on 1 July 1891 and had an undistinguished career. He was just never where the action was, until he was appointed commandant.

26. Breckinridge was appointed a second lieutenant from Arkansas on 13 April 1899. Although he was in Nicaragua in 1909, he served mainly stateside and aboard ship until appointed a naval attache to the American embassy in Moscow in 1916. During World War I, he was awarded, for some reason, a Navy Cross for service in the Scandinavian capitals Christiana, Stockholm, and Copenhagen. He was promoted to lieutenant colonel in 1916 and colonel in July 1918 still stateside. In 1930 he commanded the detachment at Peiping. He became a brigadier general in 1931 and a major general in 1935. He disappears from the records in 1942.

27. McCaughtry was an enlisted Marine before his commissioning on 1 June 1917. He was promoted to captain two days later. Interestingly, he was an enlisted Navy pilot.

28. Miller didn't last long; he was appointed a second lieutenant in 1918 and resigned in 1919.

29. Lieutenant General Edward A. Craig, USMC (ret.) Interview by Oral History unit, HQMC, 16 May 1968.

30. Metcalf, p. 365.

31. I have slightly different information relative to the *guardia*, but have used this material from a rather stronger source.

32. Oglesby joined the Marines in 1915 and was commissioned a second lieutenant on 15 August 1918 and first lieutenant the following day while serving in Santo Domingo. He made colonel on 8 July 1940 and was still in service in 1945. The only record I could find on Biebush was his resignation as second lieutenant on 19 November 1919.

33. Carpenter enrolled as a reserve Marine aviator on 18 September 1918 and was placed on the inactive list 14 November 1919. Noble resigned a first lieutenant on 19 August 1919.

34. Kenneth W. Condit and Edwin T. Turnbladh, *Hold High the Torch*, Washington, D.C., Historical Branch, G-3 Division, Headquarters, U.S. Marine Corps, 1960, pp. 81–82.

35. Carpenter was a native of New Hampshire and became a second lieutenant of Marines on 1 July 1899. He became a colonel on 6 April 1921, and commanding officer of the 1st Regiment, 2d Brigade, on 1 August 1922. He retired at that rank in 1926.

36. Second Brigade Report to Commandant, Year Ending 30 June 1922.

Chapter 13

1. Nicholson was appointed a second lieutenant 10 March 1847, first lieutenant 14 March 1856, was assigned to the Adjutant and Inspector's Office with rank of major on 6 May 1861, and retired 1 May 1894.

2. Reynolds was appointed a second lieutenant on 26 May 1824, first lieutenant 1833, captain in 1847, major, 1861, and lieutenant colonel the same year. He died in service on 2 November 1865. Stark was named second lieutenant 1 July 1831, first lieutenant 1 July 1834, captain 1847, and died in service August 1855.

3. Herring, p. 790. Ellsworth, pp. 160–61. Collum, *History of the United States Marine Corps*, pp. 104–06.

4. Neill was made second lieutenant 6 February 1865, first lieutenant in February 1869, and resigned 2 June 1873.

5. Ellsworth, pp. 161–63.

BIBLIOGRAPHY

Adams, Randolph Greenfield. *A History of the Foreign Policy of the United States.* New York: Macmillan, 1925.
Balch, Emily Greene. *Occupied Haiti.* New York: Writer's, 1927.
Bauer, K. Jack. *Surfboats and Horse Marines: U.S. Naval Operations in the Mexican War, 1846–48.* Annapolis, MD: United States Institute Press, 1969.
Beede, Benjamin R. *The War of 1898 and U.S. Interventions 1898–1934, an Encyclopedia.* New York: Garland, 1994.
Butler, Smedley D. *War Is a Racket.* New York: Round Table, 1935.
Calder, Bruce J. *The Impact of Intervention: The Dominican Republic During the U.S. Occupation of 1916–1924.* Austin: University Press of Texas, 1984.
Clark, George B. *Hiram Iddings Bearss, U.S. Marine Corps: Biography of a World War I Hero.* Jefferson, NC: McFarland, 2005.
_____. *With the Old Corps in Nicaragua.* Novato, CA: Presidio Press, 2001.
Coker, C.F.W., comp. *Henry Clay Cochrane, 1841–1947.* Manuscript Register Series, Number One. Quantico, VA: Marine Corps Museum, 1968.
Collings, Kenneth. *Just for the Hell of It.* New York: Dodd, Mead, 1938.
Collum, Richard S. *History of the United States Marine Corps.* Philadelphia: L.R. Hamersly, 1890.
Condit, Kenneth W., and Edwin T. Turnbladh. *Hold High the Torch: A History of the 4th Marines.* Washington, D.C.: Historical Branch, G-3 Division, Headquarters, U.S. Marine Corps, 1960.
Cox, Isaac Joslin. *Nicaragua and the United States.* Boston: World Peace Foundation Pamphlets, 1927.
Craige, John H. *Black Bagdad.* New York: Minton, Balch, 1933.
_____. *Cannibal Cousins.* New York: Minton, Balch, 1934.
Davis, Doris S., comp. *John Lloyd Broome, 1849–1898.* Manuscript Register Series, Number Six. Quantico, VA: Marine Corps Museum, nd (c. 1967).
_____. *Levi Twiggs, 1834–1850.* Manuscript Register Series, Number Five. Quantico, VA: Marine Corps Museum, nd (c. 1970).
Davis, H. P. *Black Democracy: The Story of Haiti.* New York: Dodge, 1936.
Denny, Harold Norman. *Dollars for Bullets: The Story of American Rule in Nicaragua.* New York: Dial, 1929.
Ellsworth, Harry Allanson. *One Hundred Eighty Landings of United States Marines 1800–1934.* Washington, D.C.: History and Museums Division, Headquarters, U.S. Marine Corps, 1974.

Frank, Benis. *A Brief History of the 3d Marines*. Washington, D.C.: Historical Branch, Headquarters, U.S. Marine Corps, 1958.

Fuller, Stephen M., and Graham A. Cosmas. *Marines in the Dominican Republic 1916–1924*. Washington, D.C.: History and Museums Division, Headquarters, U.S. Marine Corps, 1974.

Gordon, Martin K., comp. *Louis McCarthy Little, 1878–1960*. Manuscript Register Series, Number Seven. Quantico, VA: Marine Corps Museum, 1971.

_____. *Wilburt Scott Brown, 1900–1968*. Manuscript Register Series, Number Eight. Quantico, VA: Marine Corps Museum, 1973.

Harllee, John. *The Marine from Manatee*. Washington, D.C.: National Rifle Association of America, 1984.

Healy, David. *Gunboat Diplomacy in the Wilson Era: The U.S. Navy in Haiti, 1915–1916*. Madison: University of Wisconsin Press, 1976.

Heinl, Robert D., Jr. *Soldiers of the Sea: The United States Marine Corps, 1775–1962*. Annapolis, MD: United States Naval Institute, 1962.

Herring, Hubert. *A History of Latin America from the Beginning to the Present*. New York: Alfred A. Knopf, 1969.

Hopkins, J.A.H., and Melinda Alexander. *Machine-Gun Diplomacy*. New York: Lewis Copeland, 1928.

Howland, Charles P. *American Relations in the Caribbean*. New Haven, CT: Yale University Press, 1929.

Inman, Samuel Guy. *Through Santo Domingo and Haiti: A Cruise with the Marines*. New York: Committee on Cooperation in Latin America, 1919.

Johnson, Edward C. *Marine Corps Aviation: The Early Years, 1912–1940*. Edited by Graham A. Cosmas. Washington, D.C.: History and Museums Division, Headquarters, U.S. Marine Corps, 1977.

Johnstone, John H. *A Brief History of the 1st Marines*. Washington, D.C.: Historical Branch, Headquarters, U.S. Marine Corps, 1968.

Kane, Robert J. *A Brief History of the 2d Marines*. Washington, D.C.: Historical Division, Headquarters, U.S. Marine Corps, 1970.

Langley, Lester D. *The Banana Wars: An Inner History of American Empire, 1900–1934*. Lexington: University Press of Kentucky, 1983.

Leonard, John W., and Fred P. Chitty. *The Story of the United States Marines, 1740–1919*. New York: U.S. Marine Corps Publicity Bureau, n.d. (c. 1919).

McCrocklin, James H. *Garde D'Haiti, 1915–1934*. Annapolis, MD: United States Naval Institute, 1956.

Metcalf, Clyde H. *A History of the United States Marine Corps*. New York: G.P. Putnam's Sons, 1939.

Miller, William M., and John H. Johnstone. *A Chronology of the United States Marine Corps, 1775–1934*. Volume 1. Washington, D.C.: Historical Division Headquarters, 1970.

Millspaugh, Arthur C. *Haiti Under American Control, 1915–1930*. Boston: World Peace Foundation, 1931.

Munro, Dana G. *The United States and the Caribbean Republics 1921–1933*. Princeton, NJ: Princeton University Press, 1974.

Musicant, Ivan. *The Banana Wars: A History of the United States Military Intervention in Latin American from the Spanish-American War to the Invasion of Panama*. New York: Macmillan, 1990.

Niles, Blair. *Black Haiti: A Biography of Africa's Eldest Daughter*. New York: G.P. Putnam's Sons, 1926.

Perkins, Dexter. *Hands Off: A History of the Monroe Doctrine*. Boston: Little, Brown, 1943.
Pinkston, L. P. *U.S. Marines: Duties, Experiences, Opportunities, Pay*. N.p., 1913.
Quirk, Robert E. *An Affair of Honor: Woodrow Wilson and the Occupation of Vera Cruz*. New York: W. W. Norton, 1967.
Register of Commissioned and Warrant Officers of the United States Navy and Marine Corps. Washington, D.C.: Government Printing Office, 1861–1956.
Sands, William Franklin, in collaboration with Joseph M. Lally. *Our Jungle Diplomacy*. Chapel Hill: University of North Carolina Press, 1944.
Santelli, James S. *A Brief History of the 8th Marines*. Washington, D.C.: History and Museums Division, Headquarters, U.S. Marine Corps, 1977.
Schmidt, Hans. *Maverick Marine, General Smedley D. Butler and the Contradictions of American Military History*. Lexington: The University Press of Kentucky, 1987.
_____. *The United States Occupation of Haiti, 1915–1934*. New Brunswick, NJ.: Rutgers University Press, 1971.
Secretary of the Navy. *Annual Report: Includes Marine Corps Commandant's Report: 1894–1932*. Washington, D.C.: Government Printing Office, various dates.
Smith, Julian C., et al. *A Review of the Organization and Operations of the Guardia Nacional de Nicaragua*. Quantico, VA: Marine Corps Research Center, nd (c. 1936).
Stimson, Henry L. *American Policy in Nicaragua*. New York: Scribner's, 1927.
Tyson, Carolyn A., comp. *The Journal of Frank Keeler, 1898*. Marine Corps Letter Series, Number One. Quantico, VA: Marine Corps Museum, nd (c. 1967).
Venzon, Anne Cipriano, ed. *General Smedley Darlington Butler: The Letters of a Leatherneck, 1898–1931*. New York: Praeger, 1992.

Index

Adams, Capt. John Q. 153–155
Allen, Capt. Burrell O. 121
Allibone, Lt. Charles O. 21, 24–26
Archibald, Capt. Robert J. 127, 183, 197
Argentina 1, 3–5, 7, 8, 137

Badger, RA Charles J. 106, 109
Bailey, Comm. Theodorus 14
Bain, James M. 157–158, 161, 186
Bannon, Capt. Phillip M. 42, 178
Barker, Capt. Frederick A. 63, 69, 71
Barnett, George 41–44, 59, 71, 94, 95, 171
Barnette, Lt. Bradford 117
Barton, Lt. Thomas B. 140
Bassett, Lt. Frederick B., Jr. 113
Bates, 1st Lt. George T. 53
Batham, Pvt. John 138
Beach, Capt. Edward L. 55
Bearss, Hiram 108, 111, 146, 148, 153–156, 171
Bell, Cpl. Henry 138
Berkeley, Col. Randolph C. 124, 131, 183, 185
Berkley Sound 3
Berryman, 1st Lt. Ottway C., CO D 22, 25
Biebush, 2d Lt. Frederick L. 162, 186
Blaine, Sec. of State James G. 12
Blamer, Comm. Dewitt 105
Blocklinger, Comm. Gottfried 28
Bolton, 2d Lt. James K. 148, 154
Boyden, 1st Lt. Hayne D. 127, 129, 186
Bradman, Frederick L. 47, 51, 186
Brainard, Maj. Edward A. 165
Breckinridge, Col. James C. 160, 179
Breedon, Cpl. Bascome 162
Brooke, Gen. John R. 37, 38
Brown, RA George 10
Brown, Comm. Guy N. 114
Brown, Capt. Philip S., CO K 44
Brown, 2d Lt. Wilburt S. 126, 184, 206
Brownson, Lt. Willard H. 104, 105
Bruce, 1st Lt. Thomas G. 128, 130, 182, 183, 186
Bryan, Sec. of State William Jennings 53
Bullard, Col. Robert L. 45
Burton, Capt. Norman G. 32

Butler, Smedley D. 58, 59, 62, 63, 66–68, 71–73, 75–78, 82, 94–96, 98, 100, 101, 109–111, 115–118, 171, 174, 176, 179, 181
Button, 1st Lt. William R. 85–89, 172
Byrd, Capt. William C. 159, 161

Cady, Pvt. Alexander 139
Campbell, Capt. Chandler 63, 65, 66, 69, 71
Canada 1
Caperton, RA William B. 55, 56, 57, 58, 60, 61, 62, 63, 145
Carpenter, Col. Charles C. 165
Carpenter, Capt. Henry W. 101
Carpenter, 2d Lt. Manson C. 162
Catlin, Albertus W. 40–42, 44, 45, 83, 94–96, 107, 109
Chachá 154–156
Chappell, 2d Lt. Kenneth B. 121
Chile 9–12
Clarke, 2d Lt. Arthur H., CO E 21
Clary, Capt. Albert G. 15
Cochrane, Capt. Henry C., CO C 22
Coghlan, RA Joseph B. 32, 100
Colahan, Lt. Charles E. 26
Cole, Eli K. 33, 58, 59, 63, 65, 66, 67, 72, 94, 96
Collum, Capt. Richard S. 21, 23–26
Colombia 13–33
Colombia 112, 113, 143–144
Connette, 1st Lt. Charles 124, 131
corvée 76–78, 81, 83, 93–96
Cowles, RA Walter C. 105
Coyle, 1st Lt. Randolph 62
Crabb, 2d Lt. Horatio N. 141
Cromwell, Capt. Bartlett J. 27
Cuba 2, 33–52, 79, 83, 141, 150, 171–176
Cunningham, Maj. Alfred 163, 165

Daly, Sgt. Daniel J. 66, 67
Darnall, Capt. Grover C. 127, 187
Darrah, Cpl. Clyde R. 158, 184, 187
Davis, RA Charles H. 168, 169, 183
Davis, Capt. Henry C., CO M 44
Deacon, Capt. David 138
Delano, Comm. Francis H. 28, 32

205

206 Index

Denig, 2d Lt. Robert L. 42, 183, 187
Denny, 1st Lt. Frank L., CO C 22
D'Hervilly, 2d Lt. James V. 15
Diehl, Lt. Comm. Samuel W.B. 100
Dillingham, Comm. Albert C. 142, 143
Doxey, Capt. John L. 81, 95
Duncan, Comm. Silas 3, 4
Dunlap, Col. Robert H. 111, 132, 147, 155, 185

Edson, Capt. Merritt 132–133, 172, 184
Elliott, George F. 22, 23, 33, 35, 36, 172
Ellsworth, 2d Lt. Henry G. 15, 22
Entrekin, Pvt. Emery L. 90, 91
et Weir, 2d Lt. Frank D. 127

Fagan, Capt. Louis E., CO B 22
Falkland Islands 3–4
Feland, Logan 42, 43, 44, 111, 124–126, 132, 162, 163, 172, 185
Fellers, 1st Lt. William S. 119, 187
Fillette, 2d Lt. T.G., CO A 22
Finch, 1st Lt. Charles S. 120, 122, 131
Fitzgerald, Pvt. John 36
Fletcher, RA Frank F. 106, 109, 110
Florida Treaty 1
Floyd, Maj. Oliver 130, 184
Forrest, Capt. French 167–168
France 1, 5, 8, 28, 36, 50, 51, 77, 79, 80, 91, 156, 157, 159, 161–163, 168, 171–174, 176
Fuller, BGen. Ben 160, 162
Funston, Gen. Frederick 110

Gardner, 2d Lt. Daniel M., Jr. 117
Garland, Capt. Addison 14
Garrison, Pvt. Charles E. 133
Geiger, Maj. Roy 93, 181
gendarmerie 61, 72–83, 95–96, 177
Gilmer, Comm. William W. 115
Goodrich, Capt. Caspar F. 36
Great Britain 1, 28, 142, 168
Green, 2d Lt. Henry S., CO E 44
Greene, Edward A. 28, 118, 180
Gross, Pvt. Samuel 70, 71
Guardia Nacional 124, 127, 132, 133, 150–151, 174–175, 182, 185–186
Gulbranson, Lt. Comm. Clarence 121
Gulick, Col. Louis M. 130, 178, 184

Haines, 1st Lt. Henry C. 141
Haiti 2, 18, 23, 48, 50, 52, 53–99, 131, 135, 142, 145, 150, 169, 171–177
Halford, Maj. Frank 51
Hanneken, Herman H. 84–89, 173, 184, 189
Hanson, Lt. E.G. 122
Harding, Pres. Warren 163
Harllee, William C. 42, 43, 109, 152, 163
Harrington, Capt. Francis H. 21, 25
Harrington, 1st Lt. Samuel L. 156, 187

Hatch, Maj. Charles B. 54
Hatfield, Capt. Gilbert 126–130, 184, 187
Hawley, Ens. Arthur H. 105
Hebb, Capt. Clement D. 15
Henley, John R. 105, 148
Heywood, Maj. Charles 19, 20, 22, 23, 25, 27, 173
Higbee, Capt. John H. 21, 23, 24
Hill, Capt. Charles S., CO L 44
Hines, Comm. Harold K. 115
Hollins, Capt. George H. 112
Holmes, 2d Lt. George S. 5
Honduras 2, 100–102, 125–126
Hooker, Lt. Col. Richard S. 83
Hoover, Pres. Herbert 98
Horse Marines 133, 134, 156
Hubbard, Comm. John 31, 32
Hughes, Lt. Edward M. 23, 24
Hughes, Capt. John A. 114–115, 179
Huntington, Robert W. 22, 23, 34–36, 172–174

Iams, Sgt. Ross 70, 71
Impey, Lt. Robert E. 21

Jackson, Pres. Andrew 3, 175
Jones, Commo. Thomas A.C. 103
Jouett, RA James E. 20, 21, 24, 26

Kane, Theodore P. 42, 44, 58
Karmany, Col. Lincoln 46
Kautz, Capt. Austin 118
Kelly, 1st Lt. Patrick 82, 83
Kelton, 1st Lt. Allan C., QM 22
Kempff, Capt. Clarence S. 118
Keyser, Maj. Ralph S. 119
Kimball, Lt. William 21
Kincaid, 2d Lt. Gerard M. 41
Kingsbury, Capt. Ross S. 156
Kirkpatrick, 2d Lt. Edgar G. 90, 91
Klemann, Lt. John V. 40–41
Knapp, Adm Harry S. 58, 148, 150, 160
Knighton, Capt. Joseph W. 121
Knox, Sec. of State Philander 113, 116
Knox, Sgt. William R. 157

La Bounty, Comm. Selah L. 121
Lamson-Scribner, 1st Lt. Frank H. 126–127, 186
Larsen, 1st Lt. Arnold C. 118, 119
Lavoie, Capt. Ernest 95
Lee, BGen. Harry 149, 152, 163, 164, 180
Lee, 1st Lt. William A. 133, 184, 188
Lejeune, John A. 32, 47, 59, 62, 109, 110, 111, 141, 173–174
Lewis, Lt. Comm. Spenser S. 121
Little, Lt. Col. Louis McC. 89, 90, 93, 178
Long, Charles G. 106, 107, 118, 163, 173
Long, 2d Lt. Earl C. 117

Index

Long, 1st Lt. Henry D.F. 144
Long, James D. 168
Low, William W. 69, 71, 103, 104
Lowndes, Maj. Edward R. 42
Lucas, Lewis C. 33, 35, 47
Lyman, Maj. Charles H. 48
Lynch, Comm. William F. 8, 167

Magill, 1st Lt. Lewis J. 35
Mahoney, James E. 33, 35, 46, 47, 51, 111, 114, 116, 173, 178, 188
Mann, 1st Lt. Edward E. 118
Marston, 1st Lt. John 69, 93, 174, 188
Mason, Lt. Theodore B.M. 21
Mayo, Adm Henry T. 105, 106
McCalla, Capt. Bowman 18–27, 35, 174
McCaughey, Lt. JG. Scott D. 70, 71
McCaughtry, Capt. Walter E. 161
McCawley, Col Commandant, Charles G. 27, 174
McConnell, Richard G. 142
McCrea, Comm. Henry 29, 30
McCreary, Capt. Wirt 32, 44
McKeever, Comm. Isaac 5, 6, 7
McKelvey, Maj. William M. 118
McKelvey, Capt. William N. 42
McKinley, Pres. William 36, 37
McLemore, Capt. Albert S. 28, 144
McNabb, 2d Lt. Grover T. 80
Meade, Robert L. 21, 22, 85, 88, 122, 131, 184
Meeker, Capt. Edward P., CO A 22, 25
Merkel, Capt. Charles F. 157
Merriam, Lt. Greenlief 141
Mervine, Comm. William 14
Mexico 1, 2, 13, 16, 103–111, 132
Meyers, PFC William T. 97
Miller, 1st Lt. Ellis B. 156
Miller, 2d Lt. Harold N. 161
Miller, Capt. James M. 143
Miller, Lt. Comm. Marcus L. 40
Mims, Capt. Harvey B. 83
Monroe, Pres. James 1
Monroe Doctrine 1, 4, 53, 142, 145
Montevideo 4, 5, 7, 8, 167–169
Moore, Capt. James T. 157–158, 161
Moore, 1st Sgt. Philip 105
Moses, Lt. Col. Franklin J. 42, 44, 46, 113
Moulton, Cpl. F. 105
Muse, William S. 10, 25, 36
Muth, 2d Lt. Lawrence 90, 91
Myers, Maj. John T. 147

Nazro, Comm. Arthur P. 100
Neill, 2d Lt. R.R. 168
Neilson, Ens. John L. 105
Neville, Wendell C. 42, 43, 106, 107, 109, 174, 178

Nicaragua 2, 13, 16, 63, 89, 98, 99, 100–101, 112–136, 150, 166, 171–176, 178–182, 185–186, 189
Nicholas, 1st Lt. Henry T. 121, 124, 183, 188
Nicholson, 1st Lt. Augustus S. 8, 167
Nicholson, 1st Lt. Jesup, CO B. 22
Nicklin, Pvt. Deodatur 138
Noble, 2d Lt. Nathan S. 162
Norman, 2d Lt. Lawrence 126

Obleski, Pvt. Michael A. 133
Ogden, Asst. Surg. Frederick N. 22
Oglesby, 1st Lt. Donald G. 162
O'Higgins, Bernard 9
Oliver, Ens. James H. 23, 24
Ostermann, 1st Lt. Edward A. 66, 181

Pabst, Cpl. Lawrence 126
Panama 2, 13–35, 109, 112, 115–118, 122, 171–176
Paraguay 137
Parker, Comm. James P. 144
Parker, 1st Lt. William E. 41
Passmore, Sgt. William A. 90, 91
Pendleton, Joseph H. 106, 117, 118, 145–147, 159–160, 175, 180
Peralte, Charlemagne 81–89
Perkins, Capt. Jesse L. 90, 91
Perry, Capt. Thomas 28, 29
Pershing, BGen. John J. 111, 172
Peru 138–139
Pierce, Capt. Francis E. 126, 185
Pierce, Maj. Harold C. 125–127, 188
Platt, Lt. Charles T. 140
Platt Amendment 38–39
Plunkett, Cadet Charles P. 23, 25
Poe, Pvt. John M. 158
Pope, Capt. Percival C. 15
Porter, David D. 44, 140–141, 175
Potter, Capt. Hal N. 98
Potter, Comm. William P. 30
Preston, Pvt. George 138
Puerto Rico 140–141, 171
Puller, Lewis B. 93, 133, 175, 185, 188

Quick, Sgt. John H. 36

Ramsey, 2d Lt. Fred A. 32
Reeder, Lt. William H. 26
Reid, Capt. George C. 24, 25, 26
Reid, MG Robert W. 163
Reisinger, Capt. Harold C. 42
Reynolds, Capt. John G. 168
Richards, Capt. William P. 125
Riggin, PO Charles 10–11
Rixey, Lt. Col. Presley M., Jr. 152
Robertson, Comm. C. Hope 143
Robison, RA Samuel S. 149, 163

Index

Roosevelt, Pres. Franklin D. 2, 78, 98
Roosevelt, Pres. Theodore 40, 41, 45, 53, 145
Roosevelt Corollary 53, 144
Root, Sec. of State Elihu 37, 38
Rowell, Ross E. 124, 129, 130, 131, 132, 175, 185, 186
Rumsey, Lt. Comm. Henry B. 168
Rush, Capt. William R. 107
Rushforth, Pvt. Thomas J. 162
Russell, Lt. Col. Benjamin R. 30
Russell, Col. John 78, 89, 94, 95, 96, 97, 98, 110
Russia 1

Salladay, Maj. Jay McC. 153, 154
Sanderson, 1st Lt. Lawson H.M. 83
Sandino, Augusto 2, 124–132, 173
San Martín, José D. 9
Santo Domingo/Dominican Republic 2, 29, 42–44, 53, 77, 78, 79, 80, 93, 94–96, 116, 142–166, 171–176
Sargent, Lt. Comm. Nathan 28
Sawyer, Lt. JG, Frank E. 23, 25
Schley, Capt. Winfield S. 11
Schmidt, Capt. Harry 48, 185
Shaw, Col. Melville 51
Shearer, Maj. Maurice E. 126
Shepard, 2d Lt. Ralph L. 41, 179
Shinn, Asst. Surg. Herbert L. 158
Smith, Maj. Julian C. 51, 52, 185, 189
Snowden, RA Thomas 149, 160, 163
Southerland, RA William H.H. 117
Spain 1, 3, 8, 9, 34, 36–38, 46, 100, 140, 168, 171, 173, 174, 176
Stark, Capt. William B. 168
Steedman, RA Charles 15
Stingle, Sgt. B.E., CO I 44
Stowell, 2d Lt. George A. 69
Stribling, Lt. Cornelius K. 141
Symonds, Comm. Frederick M. 113

Taft, William Howard 45
Tandy, 2d Lt. Jack H. 158
Tattnall, 2d Lt. John R.F. 6, 7
Taubert, Sgt. Albert A. 90, 91
Taussig, Comm. Edward D. 28
Taylor, Brevet Capt. Algernon S. 5, 7
Tebbs, 1st Lt. John A. 131, 133
Texas 1, 51, 103, 111, 173
Thomas, 2d Lt. Gerald C. 91, 93
Thomason, Capt. John W. 121, 175, 176
Thompson, Ord Sgt. James E. 112
Thorpe, George C. 44, 150, 156–158
Thrasher, 1st Lt. Thomas E., Jr. 66, 181, 189
Tittoni, 2d Lt. Robert, CO H 44
Torrance, Asst. Surg. Robert A. 69

Townrow, Asst. Eng. Frederick W. 104
Townsend, Capt. Julius C. 121
Treadwell, Ens. Lawrence P. 102
Treadwell, Col. Thomas C., Co 1st Regt. 51, 52
Treaty of Paris 38, 39
Tupper, Capt. Charles 139
Turnage, Capt. Allen H. 93
Turner, 2d Lt. James A., CO D 22
Turner, Maj. Thomas C. 95
Turner, RA Thomas 105
Turner, Comm. William H. 142
Turrill, Col. Julius S. 96
Tuttle, Capt. Edgar S. 130

United Nations 2
Upshur, William P. 44, 66, 93
Uruguay 5–8, 166–168

Vandegrift, Alexander A. 93, 109, 110, 176
Van Orden, Capt. George 56
Vera Cruz, Mexico 2, 106–107, 171–174, 176
Villa, Gen. Pancho 111
Vogel, Lt. Col. Clayton B. 98, 189
Vulte, 1st Lt. Hermann T. 117

Wadhams, Comm. Albion V. 33
Wadsworth, Capt. Alexander S. 138, 139
Wainwright, Jonathon M. 104, 120, 143
Walker, Cpt. Asa 100
Walker, Mids. John G. 6
Waller, Littleton W.T. 41, 42, 44, 57, 58, 59, 62, 65, 73, 75, 94, 96, 108, 171, 176
Weitzel, 1st Lt. Harry W. 148
Wells, Maj. Clarke H. 78, 94, 95, 96
Wicks, Lt. JG, Homer C. 71
Williams, Lt. Col. Alexander S. 82–83, 94, 95, 96
Williams, Dion 42
Williams, Sgt. Dorcas L. 95
Willis, 1st Lt. Lauren S. 117
Wilson, Comm. John B. 100
Wilson, Pres. Woodrow W. 2, 106, 109
Winterhalter, Comm. Albert G. 101
Wise, Capt. Frederick 58, 61, 62, 107, 111, 176
Witzel, Horace M. 24, 32
Wodanczyk, CWO Michael 129
Wood, Gen. Leonard 37–38
Wood, 1st Lt. Thomas N. 22
Woods, Lt. Comm. Edward 117
Wyman, Capt. Henry L. 121

Young, Capt. K. James M.T. 23, 25

Zantzinger, Comm. John P. 4

www.ingramcontent.com/pod-product-compliance
Ingram Content Group UK Ltd.
Pitfield, Milton Keynes, MK11 3LW, UK
UKHW042003140426
5217IPUK00015B/958